# Troubleshooting Microsoft® Outlook®

Julia Kelly

Microsoft®

PUBLISHED BY
Microsoft Press
A Division of Microsoft Corporation
One Microsoft Way
Redmond, Washington 98052-6399



Library of Congress Cataloging-in-Publication Data
Kelly, Julia.
Troubleshooting Microsoft Outlook / Julia Kelly.
p. cm.
Includes index.
ISBN 0-7356-1162-9
1. Microsoft Outlook. 2. Time management--Computer programs. I. Title.

HD69.T54 K447 2000
005.369--dc21 00-048705

Printed and bound in the United States of America.

1 2 3 4 5 6 7 8 9 QWT 6 5 4 3 2 1

Distributed in Canada by Penguin Books Canada Limited.

A CIP catalogue record for this book is available from the British Library.

Microsoft Press books are available through booksellers and distributors worldwide. For further information about international editions, contact your local Microsoft Corporation office or contact Microsoft Press International directly at fax (425) 936-7329. Visit our Web site at mspress.microsoft.com. Send comments to *mspinput@microsoft.com.*



**Acquisitions Editors:** Christey Bahn, Alex Blanton
**Project Editor:** Wendy Zucker

# Dedication

*To God—my light, my guide, my life, and my breath.*

*And to all my Outlook students, without whose real-life questions and problems this book would have been a lot harder to write.*

# Quick contents

# Contents

# Acknowledgments

Thank you to everyone I worked with on this book, in order of my acquaintance with them: Christey Bahn, the delightful Acquisitions Editor who "acquired" me as the author for this book

- Jenny Benson and Wendy Zucker, kind and patient Project Editors who went to bat for me when I wanted to do things *my* way
- Allen Wyatt, a very helpful Technical Editor who helped me to write smarter than I really am
- Nancy Albright, excellent Copy Editor who cleaned up my grammatical gaffes
- Jimmie Young and Robert Place who did a wonderful job with a difficult new design

Thank you also to everyone behind the scenes whose names I never knew but who are integral to producing any book.

And, of course, perpetual thanks to my wonderful agent, Margot Maley Hutchison, at Waterside Productions, without whom I would have to get a real job.

# Troubleshooting Tips

To troubleshoot, as defined by the *Microsoft Press Computer Dictionary*, is to "isolate the source of a problem in a program, computer system, or network and remedy it." But how do you go about isolating the source of the problem in the first place? The source can be difficult to identify even for those well versed in the intricacies of an e-mail program such as Outlook or Outlook Express. When the same symptoms are caused by different problems, how do you isolate the real problem? And what if what *you* think is the source of the problem is only a symptom of another problem whose source lies deeper than you can fathom? If you can't immediately identify what's wrong, you might be tempted to quote the hardware engineer ("It's a software problem!") or the software engineer ("It's a hardware problem!") However, blame won't get your computer working properly; information and persistence will. So put on your detective hat, strap on your virtual toolbelt, and get ready to solve the problem.

## How to troubleshoot

Your primary objective is to isolate the problem. As soon as you encounter the problem, write down your observations in the greatest detail possible. (Once you start trying to fix the problem, you probably won't be able to reexamine the symptoms.) Then ask yourself questions, starting with the broadest, and gradually narrow down the scope of the problem. For example, if you can't start Windows, first make sure the computer is plugged in and the monitor is turned on—you can't get much broader than that! If you pass that test, does Windows begin starting up?

The nature of problems in Outlook and Outlook Express is such that you'll recognize direct questions about the symptoms, and the solutions to those problems are usually fairly direct, also.

Now you can start closing in (this is where you'll appreciate your notes). Go to the chapter that seems to cover your problem. Follow the questions in the flowchart until you see one that sounds like your problem, and follow the steps in the Quick Fix or go to the Solution Spread that the question points you to. If you don't see a question that sounds like your problem, look in the other chapters that are recommended in the flowchart (your problem might be covered by a different chapter topic).

Your troubleshooting might take you down a few dead ends before it leads you to the source of your problem. You're going to need patience and determination to get to the bottom of some problems. If your main method of fixing things is to experiment, be aware that sometimes your "fixes" can cause a second problem, and then you'll have two problems to troubleshoot. Keep detailed notes about what you've done so that you don't travel down the same dead end again, and so that you can reverse, if necessary, any actions you took that might have caused more problems.

## If you're still stuck

I've worked to address the most common problems you're likely to run into as you use Outlook or Outlook Express, but, obviously, I can't address every problem. There's even a remote possibility that one of my solutions won't solve your specific problem. If I haven't addressed your problem, make sure that what you've encountered is a real problem rather than your not knowing exactly how to do something in Outlook or Outlook Express. To figure out how to do things easily and quickly in Outlook 2000, you might want to take a look at my book *How to Do Everything with Outlook 2000* (Osborne, Feburary 2000).

If you do run into a dead end, you can turn to the Help file; your company's help desk; the manufacturer of your computer, hardware device, or software program; or Microsoft product support. Be cautious, however, about turning to your coworkers for help, unless you're certain they know what they're doing.

If you want to try to search out the information you need yourself, try the following web sites:

- Microsoft Support Knowledge Base: *http://search.support.microsoft.com/kb/*
- Microsoft Outlook Frequently Asked Questions at SlipStick Systems: *http://www.slipstick.com/outlook/faq.htm*
- Microsoft Outlook articles and information: *http://officeupdate.microsoft.com/articlelist/o2koutlookarticles.htm*
- Microsoft Outlook Express Frequently Asked Questions: *http://support.microsoft.com/support/IE/outlookexpress/oe5/faq/*

# Troubleshooting Web site

With the purchase of this book, you now have access to the free Microsoft Press Troubleshooting web site at *http://www.mspress.microsoft.com/troubleshooting*, which complements the book series by offering additional troubleshooting information that's updated monthly. You'll find that some of the flowcharts have been expanded to cover additional problems, and that entirely new flowcharts with accompanying solutions have been created to address some important but perhaps slightly less common problems than those addressed in this book.

You'll find the Troubleshooting web site as easy to navigate as this book, and it continues my goal of helping you identify your problem and its solution quickly and easily. To access the site, you need this code: MSO0638.

# About this book

*Troubleshooting Microsoft Outlook* presents a new way to diagnose and solve the problems you've encountered with Microsoft Outlook 2000 or Outlook Express. Whether you're a beginning user of Outlook or Outlook Express or have upgraded from an earlier version, the chances are that you bought this book because you want to fix those problems as quickly and easily as possible, without having to read pages of technical background information. I've written this book with three goals in mind: ease, simplicity, and speed. I know you'd like to figure out why your e-mail is stuck in the Outbox or why Outlook won't import your Excel contacts list, so I'll show you how to locate your problem, describe what might be causing it without going into too many specifics, and then lead you right to the solution so that you can get back to what you were doing.

## How to use this book

This book isn't meant to be read in any particular chapter order or even from cover to cover. It's designed so that you can jump in, quickly diagnose your problem, and then get the information you need to fix it, whether you've just begun to learn about computers or programs or whether you're knowledgeable enough to get right to the source of the problem. The problems you're most likely to have are grouped into chapters that are listed alphabetically; the chapter titles are kept simple so that you know at a glance what kinds of topics the chapter entails. Each chapter is broken down into two specific elements: the flowchart and the solution spread.

### Flowcharts

The first thing you'll see when you go to a chapter is a dynamic, easy-to-use flowchart. It starts by asking you a broad question about a common problem and then, as you answer a series of yes-or-no questions, helps you diagnose your problem. If the solution to your problem is a simple one involving only a step or two, you'll find a quick fix right there on the flowchart. Take a few minutes to work through the steps, and presto—your problem is solved and you'll be back to work (or play) with a minimum of downtime. If the solution to your problem requires a little more explanation and a few more steps, you'll find the page number of the solution spread and the statement of the problem it addresses. And if your problem isn't shown on the flowchart, you'll find a list of related chapters where your problem might be addressed.

## Solution spreads

The solution spreads are where the real troubleshooting takes place. I provide you with the source of the problem you're experiencing and then tell you how to fix it with clear, step-by-step instructions. The solutions contain screen shots and illustrations that show you what you'll be seeing as you move through the steps. Although our goal is to give you just the facts so that you quickly get back to what you were doing, in some cases I've also provided some background information of interest for a deeper understanding of why you might have encountered your problem. Also scattered throughout the solution spread are tips that contain additional, related material you might find interesting, and a few warnings that tell you what you should or shouldn't do in a given situation.

Because this book covers Outlook 2000 in both the Corporate/Workgroup and Internet Mail Only configurations, and Outlook Express 5, there will often be software-specific solutions in each solution spread. The software-specific solutions are identified by icons (Outlook 2000 or Outlook Express) and by headings that specify the Outlook configuration. If there's no specified configuration, the solution is for Outlook in either configuration. Be sure you read the solution that's correct for your program and configuration.

## Assumptions about operating system versions

The screen shots in this book were taken in specific operating systems and program versions: all screen shots of Outlook 2000 (Corporate/Workgroup configuration) were taken in Windows 95; all screen shots of Outlook 2000 (Internet Mail Only configuration) were taken in Windows 98; and all screen shots of Outlook Express were taken in Outlook Express 5.5 running in Windows 98.

The only differences you are likely to see are those in Outlook Express 5, which can be different in version 5.0 or 5.5, depending on whether you're running Windows 95, Windows 98, or Windows 2000. If you see an Outlook Express feature in a figure that you don't see in your copy of Outlook Express, a simple upgrade of Internet Explorer will update Outlook Express and fix the difference.

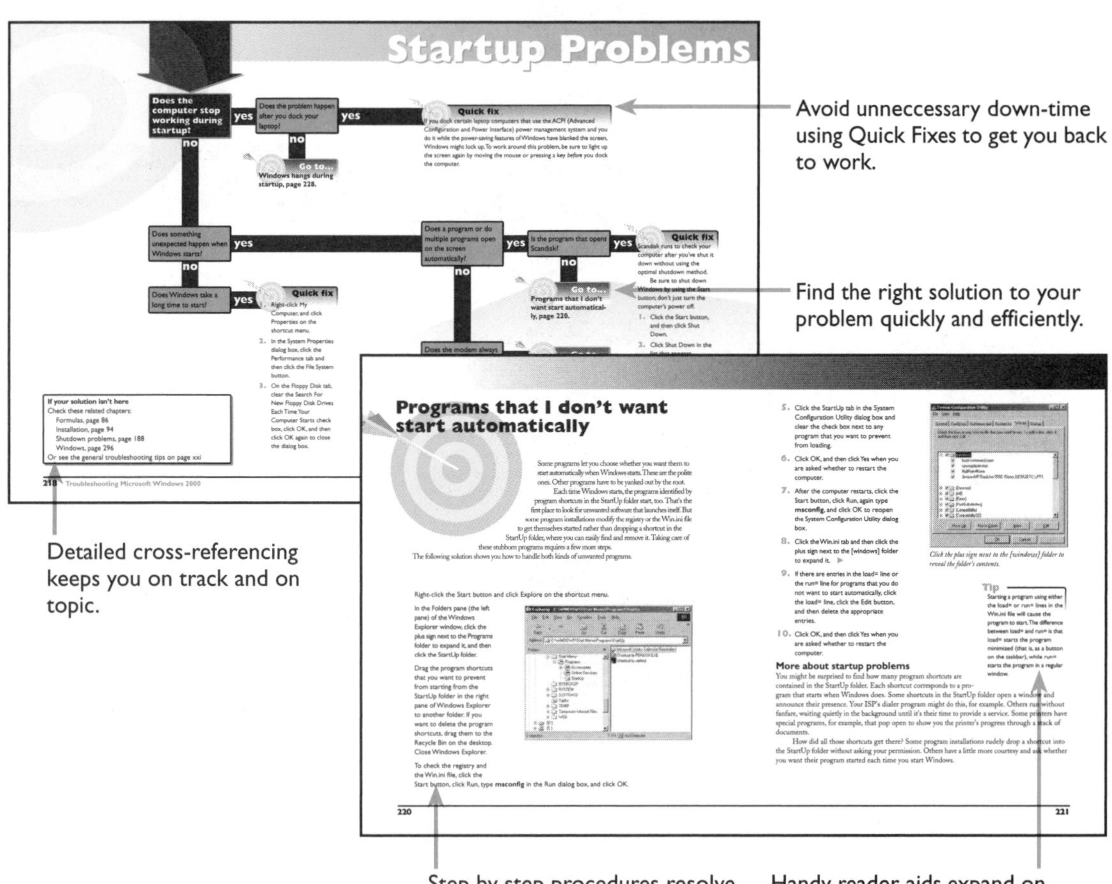


Avoid unneccessary down-time using Quick Fixes to get you back to work.

Find the right solution to your problem quickly and efficiently.

Detailed cross-referencing keeps you on track and on topic.

Step by step procedures resolve your problem as easy as 1-2-3.

Handy reader aids expand on the issue to help avoid future problems.

# Backing u

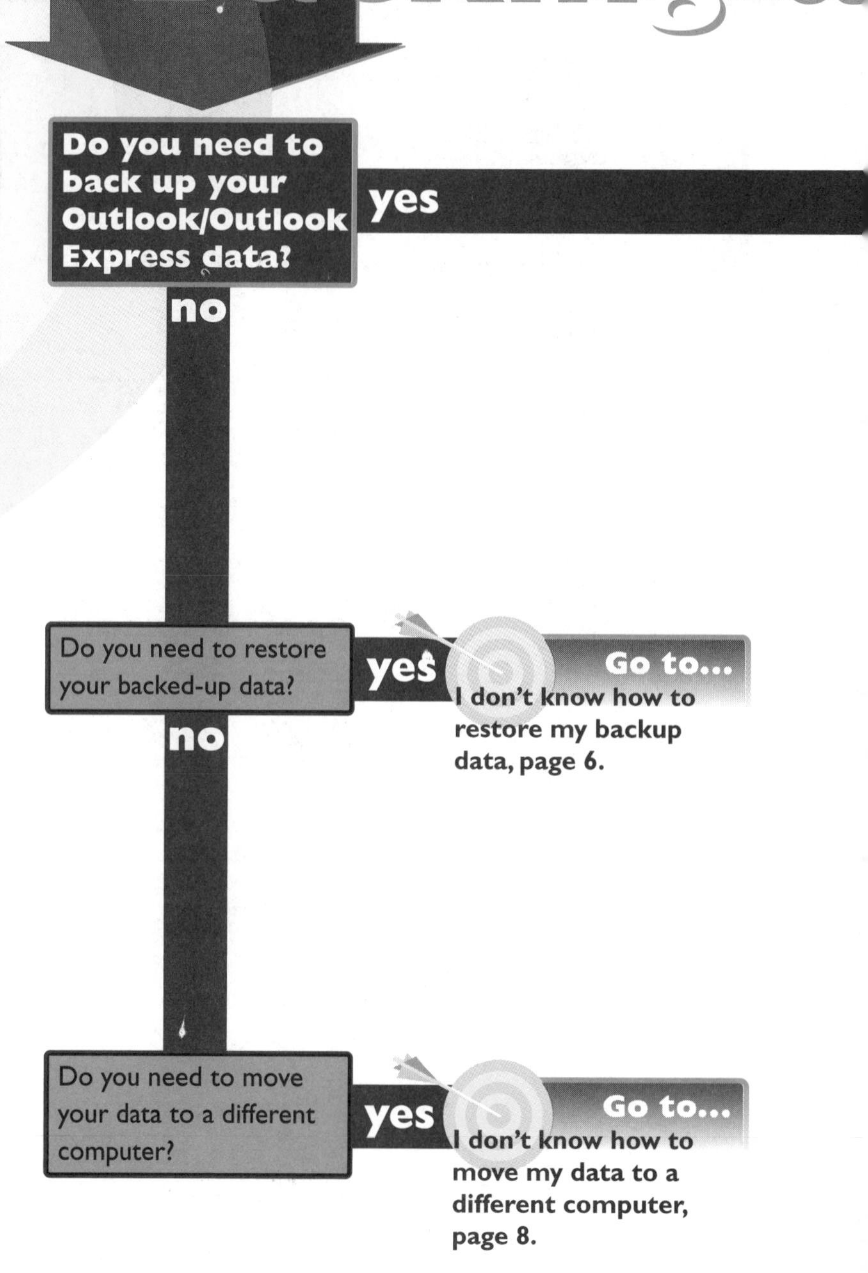

**Do you need to back up your Outlook/Outlook Express data?**

yes

no

Do you need to restore your backed-up data?

yes

**Go to...**
**I don't know how to restore my backup data, page 6.**

no

Do you need to move your data to a different computer?

yes

**Go to...**
**I don't know how to move my data to a different computer, page 8.**

Are you using Outlook on the Microsoft Exchange Server?

yes

## Quick fix

If you use Outlook on a network with the Microsoft Exchange Server, your Outlook data is most likely stored in a mailbox on the server, and your network administrator will make regular backups of your Outlook data. Even if your Outlook data is stored in a mailbox on the server, you might have a Personal Address Book (a file with a *.pab* extension) that's stored on your local hardrive. You can copy the Personal Address Book file and store the copy in your backup location.

To move the Personal Address Book file to a new computer:

1. On the new computer, click Services on the Tools menu.
2. Add the Personal Address Book to your list of Services.
3. Point the Personal Address Book dialog box to the location of the file.

no

## Go to...

**I don't know how to back up my data, page 4.**

**If your solution isn't here**
Check the general troubleshooting tips on page xiii.

# I don't know how to back up my data

## Source of the problem

Suppose that you live in a region of frequent power fluctuations (such as I do), and over time the power surges have scrambled your hard disk. Or perhaps a virus wipes out all your data…it happens when you least expect it. You need to create a backup copy of all your Outlook or Outlook Express data so you can restore the data after you get your hard disk fixed and reformatted. More likely, you might get a new computer and need to move all your existing data into the new copy of Microsoft Outlook or Microsoft Outlook Express.

## Outlook 2000 How to fix it

1. On the File menu, click Import And Export.
2. In the first wizard step, click Export To A File, and then click Next.
3. In the second wizard step, click Personal Folder File (.pst), and then click Next.
4. In the third wizard step, click the files you want to back up. To back up all your data, click Personal Folders near the top of the file list, and then select the Include Subfolders check box. To back up specific folders, click a specific folder to back up. (You need to run this procedure for each folder you want to back up.) ▶
5. Click Next. The final wizard step shows you the path where your backup file, *backup.pst,* will be saved. Feel free to click the Browse button and browse to a different folder in which to save the backup file (perhaps an easy-to-find Backups folder you create).

**Tip**

If you use Outlook on a network with the Microsoft Exchange Server, your Outlook data is most likely stored in a mailbox on the server, and your network administrator will make regular backups of your Outlook data. If you use Outlook without the Microsoft Exchange Server, your data is stored in Personal Folders on your hard disk and you can use this backup procedure.

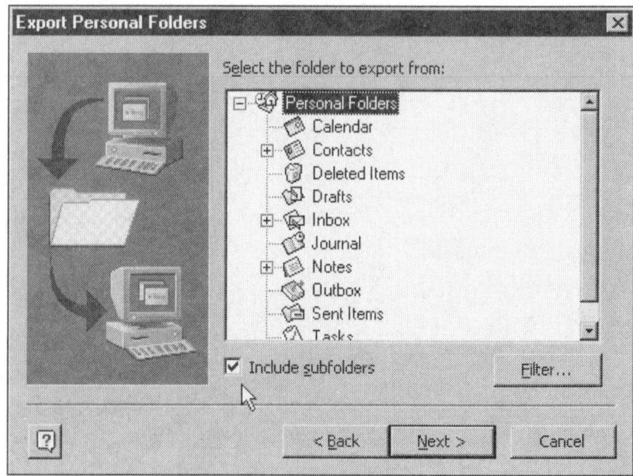

**Tip**
Storing a copy of your backup data on removable media, such as floppy or zip disks, is the only way to save the data if your hard disk crashes completely. You need to close Outlook before you can copy the *backup.pst* file.

6. Click a duplicates option. The Do Not Export Duplicate Items option speeds up the backup process, because items that were previously in this backup file won't be backed up again.

7. Click Finish. You are given the option to encrypt the file and create a password to protect it—make any choices you want (they're optional), and then click OK to complete the backup.

**Tip**
You can also use an AutoBackup utility that you can download free from this Microsoft web site: *officeupdate.microsoft.com/2000/downloadDetails/Pfbackup.htm.* This utility is easy to use, and you can copy the resulting *autobackup.pst* file without first closing Outlook.

## How to fix it

1. On the Tools menu, click Options.
2. On the Maintenance tab, click the Store Folder button.
3. In the Store Location dialog box, drag the cursor to select the entire path to the Store Folder (where your Outlook Express messages are stored), and press Ctrl+C to copy the path. ▶

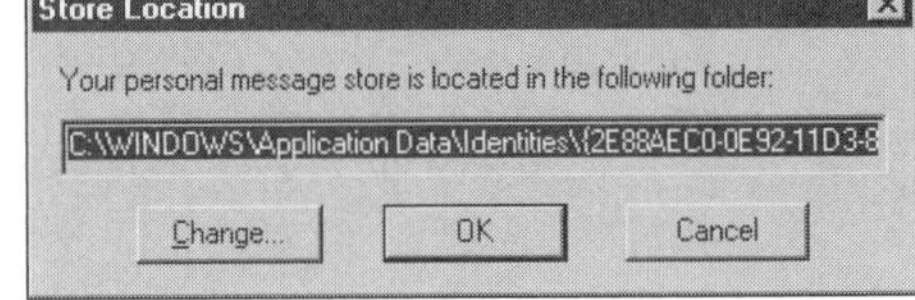


4. Click Cancel to close each dialog box.
5. Click the Start button, click Run, click in the Open box, and then press Ctrl+V to paste the path to your Store Folder.
6. Click OK to open the Store Folder.
7. Click all the files in the Store Folder, and then press Crtl+C to copy them. ▶

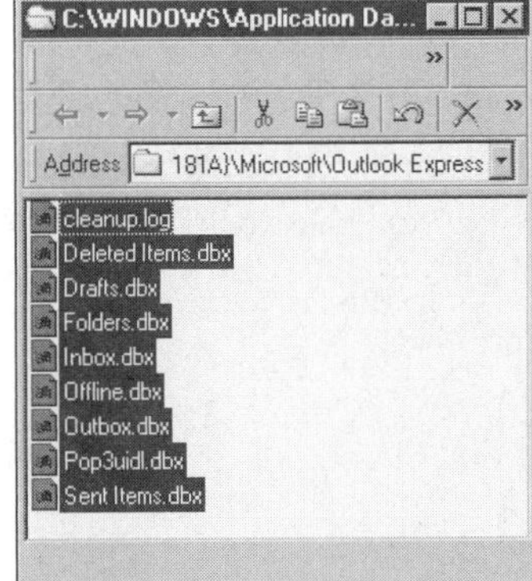


8. Paste the copied files into a different folder (a folder where you keep your backups), or onto a floppy disk—someplace where you can remember to find them if you need to restore your data.

**Warning**
Storing backup data on removable media, such as floppy or zip disks, is the only way to save the data if your hard disk crashes.

**Tip**
You can also click Copy on the Edit menu to copy the files.

# I don't know how to restore my backup data

## Source of the problem

You've dutifully backed up your data, and of course you remember (or wrote down) where you stored those backup files. Now some unforeseen event has wiped out your data—perhaps your nephew somehow deleted your *outlook.pst* file while playing with your computer. Somehow, all your Outlook data has disappeared.

Relax—you've made a backup file, so your data is safe. First, if it's a major catastrophe, get your hard disk fixed and reformatted at your local computer repair shop, and then reinstall all your programs. After Outlook is up and running, you can restore the data from your backup files.

## Outlook 2000 How to fix it

1. On the File menu, click Import And Export.
2. In the first wizard step, click Import From Another Program Or File, and then click Next.
3. In the second wizard step, click Personal Folder File (.pst), and then click Next.
4. In the third wizard step, look at the path and folder name in the File To Import box to be sure it's pointing to your backup file (click the Browse button if you need to locate the *backup.pst* file). Click an option for importing duplicates, and then click Next.
5. In the fourth wizard step, click the folder you want to retrieve backup data from.
6. In the last wizard step, click Finish.

**Tip**

This is the same dialog box that's used to import archived data, and in that case you'd want to make a decision about importing duplicates. But if you're restoring data, there won't be any duplicates, so it doesn't matter which duplicates option you click.

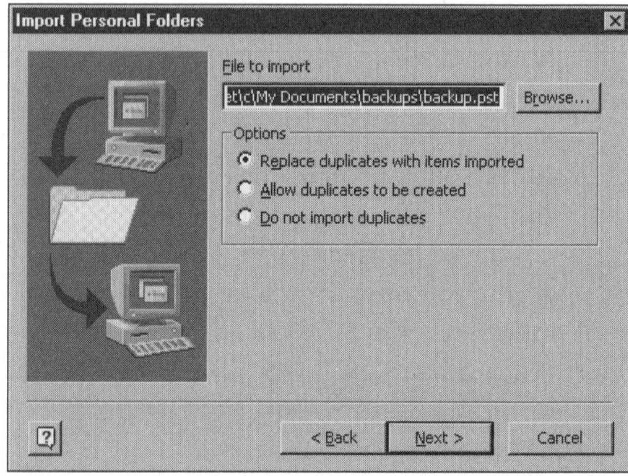

## How to fix it

1. On the File menu, click Import, and then click Messages.
2. In the Outlook Express Import dialog box, click Microsoft Outlook Express 5, and then click Next.
3. In the Import From OE5 dialog box, click the Import Mail From An OE5 Store Directory option, and then click OK. ▶

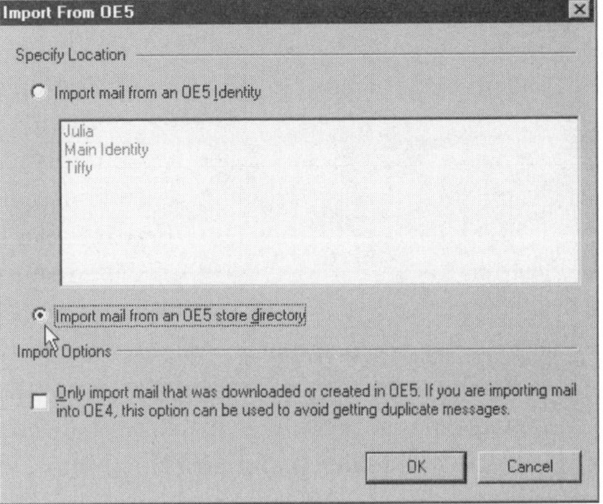


4. In the next Outlook Express Import dialog box, browse to the folder where you copied your backup files (they all have *.dbx* extensions), and then click Next.
5. In the next Outlook Express Import dialog box select the backup folders you want to import, and then click Next.
6. In the last Outlook Express Import dialog box, click Finish.

## If you want to know more about Outlook data

All your Outlook data is stored in a Personal Folder file called *outlook.pst*. Within that file, the data is separated into Inbox, Calendar, Tasks, and so forth, but it's all stored together in a single file and can be retrieved only by Outlook. When you create the backup file, *backup.pst,* it's a copy of the *outlook.pst* data that includes only the folders you choose to back up, and the backup file can be stored anywhere on your hard disk (you should save copies of backup files off your hard disk, too, to fully protect the data). Your toolbar and menu settings are stored in a file called *outcmd.dat,* which can also be backed up, restored, and moved. Your Outlook bar settings are stored in a file with the *.fav* extension, and although it can be backed up and restored, it can't be moved to another machine, because those links and shortcuts are unique to the Outlook mailbox where they were created.

You can also archive your Outlook data, which backs up and stores your aged data, on a regular basis by scheduling AutoArchive for the specific folders you want to archive.

Archived data is stored out of sight in a file called *archive.pst,* and you restore it using the same procedures as those for restoring backup files. Archived data won't be included in a backup file, because it's already in its own file.

**Tip**

To AutoArchive data, click the Tools menu, and then click the Other tab. Click the AutoArchive button, select the AutoArchive Every check box, set a number of days for your schedule, and click OK to close each dialog box. On the schedule you set, Outlook asks whether you'd like to archive your data. When you click Yes, all your old data is moved into an *archive.pst* file. You can learn more about archiving in the Outlook help files or an in-depth book about how to use Outlook.

# I don't know how to move my data to a different computer

## Source of the problem

When you get a new computer and want to move your existing Outlook and Outlook Express data into the new machine, the best way to transfer data to your new computer is to create backup files, move the files into the new computer, and then import copies of the backups into the new installation of Outlook or Outlook Express.

The files can be transferred to the new computer on a floppy disk, or by moving or copying the files over the network (if your old and new computer are on the same network), or by attaching the files to an e-mail message and mailing them to the new computer. In the new machine, you can place the files in any easy-to-find folder and import them into Outlook and Outlook Express.

**Tip**

If you've archived Outlook data, the archived data and backup data are in separate files. You need to move both files to transfer a complete set of data to the new computer.

## Outlook 2000 How to fix it

1. Copy the backup file to an easy-to-find folder in the new computer (perhaps a newly created Backups folder).
2. On the File menu, click Import And Export.
3. In the first wizard step, click Import From Another Program Or File, and then click Next.
4. In the second wizard step, click Personal Folder File (.pst), and then click Next.
5. In the third wizard step, click the Browse button and locate the backup file.
6. In the Open Personal Folders dialog box, click the name of the backup or archive file, and then click Open. The path to the backup or archive file appears in the wizard's File To Import box.
7. In the File To Import dialog box, click a duplicates option, and then click Next.
8. In the fourth wizard step, click the folders you want to import.
   - To import all the backed up data, click Personal Folders at the top of the list.

- To import a single folder or subfolder, click that folder name. ▶
- To import a subset of the data in a folder (for example, just the data accumulated during the current month), click the Filter button and create filter criteria to specify the data you want to import.

9. Click Finish. The data you specified in step 8 is imported into Outlook in the new machine.

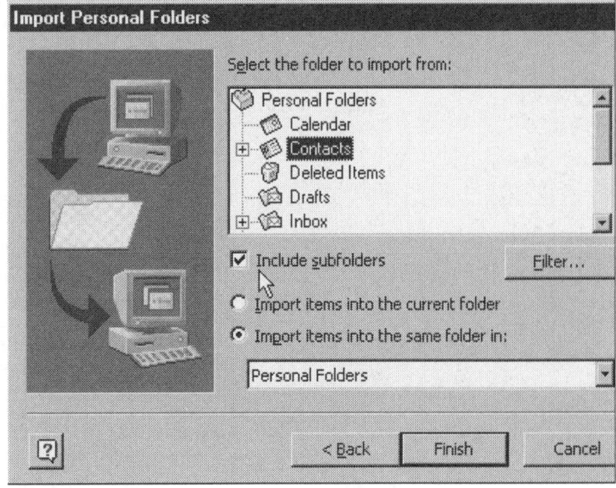


## Outlook Express How to fix it

1. Copy the backup *.dbx* files to an easy-to-find folder in the new computer (perhaps a newly created Backups folder).
2. In the Outlook Express Import dialog box, click Microsoft Outlook Express 5, and then click Next.
3. In the Import From OE5 dialog box, click the Import Mail From An OE5 Store Directory option, and then click OK.
4. In the next Outlook Express Import dialog box, browse to the folder where you copied your backup files, and then click Next.
5. In the next Outlook Express Import dialog box, click the backup folders you want to import (press Ctrl or Shift to select multiple folders), and then click Next. ▶
6. In the last Outlook Express Import dialog box, click Finish.

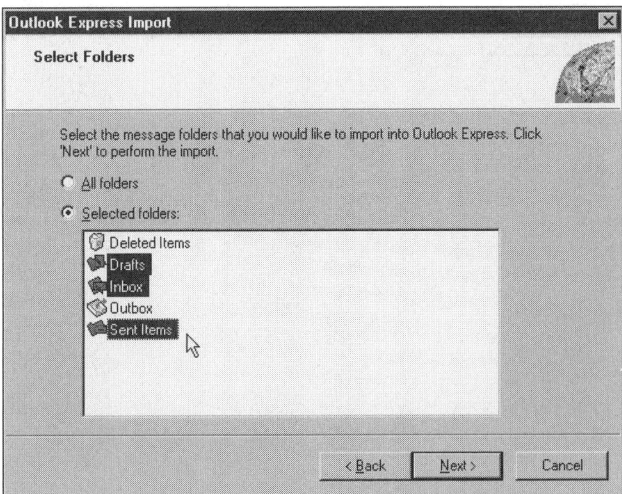

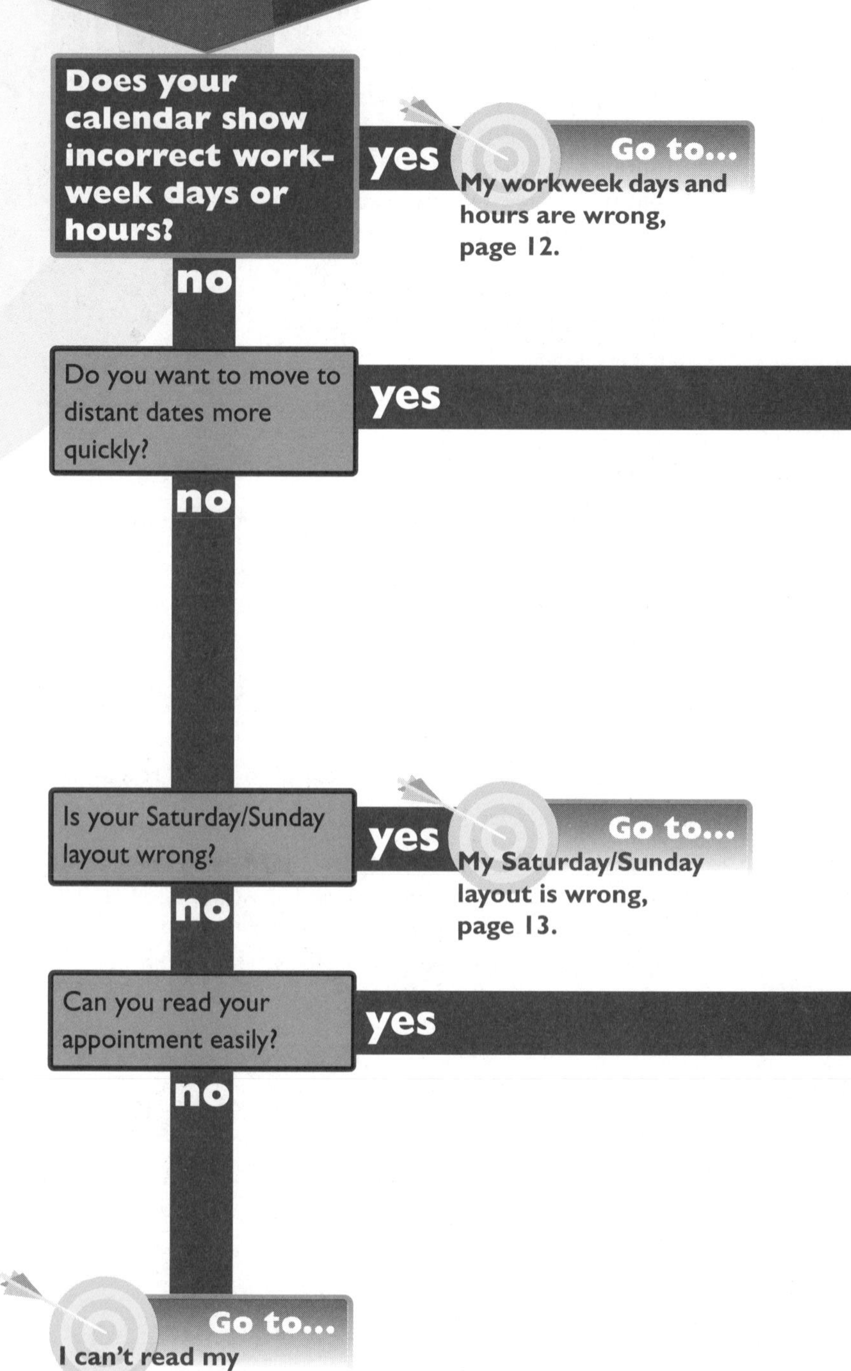
Does your calendar show incorrect work-week days or hours?
yes
Go to...
My workweek days and hours are wrong, page 12.
no
Do you want to move to distant dates more quickly?
yes
no
Is your Saturday/Sunday layout wrong?
yes
Go to...
My Saturday/Sunday layout is wrong, page 13.
no
Can you read your appointment easily?
yes
no
Go to...
I can't read my appointments easily, page 16.

## Quick fix

You can move to months that are far in the future or past more quickly:
To move the Personal Address Book file to a new computer:

1. Switch to a Daily or Weekly view so that Date Navigators (thumbnail months) are visible in the upper-right corner of the Calendar window.
2. Point to the month title of any Date Navigator and then press and hold down the left mouse button. A list of seven months appears, including three before and three after the month you're pointing to. Point to the month you want; when it's highlighted, release the mouse button.
3. To jump forward or backward further than three months: while you're pressing the left mouse button, move the pointer slightly above the list of months to scroll backward. Move the pointer slightly below the list to scroll forward. Point to the month you want; when it's highlighted, release the mouse button.

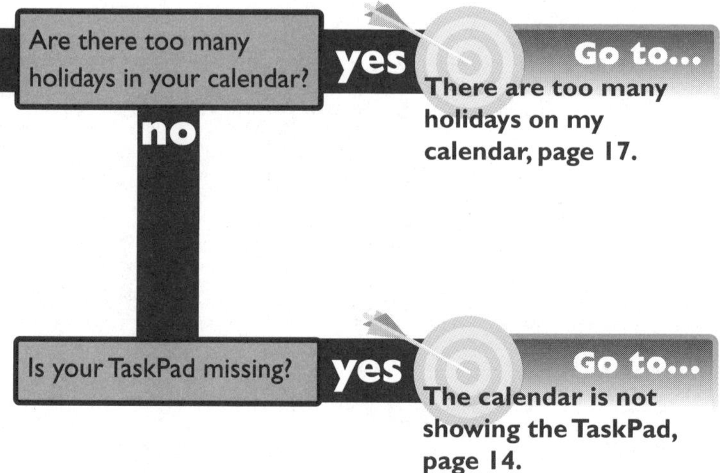
Are there too many holidays in your calendar?
yes
Go to...
There are too many holidays on my calendar, page 17.
no
Is your TaskPad missing?
yes
Go to...
The calendar is not showing the TaskPad, page 14.

**If your solution isn't here**
Check these related chapters:
Printing, page 212
Backing up and moving data, page 2
Or see the general troubleshooting tips on page xiii.

# My workweek days and hours are wrong

## Source of the problem

The Calendar folder was designed to be your *personal* calendar, to record activities and appointments for your own workdays and workhours, and when you click the Work Week button in the Calendar toolbar, it would sure be nice if it showed *your* workweek.

But the default workweek that Outlook comes with isn't everyone's workweek. It's becoming more common to work four 10-hour days each week, or to work a swing or night shift (the Calendar assumes, however, that you work the same shift on all your workdays). For the Calendar to be truly useful, you need to be able to alter the workdays and hours to show your schedule.

## How to fix it

1. On the Tools menu, click Options.
2. On the Preferences tab, click the Calendar Options button.
3. In the Calendar Options dialog box, under Calendar Work Week, select the check boxes for your work-week days (and clear the check boxes for your days off). ▶
4. Below the day check boxes, set your workday start time in the Start Time box and set your work-day end time in the End Time box.
5. Click OK to close each dialog box.

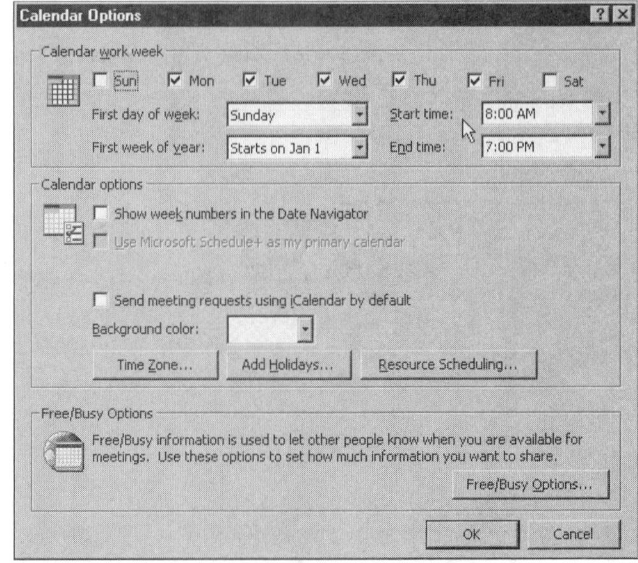

# My Saturday/Sunday layout is wrong

## Source of the problem

When you look at a monthly calendar, do you like to see Saturday and Sunday as smaller spaces that share a single column so your weekday spaces are larger and can record more events? Or would you rather show every day of the week in its own full-size space so there's room for several events on Saturday and Sunday? If the monthly calendars don't display the days the way you find them most useful, you need to change them. After all, it's *your* calendar.

## How to fix it

1. Open the Calendar folder.
2. On the View menu, point to Current View, and then click Day/Week/Month view. (It doesn't matter whether you have the Daily, Weekly, or Monthly view displayed.)
3. On the View menu, point to Current View, and then click Customize Current View.
4. In the View Summary dialog box, click the Other Settings button. ▶
5. In the Format Day/Week/Month View dialog box, select the Compress Weekend Days check box. ▶
6. Click OK to close each dialog box.

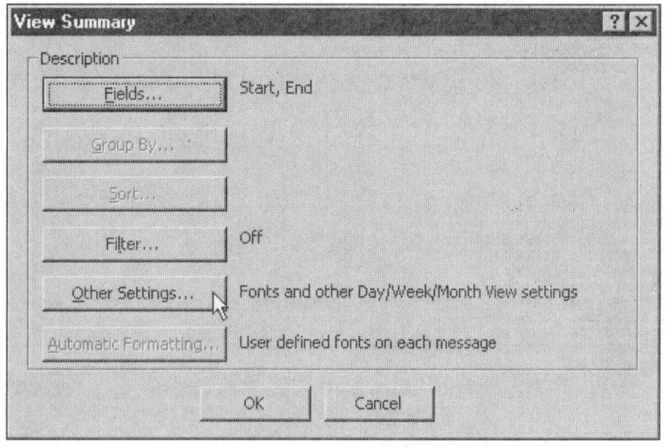


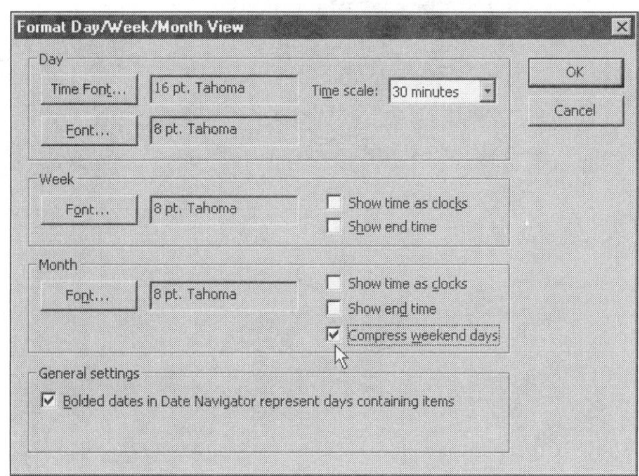


**Tip**

If you want to know what a particular check box does, select its label with the right mouse button to read a short description.

# The Calendar is not showing the TaskPad

## Source of the problem

The TaskPad is a useful little feature in Outlook, an abbreviated list of tasks that you can look at while you look at your calendar and decide where to fit each task into your schedule. But your TaskPad can disappear if you're clicking and dragging randomly while you learn to use Outlook, or if your favorite nephew is playing on your computer. You need to find it and get it back in position.

## How to fix it

1. Open the Calendar folder.
2. Click the Daily or Weekly view (TaskPad doesn't appear in the Monthly view).
3. Any of these maneuvers might bring your TaskPad back into view:
   - Maximize the Outlook window by double-clicking the Outlook title bar. ▶

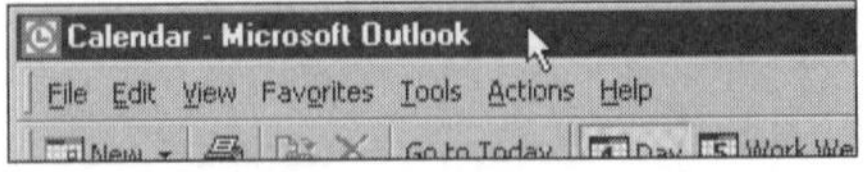


   - If the Folder List is visible, hide or resize it. To hide the Folder List, click the X button in its upper-right corner. To resize the Folder List, point to the right border of the Folder List, and when the pointer changes to a double-headed arrow, drag the border to the left to narrow the Folder List. ▶

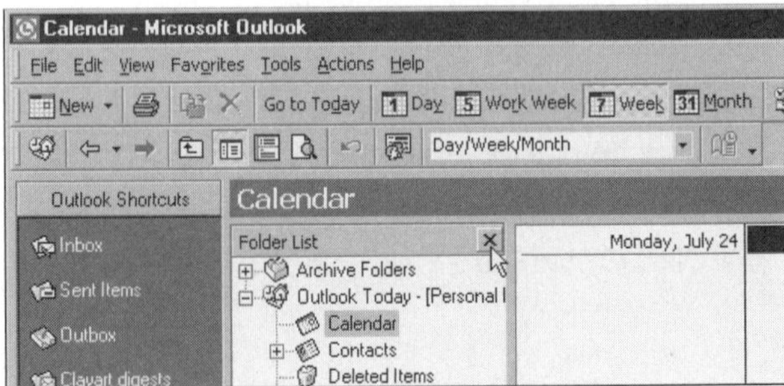

- If there are no Date Navigator months visible, point to the right border of the Outlook window, and when the pointer changes to a double-headed arrow, drag the border to the left. ▶

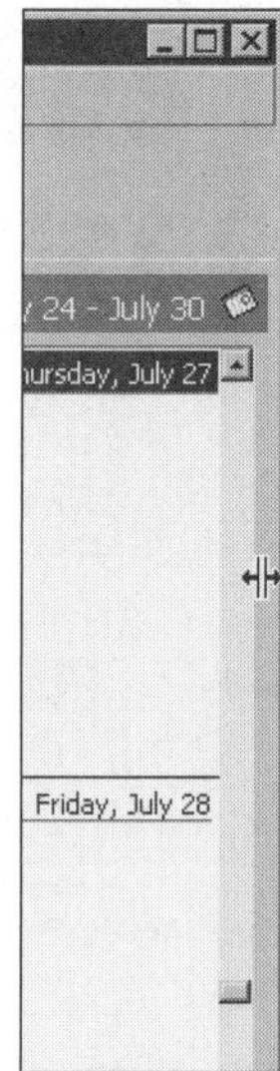


- If there are Date Navigator months down the right side of the Outlook window, point to the bottom border of the Date Navigator column, and when the pointer changes to a double-headed arrow, drag the border upward at least 2 inches. ▶

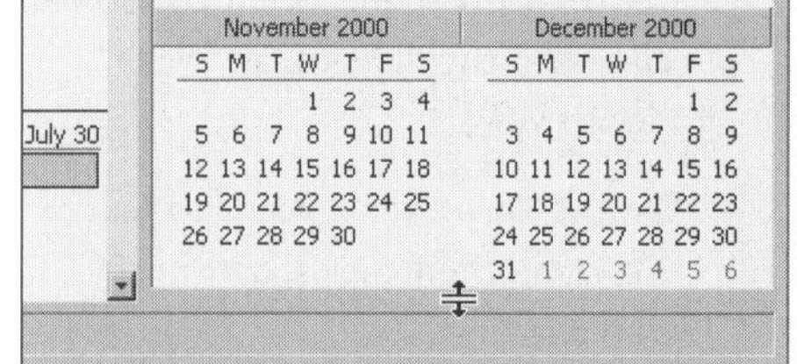


## Other reasons why your TaskPad might be missing

TaskPad might be missing for reasons other than inadvertent clicking and dragging.

If no Tasks folder is available, there won't be a TaskPad. For example, if you're looking at a Calendar folder in a backup or archive Personal Folders File that doesn't include a Tasks folder, there won't be a TaskPad in that Calendar.

If you're looking at someone else's shared Calendar but you haven't been granted access to the Tasks folder, you won't see the TaskPad. If you need to see the TaskPad, ask that person to grant you permission to the Tasks folder in his or her computer.

# I can't read my appointments easily

## Source of the problem

The default font size in all the Calendar views (Daily, Weekly, and Monthly) is 8 points, which is a mere one-ninth of an inch. For some of us, that's awfully small type to read. If you find it too small for comfort, you need to resize the font to be larger and more readable.

## How to fix it

1. On the View menu, point to Current View, and then click Day/Week/Month view.
2. On the View menu, point to Current View, and then click Customize Current View.
3. In the View Summary dialog box, click the Other Settings button.
4. In the Format Day/Week/Month View dialog box, click the Font button under the view (Day, Week, or Month) you want to resize. ▶

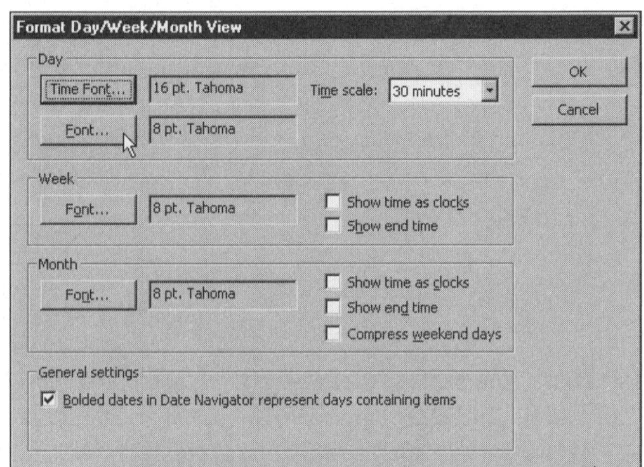


5. In the Font dialog box, under Size, click a larger font size. ▶

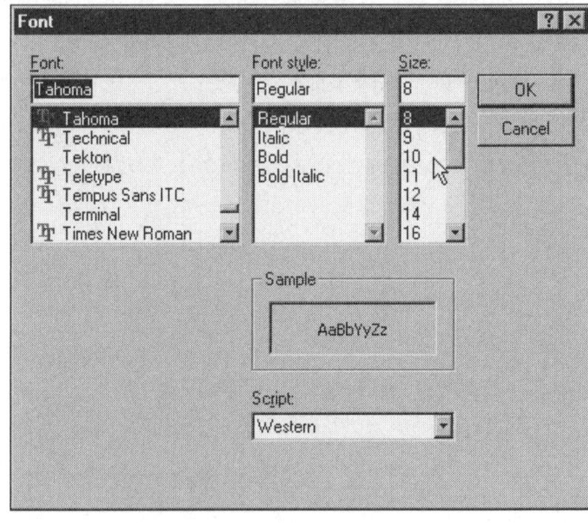


6. Click OK to close each dialog box.

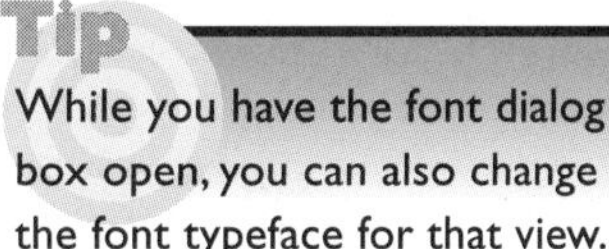

**Tip**
While you have the font dialog box open, you can also change the font typeface for that view.

# There are too many holidays in my calendar

## Source of the problem

You've just learned how to add holidays to your calendar. It was fun looking up when National Day is in Switzerland, and helpful to know when Father's Day is in the U.S. next year. But now you've got so many holidays in your calendar that there's barely room for your appointments. You need to remove lots of holidays, but removing them one-by-one is tedious and time-consuming. There is an easier way to remove holidays (it's not as automatic as adding them was, but it's pretty easy).

## How to fix it

1. In the Calendar folder, on the View menu, point to Current View, and then click Events. Your calendar switches to a table-type view.
2. In the new table view, click the Location header button to sort all the events (and holidays) by location. Each set of holidays is sorted together into a group according to the country of origin.
3. Drag down the left side to select all the holidays in the group you want to remove. ▶
4. Click the Delete button on the toolbar. That set of holidays is removed, and you can switch your view back to the view you like best.

### Tip

To add holidays, on the Tools menu, click Options. On the Preferences tab, click the Calendar Options button. In the Calendar Options dialog box, click the Add Holidays button. Select the check boxes for the countries and religious holidays you want to add (and clear any check boxes for holidays that are already in your calendar, or they'll be added a second time). Click OK to close each dialog box.

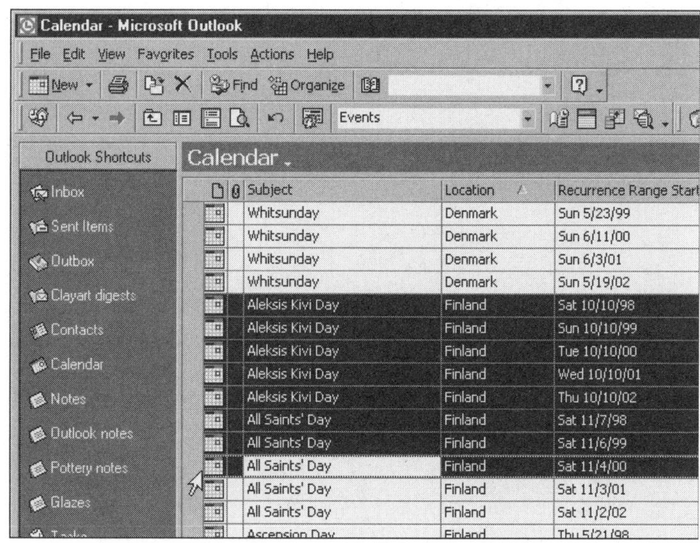

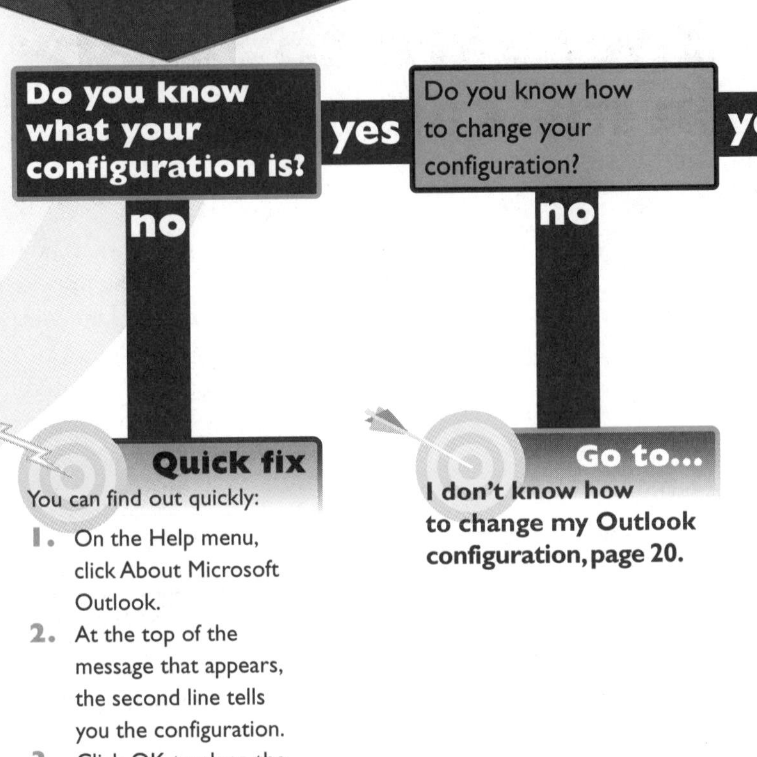
Do you know what your configuration is?
yes
Do you know how to change your configuration?
yes
no
no
Quick fix
Go to...

You can find out quickly:

1. On the Help menu, click About Microsoft Outlook.
2. At the top of the message that appears, the second line tells you the configuration.
3. Click OK to close the message.

**I don't know how to change my Outlook configuration, page 20.**

Can you find the Reconfiguration Mail Support button?

**no**

Do you have an e-mail account set up in your computer?

**yes**

## Quick fix

If there's no Reconfigure Mail Support button at the bottom of the Mail Delivery tab, and you have an e-mail account set up in another program in your computer, it's because you (or someone) chose the No E-Mail configuration when installing Outlook.

You can transfer the mail account settings from your existing account into Outlook, and then the Reconfigure Mail Support button will appear.

1. On the File menu, click Import And Export.
2. In the Import And Export Wizard, click Import Internet Mail Account Settings, and then click Next.
3. In the Internet Connection Wizard, follow the wizard steps to import your existing account information into Outlook.

**no**

## Go to...

**I don't know how to set up a new e-mail account, page 114.**

**If your solution isn't here**
Check these related chapters:

Faxing, page 128
Switching e-mail programs, page 252
Or see the general troubleshooting tips on page xiii.

# I don't know how to change my Outlook configuration

## Source of the problem

Outlook has two configurations: Internet Mail Only and Corporate/Workgroup. Each configuration offers different features and does some things better than others. For example, if you use the Internet Mail Only configuration, Remote Mail is unavailable, but you have more direct control over the list of names in your e-mail address book. On the other hand, if you're heading out of town with your laptop computer and want to use Remote Mail from your hotel room to limit your message downloads (and telephone time), you need to switch to the Corporate/Workgroup configuration. It's easy to solve the problem of wrong configuration—you just switch! And you can switch back and forth between Corporate/Workgroup and Internet Mail Only whenever you need to.

## How to fix it

1. On the Tools menu, click Options.
2. If your current configuration is Internet Mail Only, click the Mail Delivery tab. If your current configuration is Corporate/Workgroup, click the Mail Services tab.
3. Click the Reconfigure Mail Support button. ▶

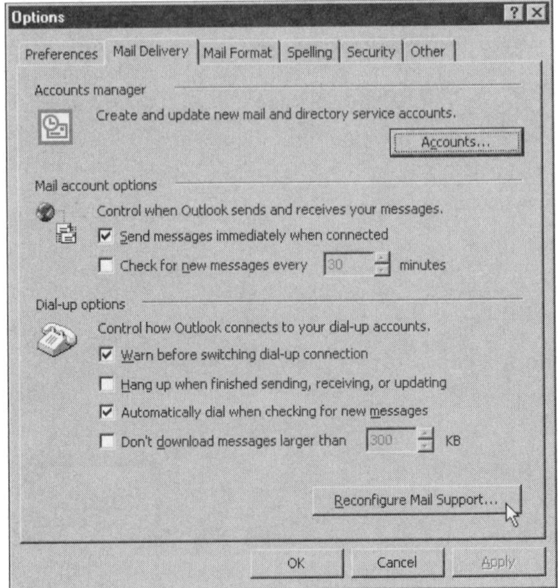

4. In the E-mail Service Options dialog box, click the option for the configuration you want. ▶

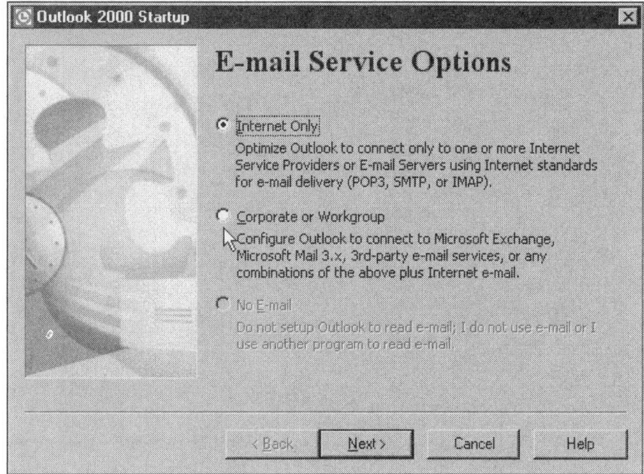


5. A message appears to warn you about some of the features you'll lose when you switch—click Yes to complete the switch.

   Outlook closes, but you can restart it immediately. When Outlook restarts, your computer will take a few moments to install files for the changed configuration, and then the new configuration will be ready to use.

## If you want to know which Outlook configuration to use

Your Outlook configuration is based on how you send and receive e-mail. If you use Outlook on a network that uses the Microsoft Exchange Server as a mail and communications server, you need to keep Outlook in the Corporate/Workgroup configuration so you can send and receive e-mail and take full advantage of all of Outlook's workgroup features (such as shared Contacts and Calendar folders). The Exchange Server exchanges e-mail with the outside world, and your e-mail messages travel to and from the Exchange Server through a Microsoft Mail mailbox. Your network administrator sets up the mailboxes and handles all your e-mail server issues.

If you use Outlook on a non-networked computer, or on a network that doesn't depend on a central mail server and mailboxes, you send and receive mail directly through a modem and a dial-up connection to an Internet service provider (ISP). In this case, you can use Outlook in either configuration and switch configurations when you want to use the features available in the other configuration. I prefer to use Outlook in the Internet Mail Only configuration because I find the Select Names dialog box easier to use in this configuration; but occasionally I switch to the Corporate/Workgroup configuration so that I can use Remote Mail to download only message headers and then choose which waiting messages to download. If I'm getting my e-mail away from home and paying for the telephone connection, Remote Mail can considerably reduce connection time and charges.

If you don't have any e-mail program on your computer when you install Outlook, or if you select the No E-mail option when you install Outlook, you won't have the option of changing the configuration. Even though you can create an e-mail message, there won't be a Send button in the message because there's no e-mail account to send it over—any messages you create accumulate in your Outbox until you set up an e-mail account.

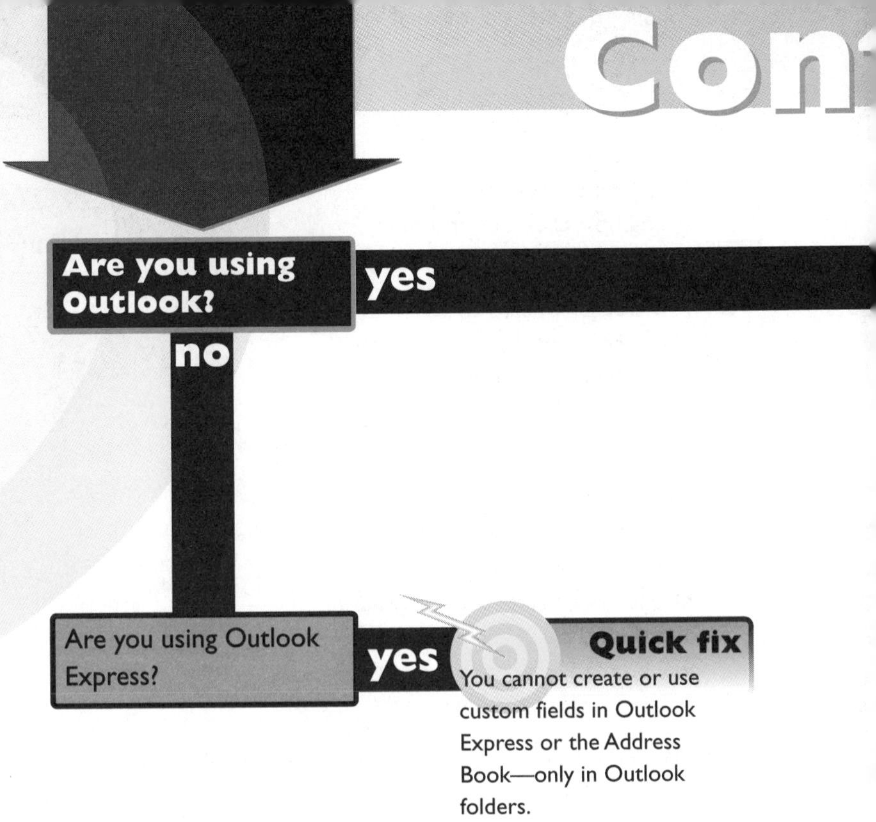

# Con

**Are you using Outlook?**

yes

no

Are you using Outlook Express?

yes

**Quick fix**

You cannot create or use custom fields in Outlook Express or the Address Book—only in Outlook folders.

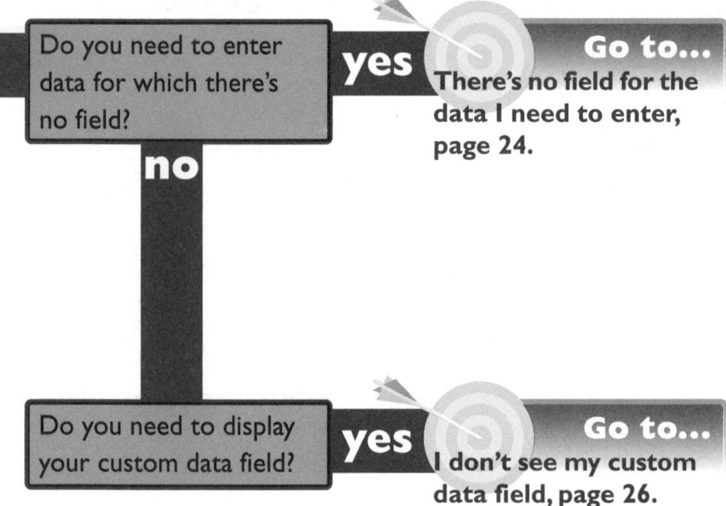
Do you need to enter data for which there's no field?
yes
Go to...
There's no field for the data I need to enter, page 24.
no
Do you need to display your custom data field?
yes
Go to...
I don't see my custom data field, page 26.

**If your solution isn't here**
Check this related chapter:
Contacts, folder display, page 28
Or see the general troubleshooting tips on page xiii.

# There's no field for the data I need to enter

## Source of the problem

Lots of us need to keep track of data for which there's no built-in field in Outlook. For example, you might need to record employee ID numbers, or perhaps you need a yes/no field to track active membership in an organization. If you can record data such as this, it's easier to filter contacts for a mail merge or organize a long list of contacts. If there's no built-in field for the data you need to record, you can create your own field.

## How to fix it

1. Open the folder or subfolder in which you want to create a custom field. (In this example, I open the Contacts folder.)
2. On the View menu, point to Current View, and then click Customize Current View.
3. In the View Summary dialog box, click the Fields button.
4. In the Show Fields dialog box, click the New Field button.
5. In the New Field dialog box, in the Name box, type a name for the new field. ▶
6. In the Type list box, select the type of data the field will contain. For most data, the appropriate type is Text.
7. In the Format list box, select a display format for your data. (If you selected Text in the Type box, the only Format option is Text.)

**Tip**

You can show the Show Fields dialog box more quickly if you right-click an empty space in the window and then click Show Fields on the shortcut menu.

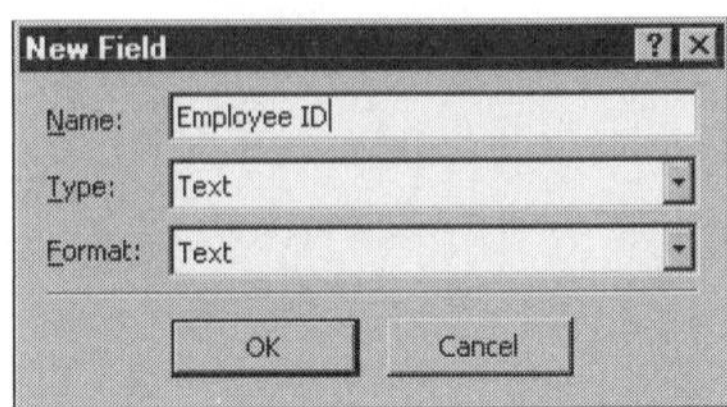

8. Click OK. In the Show Fields dialog box, the new custom field appears in the Show These Fields In This Order box. ▶

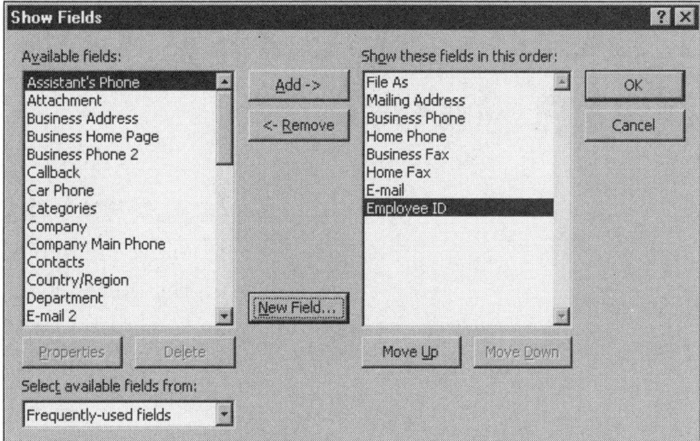


9. Click OK to close the Show Fields dialog box, and then click OK to close the View Summary dialog box. Whichever view is displayed in your folder, the new custom field is also displayed. You can click an empty field to select it and then type an appropriate entry. ▶

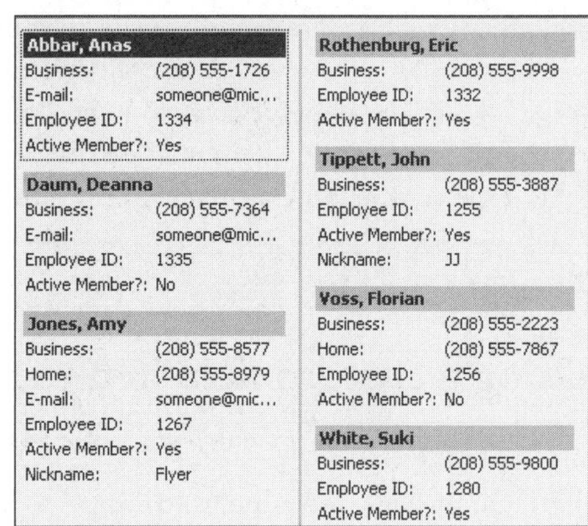


## If you want to know more about custom fields

You might not really need a custom field. There are many more built-in Contacts fields than are displayed in any default view.

Open the Show Fields dialog box (shown in step 9 ) and select different field categories in the Select Available Fields From box. In each category you select, look at the fields in the Available Fields list above the box. You might find exactly the field you need.

There are four generic text-type fields in the Miscellaneous Fields category: User Field 1, User Field 2, User Field 3, and User Field 4. You can't rename them, but they're ready to use if you need them (you should write, perhaps in an Outlook note, what kind of data the field holds).

# I don't see my custom data field

## Source of the problem

If you've created a custom data field, it won't be displayed on the built-in Contact form. Although it's possible to create a custom Contact form that displays custom fields, you don't need a custom form to display and use your custom data fields. You can display custom fields right away in a table-type view of your Contacts folder as well as in the Card view of your Contacts folder. Table-type views often make data entry and sorting easier, and the Card view makes it easier to see all the data for each contact.

In this example, I demonstrate displaying and using a custom field, Employee ID, in both a table-type view and a Card view in my TS Contacts subfolder.

## How to fix it

### Using a custom field in a table-type view

1. Open the folder in which you created the custom field.
2. On the View menu, point to Current View, and select a table-type view. In a Contacts folder, the Phone List view is a simple table-type view.
3. Right-click the column heading row, and then click Field Chooser.
4. In the Field Chooser dialog box, select User-Defined Fields In Folder in the box at the top.
5. Drag the custom field from the Field Chooser dialog box to the column heading row. ▶
6. Close the Field Chooser by clicking its Close button.

   With your custom field displayed, you can enter or edit data, and you can use the custom field to sort and filter the list.

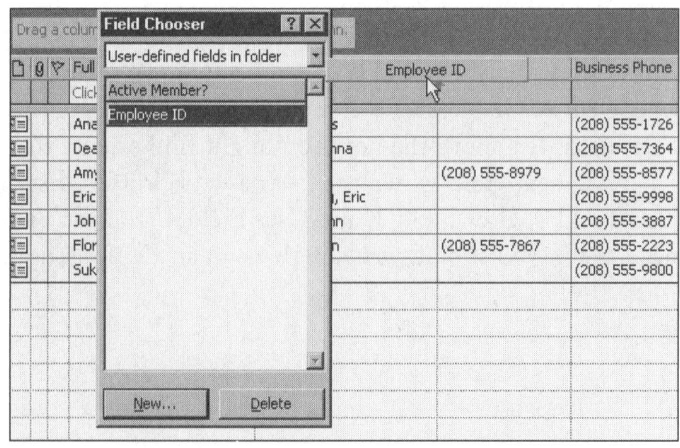

## Using a custom field in the card view

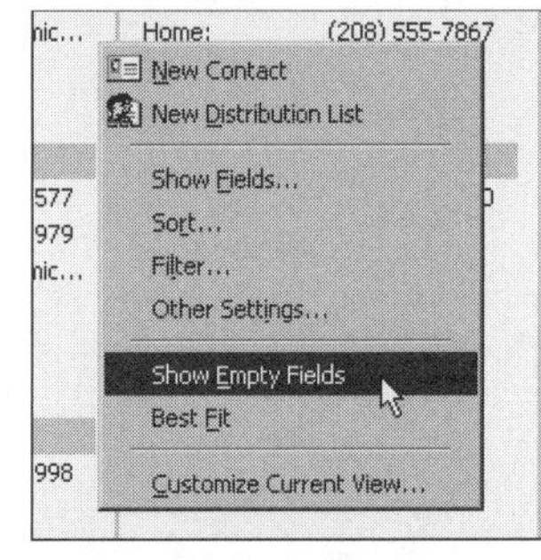


1. On the View menu, point to Current View, and then click Address Cards.
2. Right-click any empty space in the window, and then click Show Empty Fields. ▶
3. If the field you need to enter or edit isn't displayed, right-click an empty space in the window, and then click Show Fields.
4. If the field you want to display is a custom field you created, in the Select Available Fields From box, select User-Defined Fields In Folder.
5. In the Available Fields list (on the left side of the dialog box), double-click each field you want to add to the view. ▶

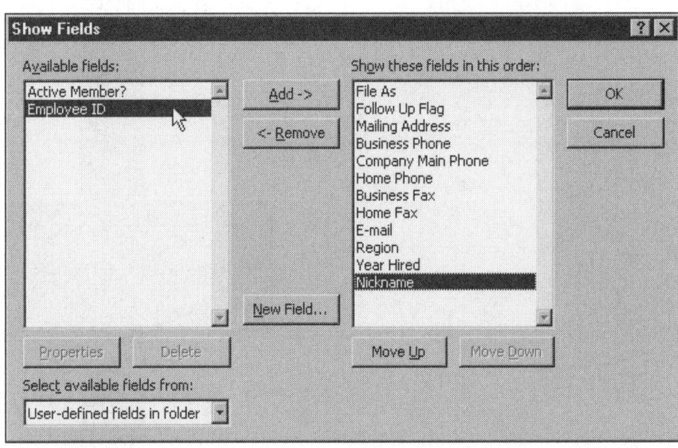


6. To move a field to a different position in the card view, drag it up or down in the Show These Fields In This Order list (on the right). ▶
7. Click OK to close the Show Fields dialog box.

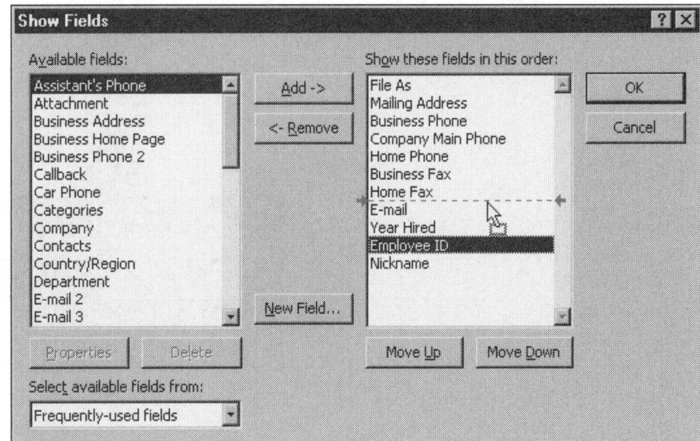


8. In a contact for which you need to enter or edit data in the custom field, click in the custom field and type or edit the entry. ▶

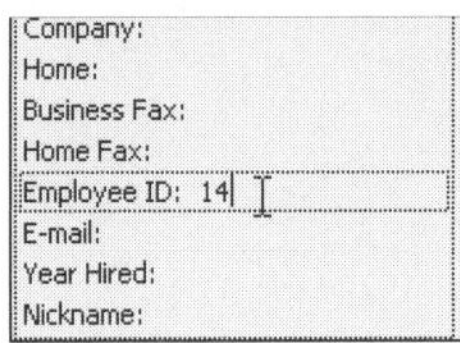

# Cont

**Do you need to sort your Contacts card view by a field other than "File As"?**

yes

no

Are letter buttons missing from your Contacts window?

yes

**Quick fix**

Check your sort order—if Contacts cards are sorted by a non-text field (such as birthday or anniversary, which are date fields), there won't be any letter buttons.

no

Do you need to separate a group of contacts from the rest of the list on a regular schedule?

yes

**Go to...**

I don't know how to sort my Contacts card view, page 30.

**Go to...**

I need to segregate a group of contact entries efficiently, page 31.

**If your solution isn't here**

Check this related chapter:

Contacts, custom data, page 22

Or see the general troubleshooting tips on page xiii.

# I don't know how to sort my Contacts card view

## Source of the problem

Your Contacts card view is sorted by the File As field, which is an easy way to locate a contact's phone number—click a letter button on the right side of the Contacts window to jump to the correct part of the alphabetical list, and then scroll to the contact entry you want to see. But what if you have a Contacts list that's hundreds of entries long, and the only thing you remember about a contact is the company name? You can sort your card view by the Company field and scan the contact names in the company to locate the person you need to find.

## How to fix it

1. On the View menu, point to Current View, and then click Customize Current View.
2. In the View Summary dialog box, click the Sort button. ▶

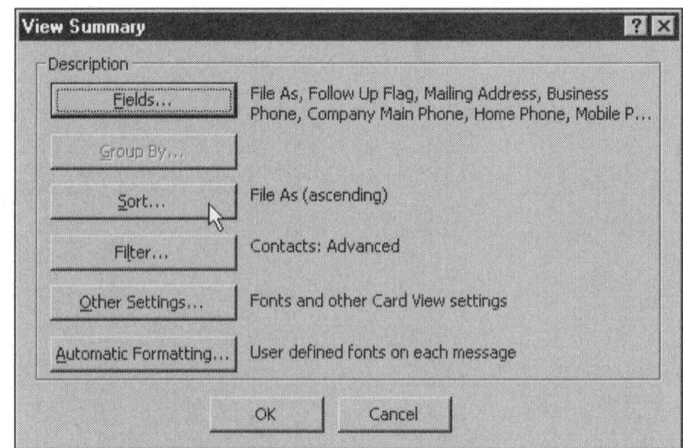


3. In the Sort dialog box (shown in the lower figure on the right), in the Sort Items By list box, select Company. ▶
4. Click OK.
5. If you see a message telling you that the field named Company is not shown, and asking whether you want to show it, click Yes. (If you click No, the cards will be sorted by company, but you won't know which contacts belong to which company.)

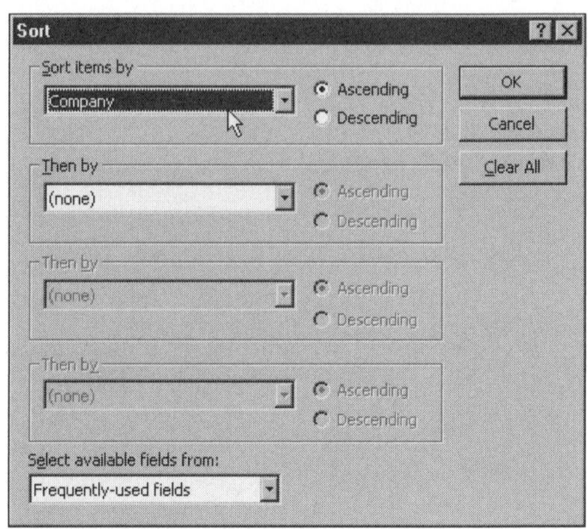

# I need to segregate a group of contact entries efficiently

## Source of the problem

Part of your job requires that you send a weekly update fax to all your contacts, which you know you can do using the mail-merge capabilities of Outlook. Segregating your contacts by fax numbers, and doing so quickly, would make your job much easier. The solution is to define a new view of your Contacts list that filters those entries that have business fax numbers; then all you have to do each week is select that view and run your mail merge.

## How to fix it

1. On the View menu, point to Current View, and then click Define Views.
2. In the Define Views dialog box, click the New button.
3. In the Create A New View dialog box, type a name for the view (something easy to recognize, such as Fax Merge) and select the Card type of view.

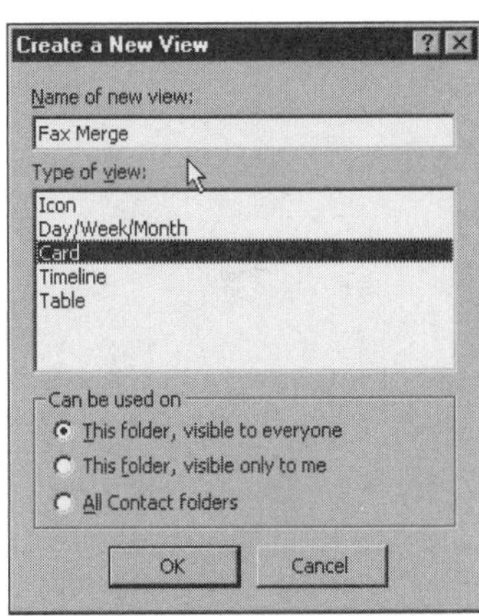


4. Click OK.
5. In the View Settings dialog box, click the Filter button.
6. In the Filter dialog box, set up the filter for the view. For my fax-merge view, I set a criterion on the Advanced tab that reads Business Fax Is Not Empty. (Be sure you click the Add To List button to add the filter criteria to the Find Items That Match These Criteria list.)

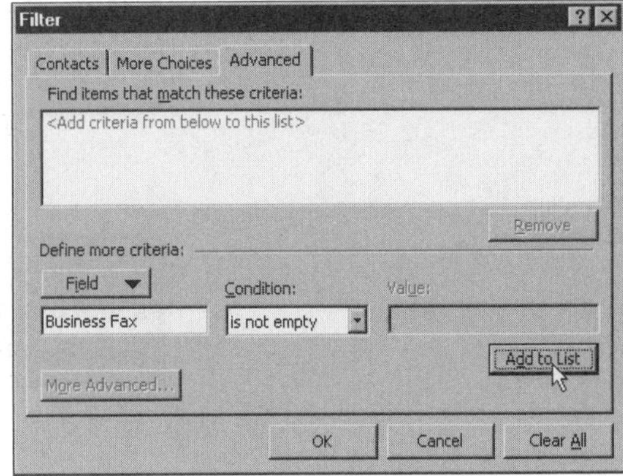


7. Click OK twice, and then click Close to close the dialog boxes.

   Now you can display your new view and then run the mail merge for the contacts in the current view.

**Do you need a quick way to change the same company address for many contacts?**

yes

no

Is you Contacts folder accessible to too many people on your network?

yes

no

Does your search for a contact containing a specific word come up empty?

yes

**Quick fix**

In the Find Items In Contacts pane, be sure the Search All Text In The Contact check box is selected.

no

When you click the Display Map Of Address button in a Contact form, do you get the wrong map?

yes

no

Do you have problems importing a contacts list from Excel?

yes

**Go to...**

**I can't import my contacts from Excel, page 39.**

**Go to...**

**I need a quick way to change the same company address for many contacts, page 34.**

Does the folder have to be a public folder?

**yes**

**Go to...**

**My contacts are accessible to too many people on my network, page 38.**

**no**

**Quick fix**

Place the Contacts folder in the Personal Folders file, rather than a Public Folders file.

1. On the View menu, click Folder List.
2. Open both the Public Folders file and Personal Folders file by clicking the small plus symbols next to each one.
3. Drag your Contacts folder from the Public Folders file and drop it on the Personal Folders file. (If you drop it on the Personal Folders folder, it will become a first-level folder under Personal Folders.)

**Quick fix**

The problem is in the Microsoft Expedia map web site. The map search engine occasionally goofs—there's nothing you can do to fix it except send Microsoft a message pointing out the particular problem.

**If your solution isn't here**

Check the general troubleshooting tips on page xiii.

# I need a quick way to change the same company address for many contacts

## Source of the problem

You've got several business associates at the same company—perhaps ten, perhaps 200—and the company they work for has moved to a new location across town. You need to update the business address for all these contacts. You can copy and paste the changed address into each individual contact, but what a tedious waste of time! There are faster ways to change an identical address (or any other data) for a group of contacts, and which method is best for you depends on the size of the group of contacts that needs to be changed and your skills in other software programs (such as Microsoft Excel).

There are a couple of good ways to make the same change to several contacts. For a small group of contacts, you can use the "group and move" technique in Outlook. For a large group of contacts, I'd recommend exporting the entire group to Excel, then using either Search and Replace or AutoFill in Excel to change the data, and then importing the changed contacts back into Outlook.

## How to fix it

### Change the address for a small number of contacts

This method is useful for changing up to a couple of dozen contacts, but for more than that it becomes unwieldy.

1. Open the Contact dialog box for one of the contacts in the group you need to change, change the business address, and then save and close the contact.
2. On the View menu, point to Current View, and then click By Company.
3. Display the Advanced toolbar and click the Group By Box button. ▶

4. If the Business Address field is not displayed, add it to the view.

**Tip**

To add a field to a view, right-click in the row of column headings and click Field Chooser. Drag the field from the Field Chooser to the row of column headings.

5. Drag the Business Address column heading up into the Group By box and onto the right side of the Company heading. ▶

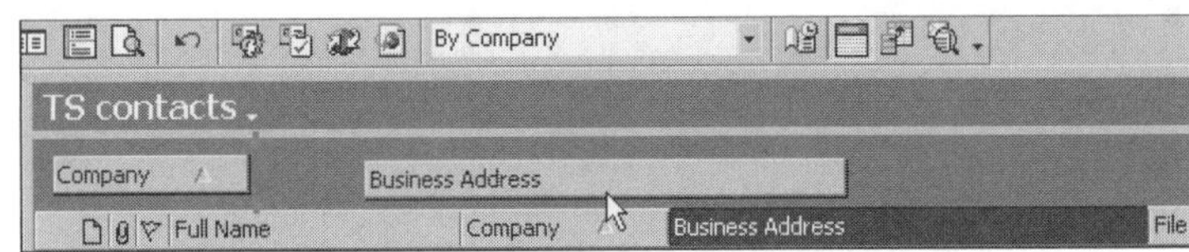


The contacts are now grouped by Company and then by Business Address.

6. Create a filter for the list that hides all contacts except those in the company whose address you want to change. Right-click an empty space in the data area of the window and click Filter. In the Contacts tab, in the Search For The Words box, type the company name and then select Company Field Only in the In list box. Click OK to run the filter; you should have two groups displayed—one with the company name and the old address, and one with the company name and the new address (which you entered in step 1). ▶

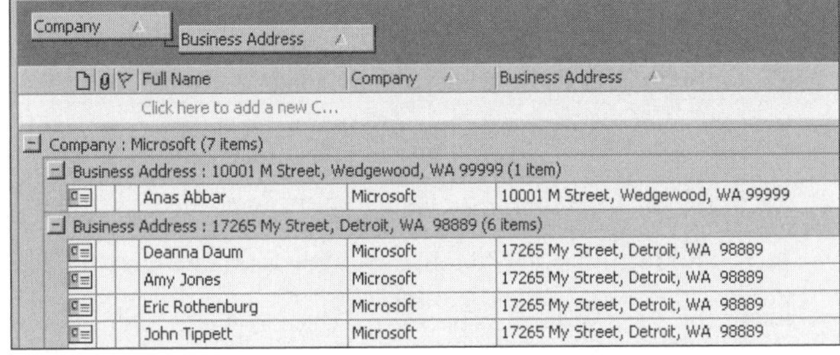


7. Select all the items in the group with the old address, and drag them to the group with the new address. When the screen tip next to the mouse pointer reads Change Company To the company name and the new business address, drop the items. ▶

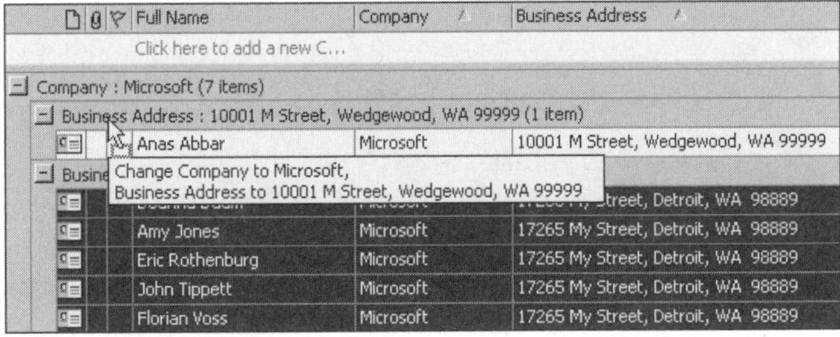


All the items you moved now have the new business address. You can remove the filter and switch your view, and get back to your normal tasks.

**Tip**

To remove the filter, right-click in an empty space in the data area of the window and click Filter. In the Filter dialog box, click the Clear All button, and then click OK.

*If this solution didn't solve your problem, go to the next page.*

# I need a quick way to change the same company address for many contacts

(continued from page 35)

## Change the address for a large number of contacts

The Excel method is useful when you need to change more than a couple of dozen contacts, because Excel is better at changing large quantities of data at once. In this technique, you export your contacts to an Excel worksheet, change the addresses that need changing (using any of Excel's data-manipulation features, such as Search and Replace or AutoFill), and then import the contacts back into Outlook.

1. Open the Contacts folder in any view.
2. On the File menu, click Import And Export.
3. In the first wizard step, select Export To A File, and then click Next.
4. In the second wizard step, click Microsoft Excel, and then click Next.
5. In the third wizard step, be sure the Contacts folder you want to export is selected, and then click Next.
6. In the fourth wizard step, click the Browse button. Navigate to an easy-to-locate folder, and type a name for a new Excel workbook to export the contacts into.
7. Click OK to return to the Export To A File Wizard, and then click Next.
8. In the fifth wizard step, click the Map Custom Fields button.
9. In the Map Custom Fields dialog box, click the Default Map button, and then click OK to return to the Export To A File Wizard.
10. Click the Finish button. Copies of your contact data are exported to the Excel workbook.

**Tip**

It's important to click the Default Map button and export *all* your contact fields, because any data you don't export won't be available when you re-import.

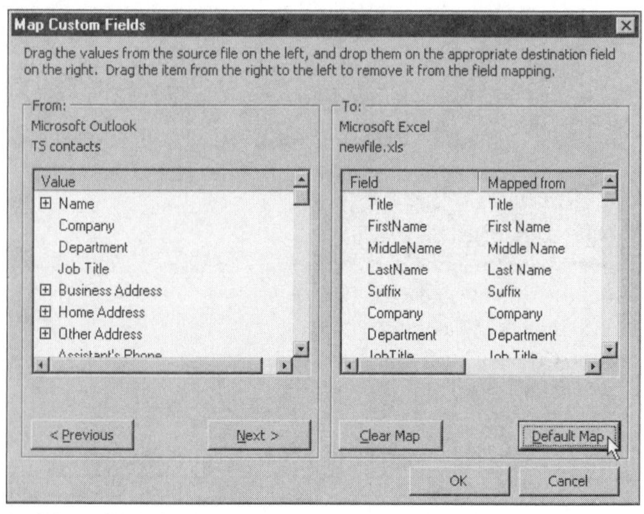


Next, make the changes to the data in the Excel workbook.

11. Open the Excel workbook.

12. Use any of Excel's features to change all the data at once, such as Search And Replace, copy and paste, AutoFill, or any technique you're comfortable with.

13. Save and close the Excel workbook.

14. Finally, import the changed contacts back into Outlook. On the File menu, click Import And Export.

15. In the first wizard step, click Import From Another Program Or File, and then click Next.

16. In the second wizard step, click Microsoft Excel, and then click Next.

17. In the third wizard step, make sure the path and file name in the File To Import box are correct, click the Replace Duplicates With Items Imported option, and then click Next. ▶

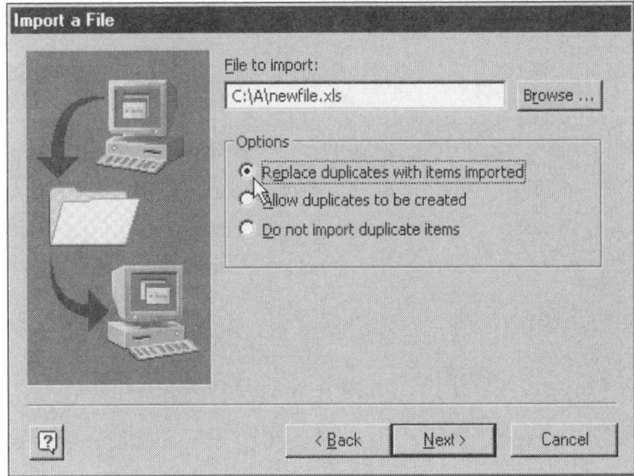


18. In the fourth wizard step, make sure the correct Contacts folder is selected, and then click Next.

19. In the fifth wizard step, click Finish.

    All the existing contacts in your folder are replaced with the contacts imported from Excel.

## If you want to know more about changing your data in Excel

There are several easy ways to change data after you export it to an Excel workbook:

- You can change the data in a single cell (for example, a street address), and then click away from the cell. Then select that cell and press Ctrl+C to copy it. Select all the rest of the cells in the column (the cells where you want to paste the copied data), and press Enter to paste the copied data into all the cells at once.
- You can change the data in a single cell at the top of a column, and then click away from the cell. Then select the cell you changed and all the cells beneath it (where you want to paste the changed data), and press Ctrl+D to copy the data in the top cell to the selected cells below.
- You can change the data in a single cell at the top of a column, and then click away from the cell. Then select the cell with the changed data, and drag the small black box in the lower-right corner of the selected cell (the *fill handle*) to copy the data in the selected cell to the cells below. (This works well with text, but not with numbers—you could end up pasting a number series instead of copying the same number.)
- You can also copy the top cells in several adjacent columns and use any of the techniques in this list to paste the data to the cells below in several columns at once, which is even more efficient.

# My contacts are accessible to too many people on my network

## Source of the problem

You use Outlook in a network environment and your Contacts folder is public, which means it's open to everyone on the network. Some of your networked associates need to have access to your Contacts folder, but you don't want *everyone* to have access to your confidential contact data. The answer is to change permissions for your public Contacts folder so that you decide who has access to your data.

## How to fix it

1. On the View menu, click Folder List.
2. In the Folder list, right-click the folder name and click Properties.
3. In the Properties dialog box, click the Permissions tab.
4. In the Name list, click the Add button and add to the list the names of all the people who should have access to your Contacts folder.
5. In the Name list, select one or more names.
6. In the Roles list box, select a role that grants the selected name(s) permission to at least read items in your Contacts folder.
7. Below the Roles list box is a set of options and check boxes for specific activities the select names can be granted or denied permission for. Make sure that (at least) the Read Items and Folder Visible check boxes are selected.
8. Click OK.

**Tip**

You can apply the same permissions to several names at once by selecting several names in step 5—use the Ctrl or Shift key to select multiple names.

**Tip**

You can mark individual contacts as Private (select the Private check box in the lower-right corner of the Contact form) so they won't appear to others who open your public Contacts folder, regardless of their permission level.

# I can't import my contacts from Excel

## Source of the problem

You've got a list of contacts in an Excel workbook, and you need to get that list into your Contacts folder in Outlook, but every time you try to import the list, you get an error message that includes the words "ODBC" and "too many fields." It's very frustrating—but it's easy to fix.

The problem is that the Excel worksheet from which you're importing must be set up correctly, with column headings and a named range, so that Outlook can identify the data you want to import.

## How to fix it

**Tip**

This solution is *not* for importing a list that you previously exported from Outlook, as covered to "I need a quick way to change the same company address for many contacts." This solution is for importing a fresh list from Excel that's never been in Outlook.

1. In the Excel worksheet, make sure that all your contact data is in a neat, rectangular table, with no completely blank rows or columns.
2. In the row immediately above the table, give each column a heading (such as FirstName, LastName, Street, City, and so forth).
3. Select the entire table, including the headings row (not the entire worksheet, just the entire data table).
4. Click in the worksheet's Name box, type a one-word name that's not identical to any column headings, and press Enter. (Don't click away or press Tab—just press Enter.) ▶

   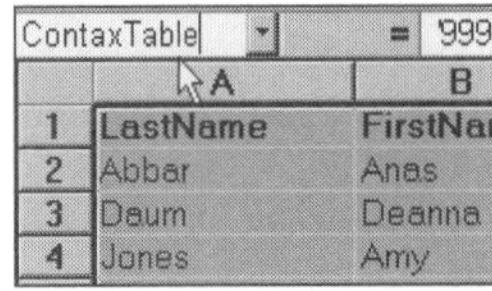
   

   You can tell the data range has been correctly named by clicking the arrow next to the Name box—the range name you created appears on the list, and when you click the range name, your data table is selected.
5. Save and close the Excel workbook.
6. Import the workbook into Outlook. Outlook recognizes the range name, and in the fifth wizard step you can map the Excel column headings to match Outlook's field names.

# E-mail, ac

**Can you find the correct Contacts folder when you address a message?**

yes

In the Select Names dialog box, are your contact names in the order you want?

yes

no

**Go to...**

**Contact names are out of order in the Select Names dialog box, page 43.**

no

**Go to...**

**When I address a message, my Contacts subfolder isn't there, page 44.**

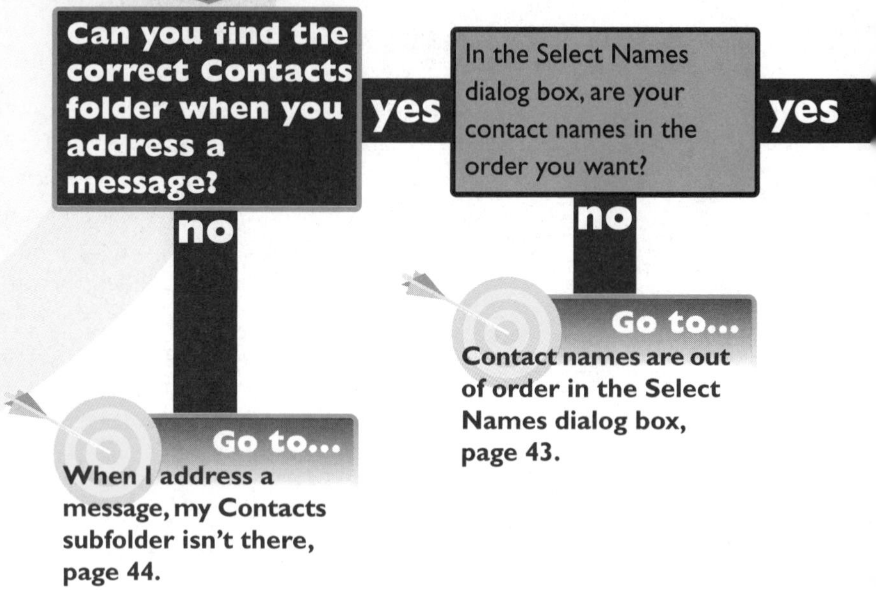

**If your solution isn't here**

Check these related chapters:

Switching e-mail programs, page 252
E-mail, automatic addresses, page 48
E-mail, importing addresses, page 68
E-mail, sending, page 92
Or see the general troubleshooting tips on page xiii.

Are you unable to create a long distribution list?

yes

**Quick fix**

Distribution list have a limit of 107 names. Also, some mail servers won't send a message to more than perhaps 50 names in an attempt to prevent spamming and virus threats from traveling through the server. Rather than creating one very long distribution list, create multiple shorter distribution lists, and send each in a separate copy of the message so that you don't run into any server limits.

no

Are your contact names shared between Outlook and Outlook Express?

yes

Do you want a different Contacts subfolder to be your default address book?

yes

**Go to...**

**My default e-mail address book is the wrong Contacts subfolder, page 42.**

no

Can you find your contact's name in the Select Names dialog box?

no

**Quick fix**

Make sure you're looking in the correct Contacts folder or subfolder (select the folder name from the list box above the names in the Select Names dialog box).

If you're working in Outlook, in Corporate/Workgroup configuration, contacts with no e-mail address or fax number aren't displayed in the Select Names dialog box.

no (Are your contact names shared between Outlook and Outlook Express?)

**Go to...**

**Outlook and Outlook Express have different address lists, page 70.**

# My default e-mail address book is in the wrong Contacts subfolder

## Source of the problem

You're working on a project that has you in constant e-mail communication with clients whose e-mail addresses are in a special Contacts subfolder. Every time you address a message to one of those clients, you have to take the extra step of clicking the subfolder name in the Select Names dialog box before you can click the client name. This is inefficient—you'd rather have that special Contacts subfolder be your default e-mail address book.

## How to fix it

### In Outlook, Internet Mail Only configuration, and in Outlook Express

In Outlook, Internet Mail Only configuration and in Outlook Express, the default address book is always the main Contacts folder. You can click other available folders from the box, but you can't change the default.

## How to fix it

### In Corporate/Workgroup configuration

In Outlook 2000, Corporate/Workgroup configuration, you can set a different default Contacts subfolder.

1. On the Tools menu, click Services.
2. Click the Addressing tab.
3. In the Show This Address List First box, click the name of the Contacts subfolder you want to use as your default address book. ▶

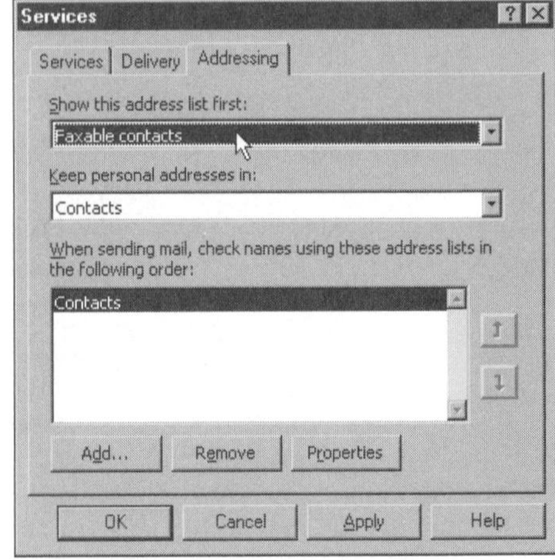


4. Click OK.

The Contacts folder you set as the default will appear first in the Select Names dialog box when you address a message (you can click other available folders from the box).

# Contact names are out of order in the Select Names dialog box

## Source of the problem

It seems as if every time you address a message using the Select Names (or Select Recipients) dialog box, the contact names are out of order—and it's very difficult to locate a contact name in a list of hundreds when the names are listed first-then-last. Fortunately, this is very easy to fix.

## How to fix it

### In Outlook, Internet Mail Only configuration, and in Outlook Express

You can sort by Name or you can sort by E-mail (which moves all the e-mail addresses into a group at the bottom or top of the list).

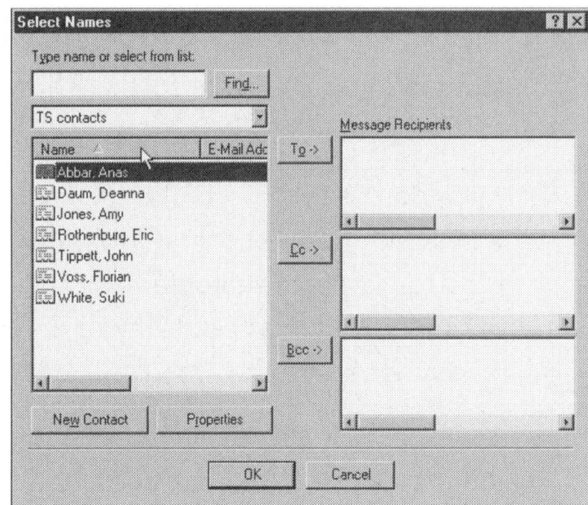


1. To sort the list, click the column header you want to sort. ▶
2. If you click the Name column header repeatedly, the names cycle through four sort orders (first, last A–Z; first, last Z–A; last, first A–Z; last, first Z–A). Click until you get the sort order you want.

## How to fix it

### In Corporate/Workgroup configuration

1. On the Tools menu, click Services.
2. On the Services tab, click Outlook Address Book, and then click the Properties button.
3. In the Properties dialog box, click the Show Names By option you want.
4. Click Close, and then click OK to close both dialog boxes. ▶

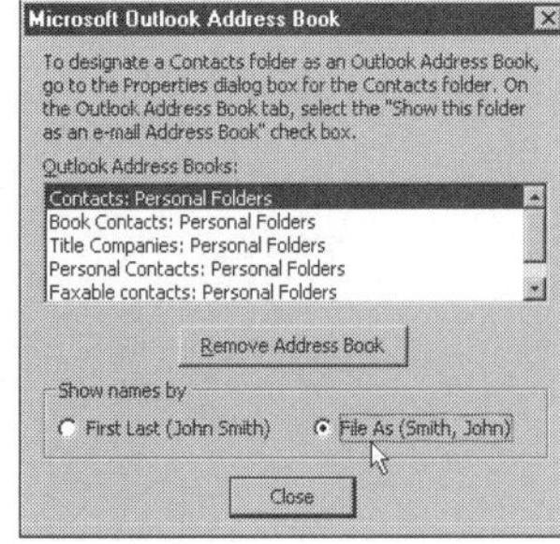

# When I address a message, my Contacts subfolder isn't there

## Source of the problem

You've got an important message to send to a client whose name and e-mail address you keep in a special Contacts subfolder so that it's always easy to find—but when you click the To button in your message, the Select Names (or Select Recipients) dialog box doesn't list the special Contacts subfolder you created. Not a problem—you need to tell Outlook that your special subfolder is an Outlook address book. Your configuration determines the method.

## How to fix it

### In Corporate/Workgroup configuration

Click the subfolder you want in the Show Names From The box. ▶

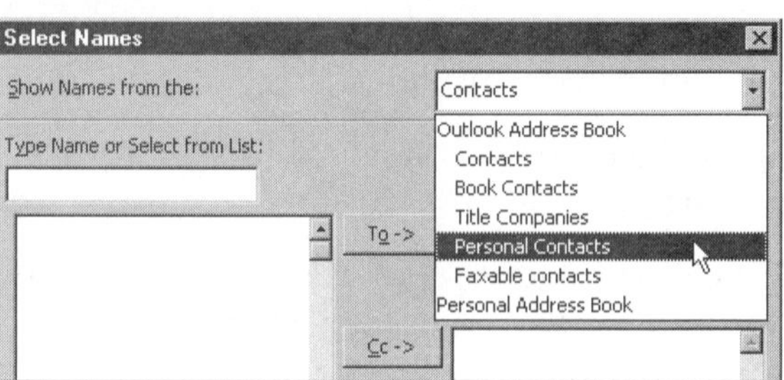


1. If you don't see the subfolder listed beneath Outlook Address Book, you need to make the subfolder available as an Outlook address book. If you don't see Outlook

   Address Book in the list, you first need to add the Outlook Address Book as a service, and then make your Contacts subfolder available as an Outlook address book.

## Install the Outlook Address Book service

If you don't see Outlook Address Book listed when you open the Show Names From The box, follow these steps to install it:

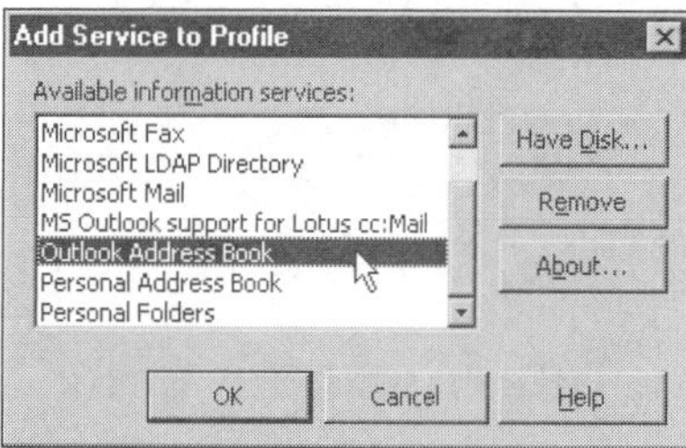


1. On the Tools menu, click Services.
2. On the Services tab, click the Add button.
3. Click Outlook Address Book, and click OK twice to close both dialog boxes. ▶

## Make a Contacts subfolder available as an Outlook address book

If you see Outlook Address Book listed when you open the Show Names From The box, follow these steps to make your Contacts subfolder available as an Outlook address book:

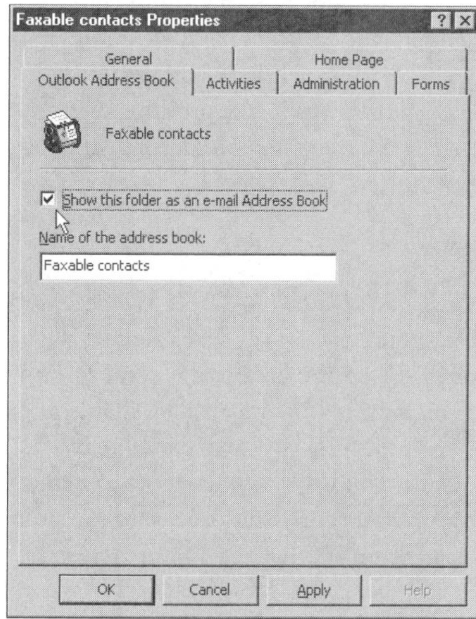


1. Cancel the Select Names dialog box.
2. On the View menu, click Folder List to open the Folder list.
3. In the Folder list, right-click the subfolder name and click Properties.
4. In the subfolder Properties check box, click the Outlook Address Book tab.
5. Select the Show This Folder As An E-mail Address Book check box, and then click OK. ▶

Now the subfolder can be clicked in the Select Names dialog box.

**Tip**

In Outlook, Corporate/Workgroup configuration, the only names that appear in any address book subfolder are those that have e-mail or fax numbers entered in the Contacts subfolder.

***If this solution didn't solve your problem, go to the next page.***

# When I address a message, my Contacts subfolder isn't there

*(continued from page 45)*

## How to fix it

### In Internet Mail Only

In the Internet Mail Only configuration, all Contacts subfolders are available by default in the Select Names dialog box—but it's possible that someone made your Contacts subfolder unavailable.

Click the subfolder you want in the folder box, above the list of names. ▶

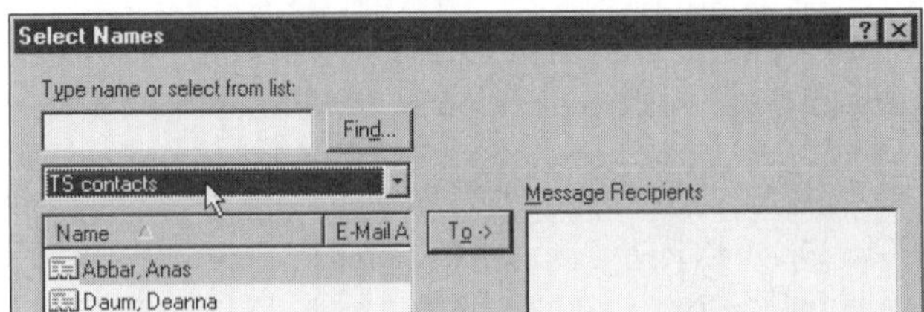


If you don't see the subfolder listed, you need to make the subfolder available as an Outlook address book. Follow the steps in the previous section, "Make a Contacts subfolder available as an Outlook address book."

## Outlook Express How to fix it

Outlook Express can share contact data with Outlook in Internet Mail Only configuration. If Outlook Express is sharing contact data with Outlook, all changes to any Contacts subfolder (such as making it available or unavailable as an e-mail address book in the Select Recipients dialog box) must be made in Outlook.

If you want to know how to make Outlook Express share contacts with Outlook (in Internet Mail Only configuration), go to the problem "Outlook and Outlook Express have different address lists," page 70.

# E-mail, au

**When you type a name or partial name in the To box, is it recognized automatically?**

yes

no

## Quick fix

If a name isn't recognized automatically, click in the address box and press Ctrl+K or Alt+K to give AutoName a wake-up call. This works in Outlook and Outlook Express, in both the Contacts Folders and the Address book. You won't have to press Ctrl+K or Alt+K if AutoName is turned on. To turn on AutoName in Outlook:

1. On the Tools menu, click Options.
2. On the Preferences tab, click the E-mail Options button.
3. Click the Advanced E-mail Options button.
4. Select the Automatic Name Checking check box.
5. Click OK to close each dialog box.

To turn on AutoName in Outlook Express:

1. On the Tools menu, click Options.
2. On the Send tab, select the Automatically Complete E-mail Addresses When Composing check box.
3. Click OK.

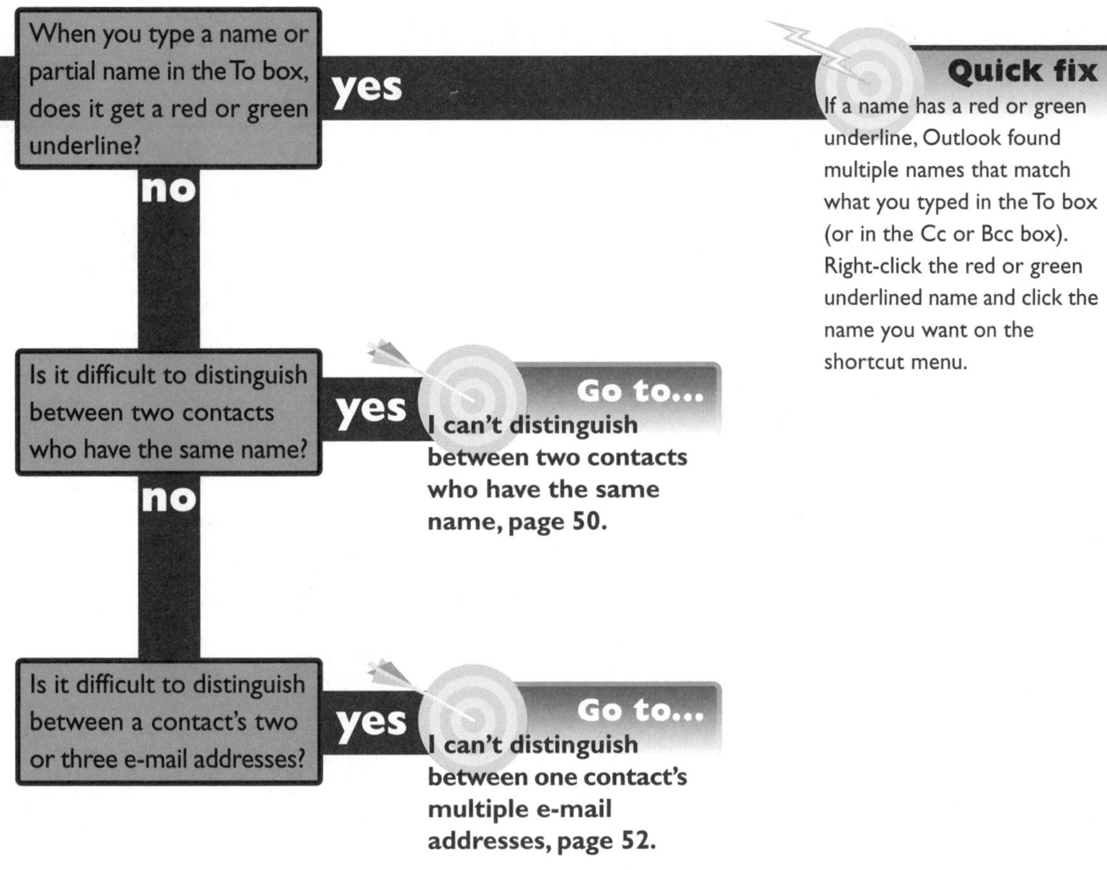

When you type a name or partial name in the To box, does it get a red or green underline?
yes
no
Quick fix
If a name has a red or green underline, Outlook found multiple names that match what you typed in the To box (or in the Cc or Bcc box). Right-click the red or green underlined name and click the name you want on the shortcut menu.
Is it difficult to distinguish between two contacts who have the same name?
yes
no
Go to...
I can't distinguish between two contacts who have the same name, page 50.
Is it difficult to distinguish between a contact's two or three e-mail addresses?
yes
Go to...
I can't distinguish between one contact's multiple e-mail addresses, page 52.


**If your solution isn't here**

Check these related chapters:

Switching e-mail programs, 252

E-mail, addressing messages, 40

E-mail, sending, 92

Or see the general troubleshooting tips on page xiii.

# I can't distinguish between two contacts who have the same name

## Source of the problem

You've got two different contacts who are both named Amy Jones. When you type the name in the To box of a message, Outlook's AutoName feature doesn't know which one you want to use.

## How to fix it

You have three options, depending on your configuration. If you work in Outlook Express or in Outlook, Internet Mail Only configuration, you can use nicknames to tell AutoName which Amy Jones you want. In any Outlook configuration and in Outlook Express, you can use AutoName without nicknames and choose which name you want after AutoName finds them; or you can forget about AutoName because it's too much trouble and just use the Select Names dialog box.

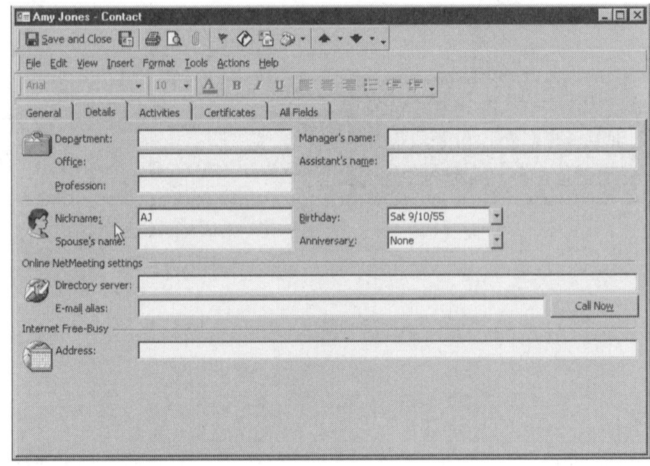

### Use nicknames to identify the contacts

1. In each contact's dialog box, on the Details tab, type a Nickname that you can remember and associate with that contact, and then click Save And Close. ◀

2. When you enter a second contact with the same name, you'll see a Duplicate Contact Detected dialog box. Click the Add This As A New Contact Anyway option, and click OK. ▶

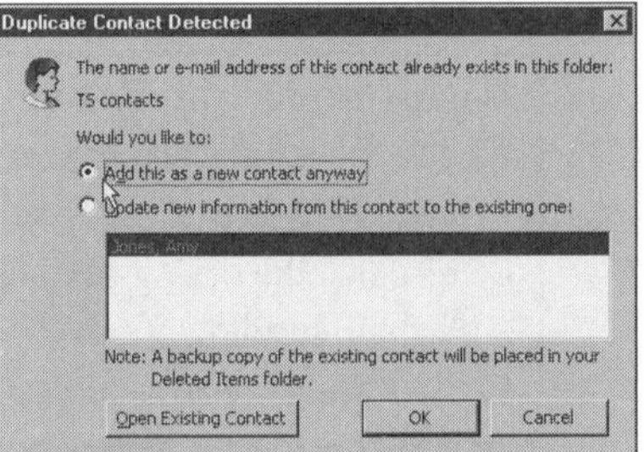

**Tip**

If you use Outlook Express and your contacts are not shared with Outlook, you can use nicknames on the Name tab in the Address Book to identify different contacts.

3. To address a message, type the appropriate nickname (or at least part of the nickname) in the To box. Outlook (or Outlook Express, if your contacts are shared) looks up the nickname and fills in the corresponding e-mail address.

**Tip**

If the message doesn't fill in the contact's name with a black underline, click in the To box and press Ctrl+K or Alt+K to wake up AutoName.

## Use AutoName without nicknames

If you don't use nicknames to enter the To address, or if you're working in Outlook, Corporate/Workgroup configuration, the contact name is underlined in red (which means there are multiple contacts with the same name).

1. Right-click the name, and click one of the names on the shortcut menu (you won't be able to tell which is which).

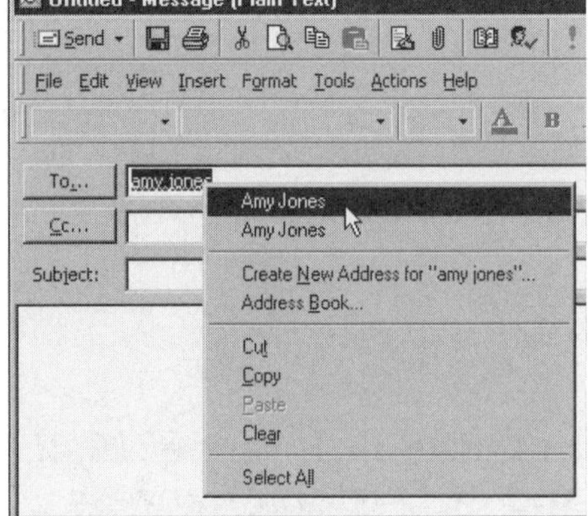


2. Right-click the black underlined name in the To box and click Properties to see which e-mail address was entered. If it's the wrong address, delete it and enter it again; but when you right-click the red-underlined name, click the other name on the shortcut menu. If this seems grossly inefficient, use the Select Names dialog box to address your message.

**Tip**

AutoName takes a lot longer to work in Corporate/Workgroup configuration (and nicknames don't work at all), so if you work in Corporate/Workgroup configuration, you might find it easier to click the To button and use the Select Names dialog box.

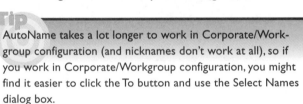

## Use the Select Names (or Select Recipients) dialog box

Although the Select Names and Select Recipients dialog boxes are slightly different between the two Outlook configurations and Outlook Express, they work the same way. Each contact's name is listed on the left, with the e-mail address to the right of the name.

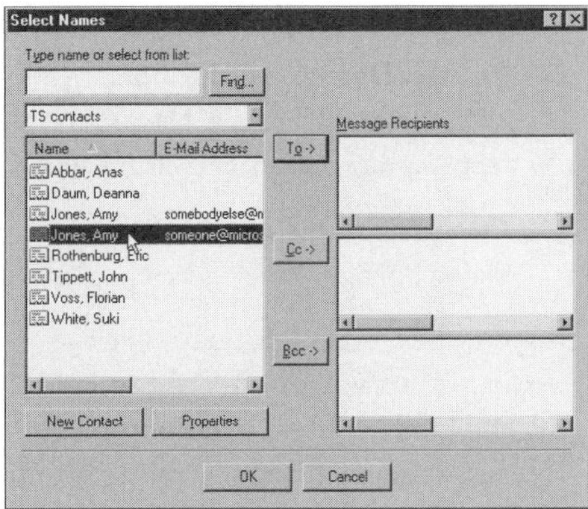


Double-click the name with the correct e-mail address. If you want to add the name to the Cc box or the Bcc box instead, click the name once and then click the Cc or Bcc button.

# I can't distinguish between one contact's multiple e-mail addresses

## Source of the problem

Some of your contacts have multiple e-mail addresses. When you send one of them a message, it's important that the message go to the correct e-mail address so that the recipient receives it in a timely manner. But Outlook doesn't know the difference between the addresses, so how can you choose the correct address efficiently every time?

The techniques you can use depend on (as usual) whether you're using Outlook or Outlook Express and which Outlook configuration you're using.

If you use Outlook Express and your contacts are not shared with Outlook, you can use nicknames in the Address Book to identify contacts with different e-mail addresses.

## How to fix it

### In Outlook, Internet Mail Only configuration, and in Outlook Express

Create a contact for each e-mail address, and use nicknames to help AutoName identify them.

1. Create a separate contact dialog box for each of your recipient's e-mail addresses.

   When you see the Duplicate Contact Detected dialog box, click the Add This As A New Contact Anyway option, and click OK.

2. Open one of the contact dialog boxes.

3. On the Details tab, type a Nickname that you can remember for the e-mail address that's entered in that contact, and then click Save And Close. ▶

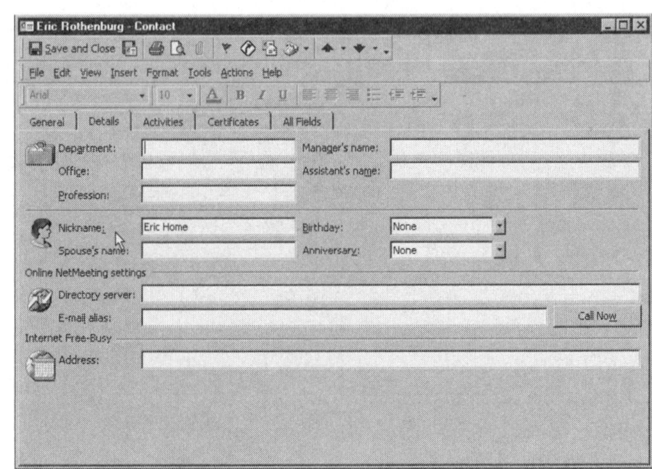

4. Repeat steps 2 and 3 to create a memorable nickname in each of the contact dialog boxes for that contact. Nicknames such as **Eric Work** and **Eric Home** are memorable and functional. (Your correspondents never see the nicknames you use to identify them.)

To address a message, type the appropriate nickname (or at least part of the nickname) in the To box. Outlook (or Outlook Express, if your contacts are shared) looks up the nickname and fills in the corresponding e-mail address.

Nicknames make it easier for AutoName to locate the correct e-mail address. Even if you don't use nicknames, you can still locate the correct e-mail address in the Select Names (or Select Recipients) dialog box easily when you create a separate contact for each e-mail address, because each contact and the default e-mail address are listed in the dialog box. ▶

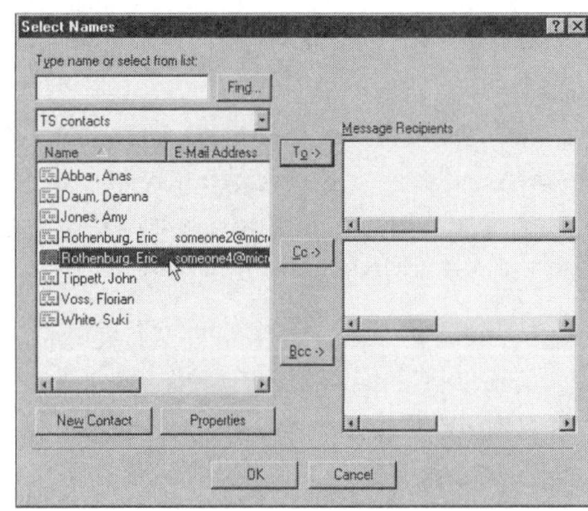


**Tip**

If the message doesn't fill in the contact's name with a black underline, click in the To box and press Ctrl+K or Alt+K to wake up AutoName.

**Tip**

If the address you choose isn't the default address for that contact, you'll see the contact's address in the message's To box instead of the contact's name—but that's okay.

## How to fix it

### In Outlook, Internet Mail Only configuration

If you prefer not to create separate contacts for each e-mail address, use this technique to choose the correct e-mail address for the message.

1. In the message, click the To button (or the Cc or Bcc button) to open the Select Names dialog box.
2. A contact's name is listed only once in the Select Names dialog box, so add the name to your message. In the message, right-click the name you added. If there are two or three addresses for that name, they're listed in the shortcut menu. ▶
3. Click the address you want.

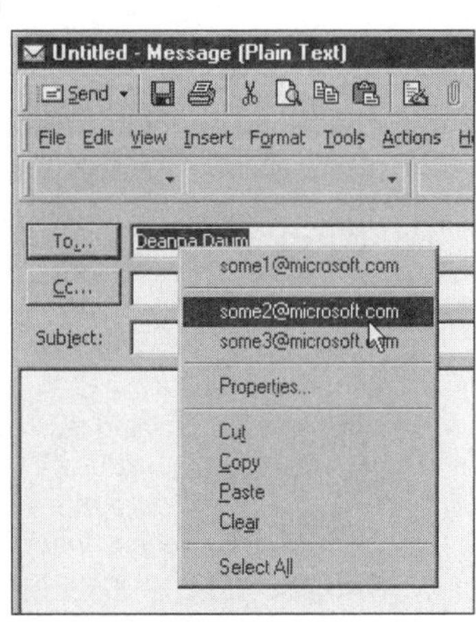


*If this solution didn't solve your problem, go to the next page.*

# I can't distinguish between one contact's multiple e-mail addresses

*(continued from page 53)*

## Change the default e-mail address for a contact

If you find that you're constantly switching a contact's address in the To box because the address that's entered isn't the address you usually want to use, you can make the address you usually use the default address (and not have to switch addresses so often).

1. Open a new message and click the To button to open the Select Names dialog box.
2. Right-click the name of the contact, and click Properties.
3. In the Properties dialog box, click the Name tab. The e-mail addresses are listed, and the default address is in bold type.
4. To switch the default to a different address, click the address, click the Set As Default button, and then click OK. ▶

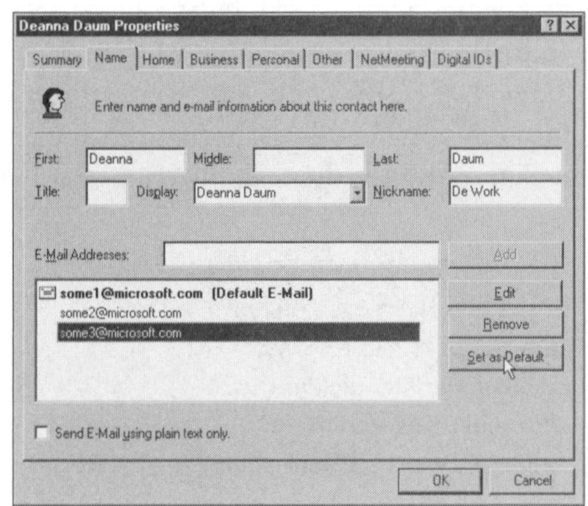


# How to fix it

## In Outlook, Corporate/Workgroup configuration

In the Corporate/Workgroup configuration, a contact's name is listed with each e-mail address (E-mail, E-mail 2, and E-mail 3) in the Select Names dialog box—but you can't tell which e-mail address is the correct one from a not-so-helpful label such as "E-mail 2."

If you can't remember which listing you need:

1. Right-click one of the listings (for example, "Julia Kelly (E-mail 2)").
2. Click Properties.
3. Click the SMTP-Address tab to see the actual address for that listing. ▶
4. If that's the one you want, click Cancel in the Properties dialog box, and double-click that listing to add it your list of recipients.

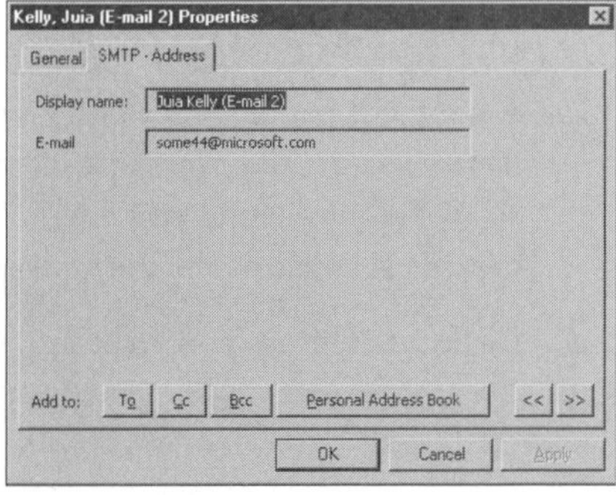

## How to fix it

In Outlook Express, you can't select from multiple e-mail addresses for a single contact—you can only enter the default address. So your choices are: type the nondefault address in the message's To box, or change the default e-mail address for the contact. If you have Outlook Express sharing addresses (Contacts folders) with Outlook, changing the default address in Outlook Express also changes it in Outlook.

1. In the Select Recipients dialog box, double-click the recipient's name. Names are listed only once, even if you've entered more than one e-mail address.
2. In the message To box, right-click the name you added, and click Properties. ▶

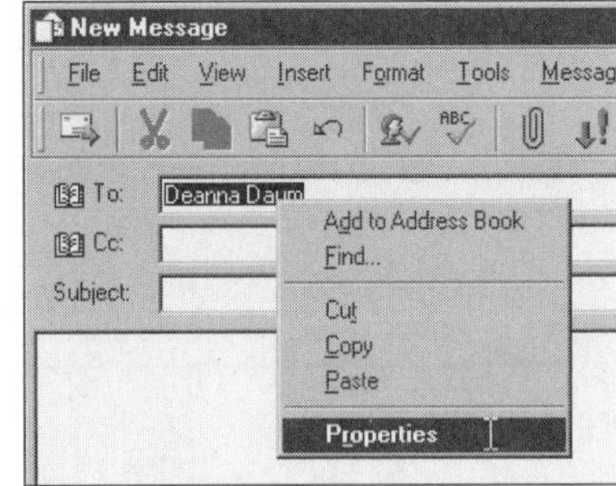


3. In the contact's Properties dialog box, click the Name tab.
4. Under E-mail Addresses, double-click the address you want to use in your message, and click OK. ▶

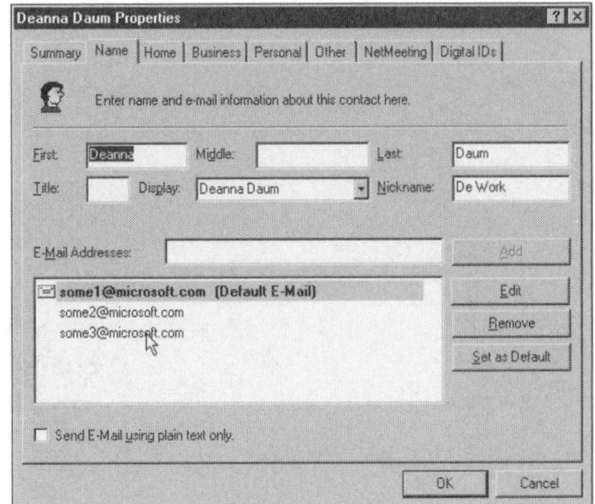


The address you double-clicked becomes the default address for the contact, and it is the address to which the message is sent.

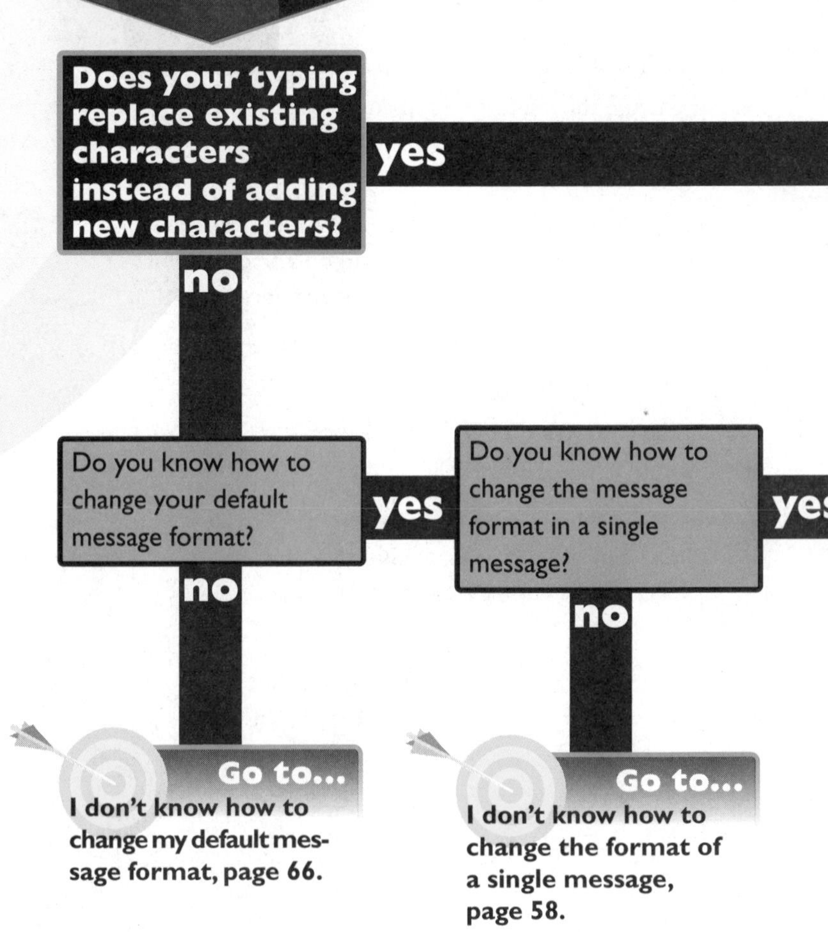

Does your typing replace existing characters instead of adding new characters?
yes
no
Do you know how to change your default message format?
yes
no
Do you know how to change the message format in a single message?
yes
no
Go to...
I don't know how to change my default message format, page 66.
Go to...
I don't know how to change the format of a single message, page 58.

# E-mail, creating

**Quick fix**

When you type a new word in the middle of an existing sentence, if your typing replaces existing characters instead of adding new characters, you're typing in Overtype mode. It's easy to switch to Overtype mode by inadvertently hitting the Insert key on your keyboard while you type.

To switch back to Insert mode, press the Insert key again.

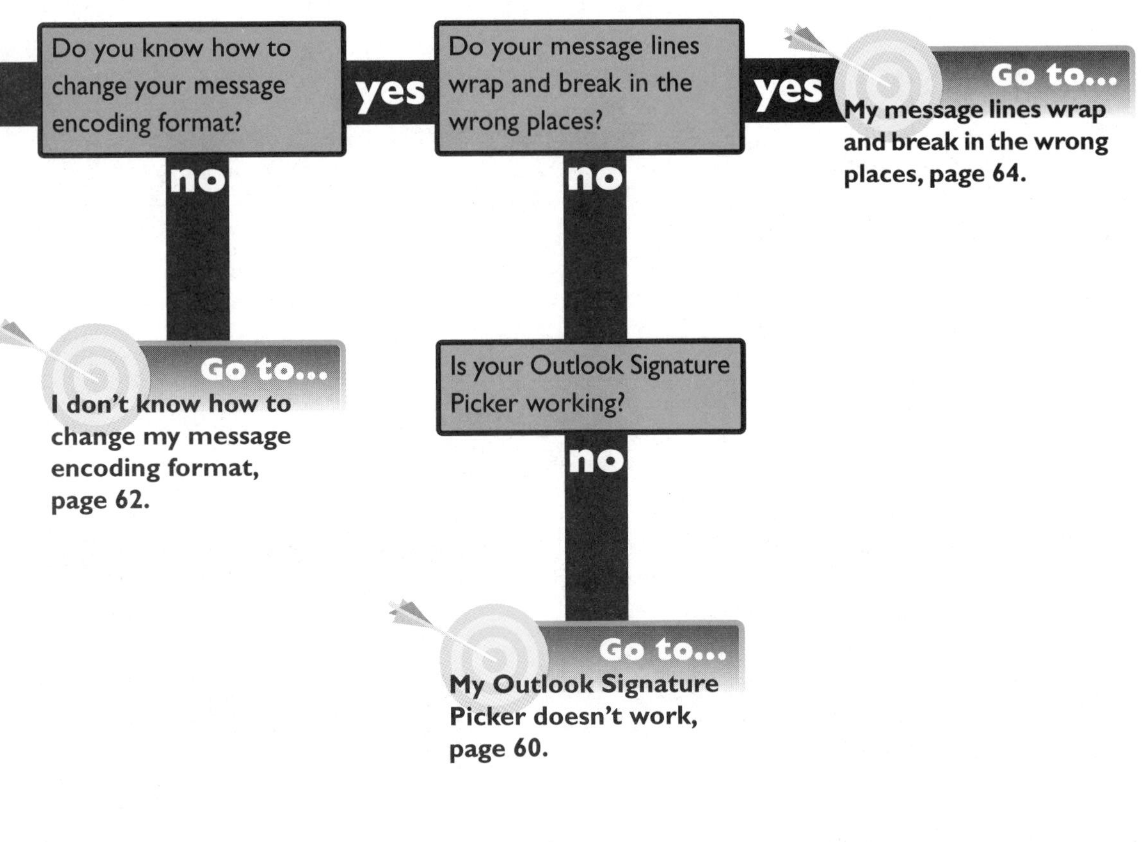

Do you know how to change your message encoding format?
yes
Do your message lines wrap and break in the wrong places?
yes
Go to...
My message lines wrap and break in the wrong places, page 64.
no
Go to...
I don't know how to change my message encoding format, page 62.
no
Is your Outlook Signature Picker working?
no
Go to...
My Outlook Signature Picker doesn't work, page 60.

**If your solution isn't here**

Check the general troubleshooting tips on page xiii.

# I don't know how to change the format of a single message

## Source of the problem

You normally send e-mail in the very businesslike Plain Text message format, but your grandmother (who recently discovered the joy of using e-mail) likes to exchange e-mail in HTML format with fancy stationery. You don't want to change your default Plain Text format, but you want to send messages to your grandmother in the HTML format. How do you change the format of a single message?

## Outlook 2000 How to fix it

In the message, on the Format menu, click the message format you want—Plain Text, Rich Text, or HTML. ▶

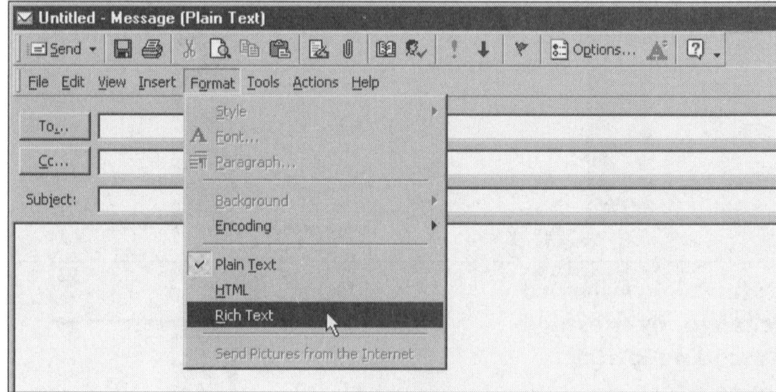


If your open message is already formatted as Rich Text, you can't choose HTML; and if your open message is already formatted as HTML, you can't choose Rich Text. ▶

Here's a trick you might find useful: if you click Plain Text, and then open the Format menu again, you can click the message format you want.

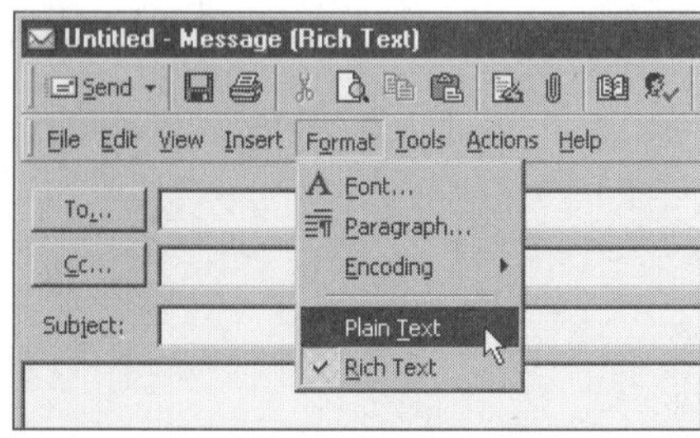


**Tip**

If you use Word as your e-mail editor, you can't change the message format in an open message. You must close the message, change the default message format in Outlook, and then create your message.

## How to fix it

In the message, on the Format menu, click the message format you want.

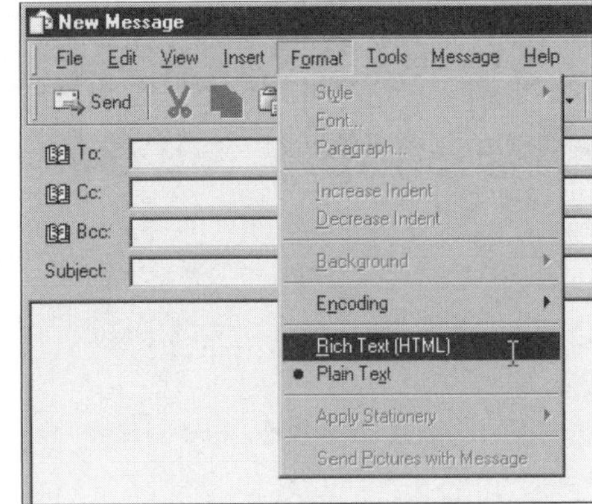


### Tip

In Outlook Express, Rich Text (HTML) is really just HTML, which is web-page–style formatting. In Outlook, Rich Text and HTML are two different kinds of format coding, but Outlook Express doesn't have real Rich Text formatting (it's just a descriptive label).

# My Outlook Signature Picker doesn't work

## Source of the problem

You've got three different signatures for your Outlook messages, and you normally use the Signature Picker to insert a signature appropriate for each recipient.

**Tip**

If you click the message's Insert menu, point to Signature, and click the name of the signature you want, you're using the Signature Picker.

Recently you started using Word as your e-mail editor, and your detailed signatures have all disappeared!

**Tip**

To turn Word on or off as your e-mail editor, click Outlook's Tools menu. Click Options, click the Mail Format tab, and select or clear the Use Microsoft Word To Edit E-mail Messages check box.

When Word is your e-mail editor, you can't use e-mail signatures that you created in Outlook—you have to create separate signatures in Word. Your Outlook signatures are still available in Outlook, and if you turn off Word as your e-mail editor, you get to use your Outlook signatures again.

But you like using Word as your e-mail editor—how do you create an e-mail signature in Word?

## How to fix it

1. Open a new message or a document in Microsoft Word.
2. On the Tools menu, click Options.
3. On the General tab, click the E-mail Options button.
4. In the E-mail Options dialog box, click the E-mail Signature tab.
5. Click the New button, and type a short name for your signature in the box at the top. Then type and format your signature in the box at the bottom. ▶

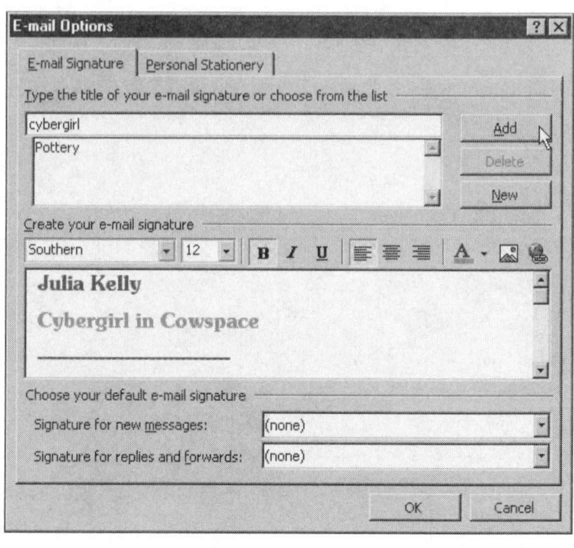

6. Click the Add button to add the new signature to your list of available signatures when Word is your e-mail editor.
7. If you want specific signatures to be added by default to outgoing messages and to replies and forwarded messages, choose those signature names in the boxes at the bottom of the dialog box.
8. Click OK to close each of the dialog boxes.

## Insert a signature when Word is your e-mail editor

In Word, signatures are saved as AutoText entries. To insert a signature in an e-mail message, on the message's Insert menu, point to AutoText, point to E-mail Signature, and then click the signature you want. ▶

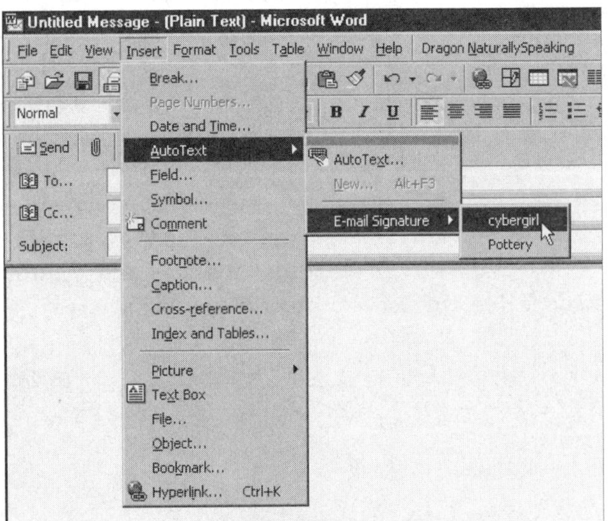


## Switch a signature when Word is your e-mail editor

If you want to change the default signature that's already in a new message, a quick way is to right-click the signature and then click the name of the replacement signature you want. ▶

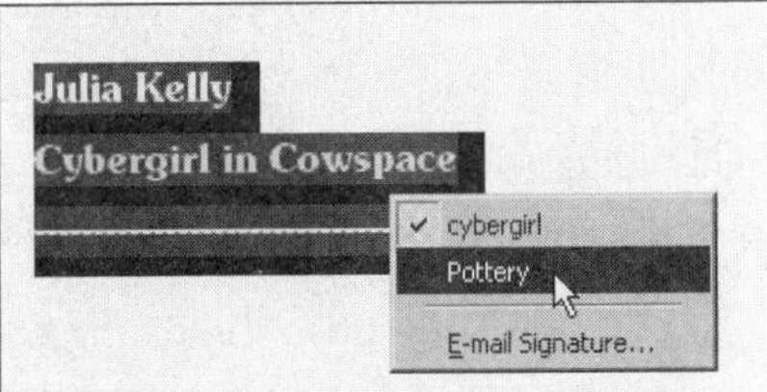


## If you want to know more about signature formatting

You can create great signatures with dynamic formatting in both Outlook and Word, but if you send them in messages that are formatted as Plain Text, only the text characters appear to your recipients. None of the colorful, vibrant formatting is transmitted with the message.

Even worse is that if you send the well-formatted signature to recipients as Rich Text or HTML, and their mail programs can't read Rich Text or HTML, all your formatting work appears to your recipients as long strings of annoying gibberish.

The solution is to create duplicate signatures—one fully formatted for those recipients to whom you send Rich Text or HTML messages, and one completely unformatted for those recipients to whom you send only Plain Text messages.

# I don't know how to change my message encoding format

## Source of the problem

An associate at a company you do business with has told you that the company's mail server is having problems transmitting the messages you send, and has asked you to switch your message encoding format for messages you send to that company. It's easy enough to do, if you can just remember how to do it.

**Tip**

The two most common message encoding formats are MIME and Uuencode. Uuencode is the old standard and is readable by most mail servers; MIME is the new standard and supports the transfer of a wider range of file types. The "best" encoding format is whichever one works between you and your correspondent.

## Outlook 2000 How to fix it (Corporate/Workgroup configuration)

1. On the Tools menu, click Options, and then click the Internet E-mail tab.
2. Under Internet E-mail Sending Format, click MIME or UUENCODE.
3. Click OK to close the dialog box.

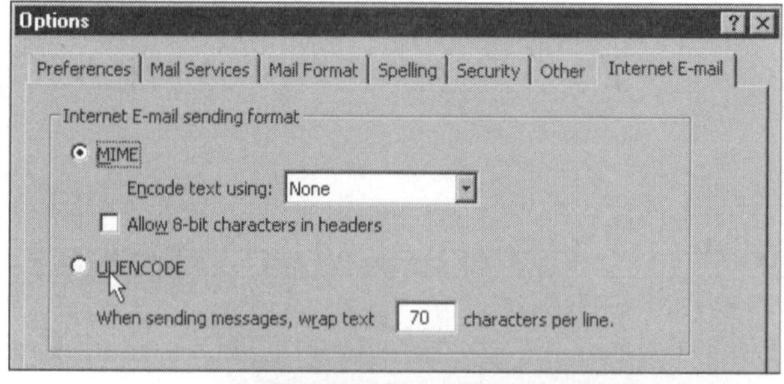


If you used the preceding steps to switch your default encoding format at the request of a specific associate, remember to switch to your normal encoding format after you send the message to that associate.

In the Corporate/Workgroup configuration, you can change the encoding format for a single message without changing your default encoding format: click the message's File menu, click Properties, and then click the Internet E-mail tab. Click the Override The Default Setting And Use option, click the encoding option you want, and then click OK.

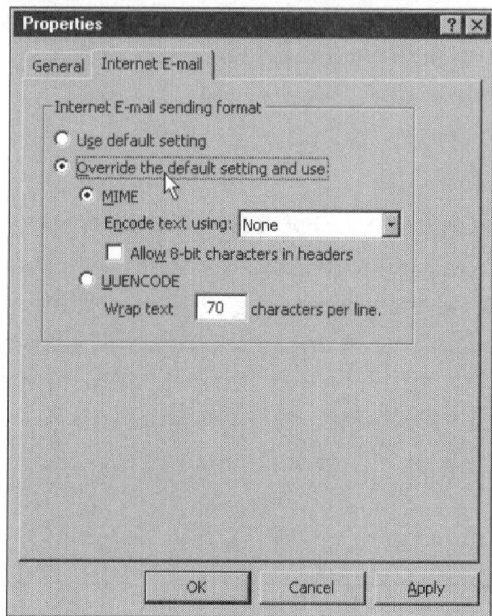

## How to fix it (Internet Mail Only configuration)

1. On the Tools menu, click Options, and then click the Mail Format tab.
2. Under Message Format, in the Send In This Message Format box, click Plain Text.
3. Click the Settings button. ▶
4. In the Plain Text Settings dialog box, click MIME or Uuencode, and then click OK to close each of the dialog boxes. ▶

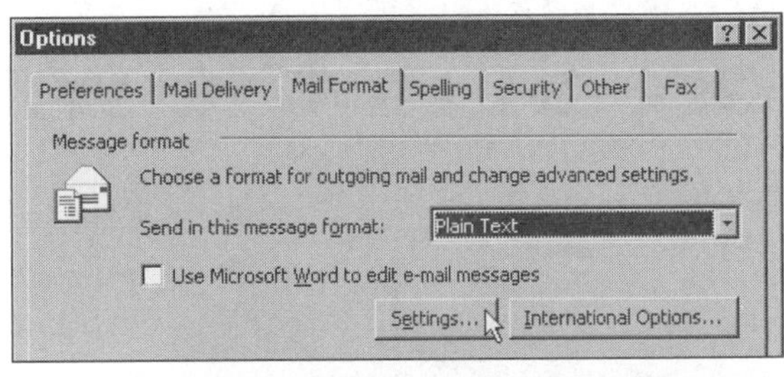


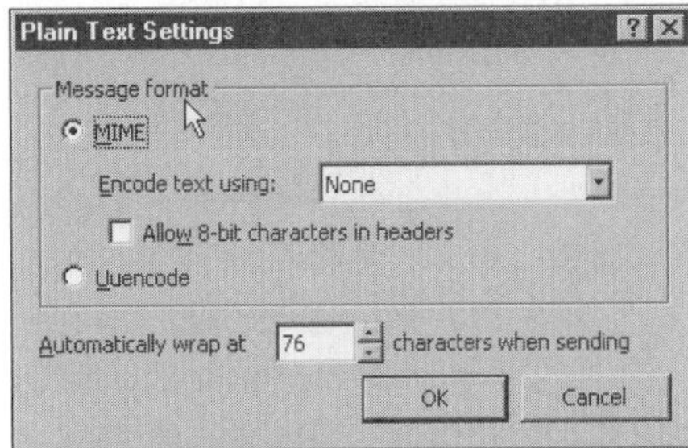


## Outlook Express How to fix it

1. On the Tools menu, click Options, and then click the Send tab.
2. Under Mail Sending Format, click the Plain Text Settings button. ▶

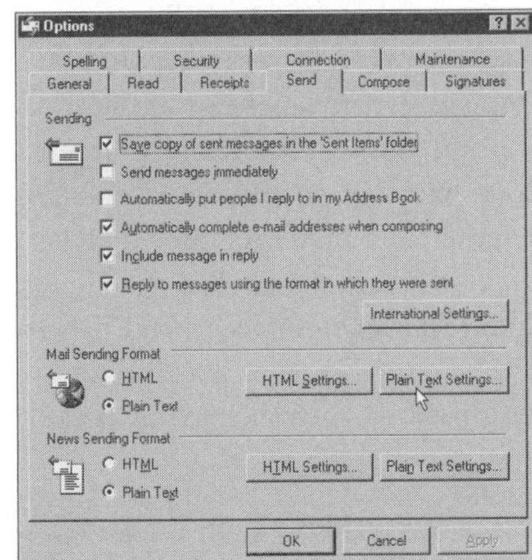


3. In the Plain Text Settings dialog box, click the message encoding format you need—MIME or Uuencode—and then click OK to close each of the dialog boxes. ▶

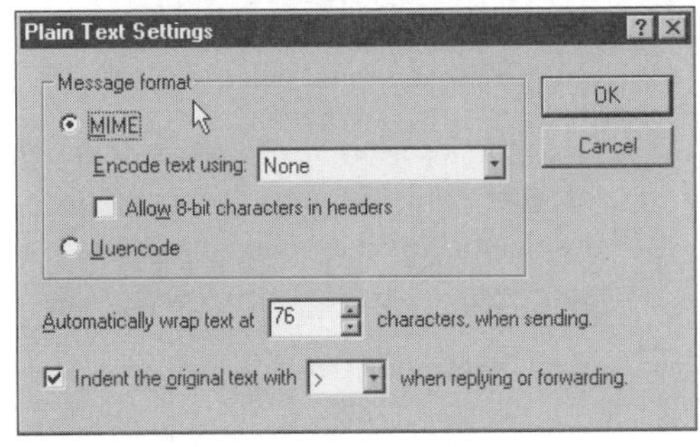


**Tip**

If you need to change your message encoding format for messages that you post to a newsgroup, click the Plain Text Settings button under News Sending Format and change the encoding format.

# My message lines wrap and break in the wrong places

## Source of the problem

You got a message that was forwarded to you, and the text of the message was broken up into lots of short lines (which makes it hard to read). Or perhaps you posted a message to a newsgroup or a list server, and when you received the digest of posted messages the next day, you saw to your dismay that the last word or two of every line in your message was missing.

The problem is the wrap length of lines in those messages, and wrap length is controlled by the mail program that sent the message out. You can't fix this problem completely, because you can't control others' mail programs, but you can control the wrap length of the messages you send out.

A forwarded or replied message that you receive is broken up into short lines because the sender's mail program wrapped the original longer lines into shorter pieces for sending. This often happens when a message has been forwarded several times.

If you sent a message that got truncated at the end of every line, you sent the message with a long wrap length and the receiving mail program cut the lines short rather than wrapping them. (Some older mail programs do that.)

You can change the wrap length of the text in your outgoing messages. Shorter lines are more likely to remain intact when others reply or forward your message, but shorter lines also break up the lines in messages that you reply to or forward. If the default wrap length of 76 characters doesn't work for you, experiment until you find a length that works better.

## How to fix it

### In Corporate/Workgroup configuration

1. On the Tools menu, click Options.
2. Click the Internet E-mail tab, and under Internet E-mail Sending Format, type the number of characters at which you want your message lines to wrap. ▶
3. Click OK to close the dialog box.

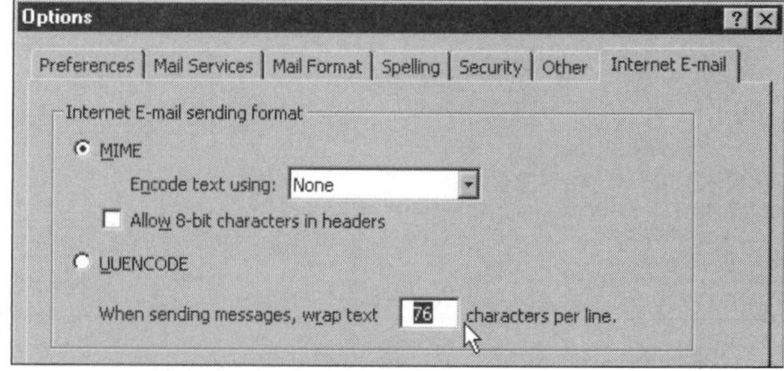

## How to fix it (Internet Mail Only configuration)

1. On the Tools menu, click Options.
2. Click the Mail Format tab, and under Message Format, in the Send In This Message Format box, click Plain Text, and then click the Settings button. ▶

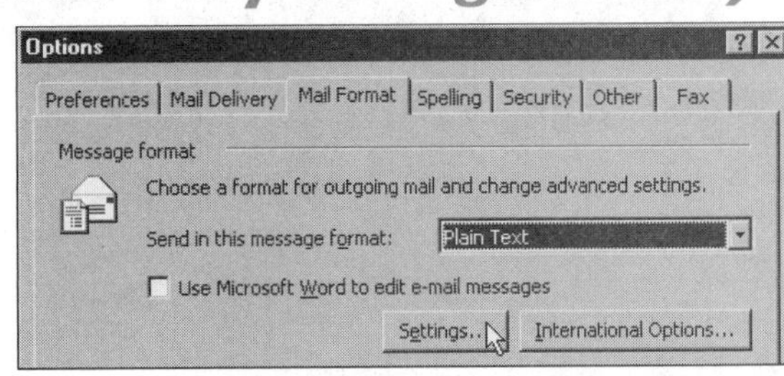


3. In the Plain Text Settings dialog box, in the Automatically Wrap At box, type the number of characters at which you want your message lines to wrap, and then click OK to close each of the dialog boxes. ▶

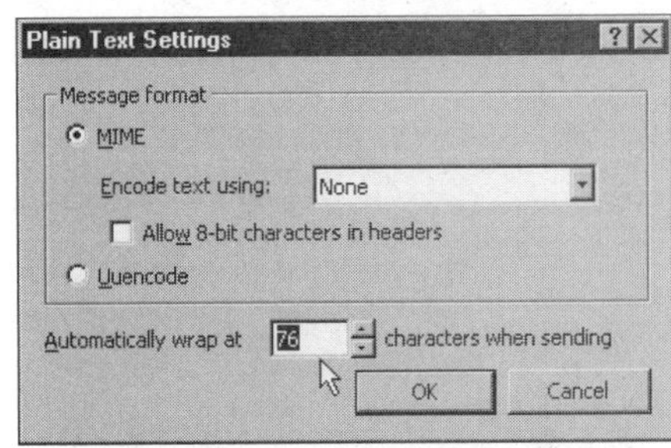


## How to fix it

1. On the Tools menu, click Options, and then click the Send tab. Under Mail Sending Format, click the Plain Text Settings button. ▶

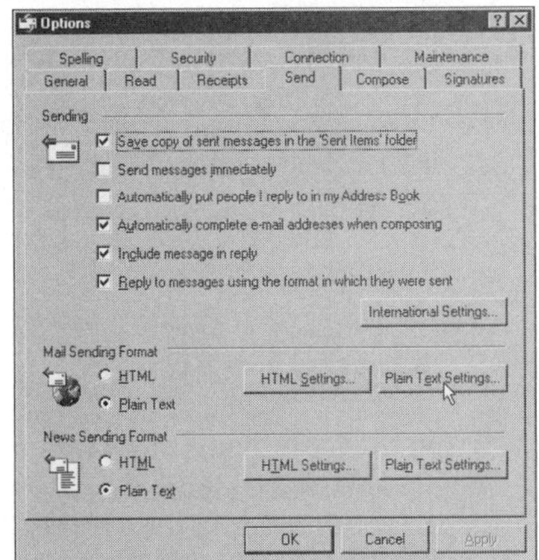


2. In the Plain Text Settings dialog box, in the Automatically Wrap Text At box, type the number of characters at which you want your message lines to wrap, and then click OK to close each of the dialog boxes. ▶

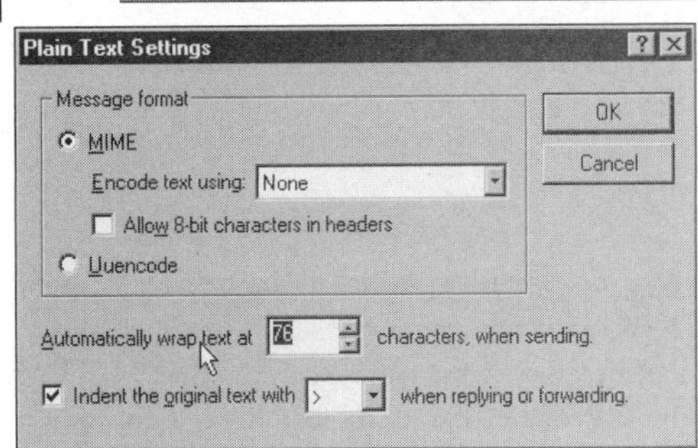


**Tip**

If you need to change your line wrap length for messages that you post to a newsgroup, click the Plain Text Settings button under News Sending Format and change the wrap length.

# I don't know how to change my default message format

## Source of the problem

You normally send e-mail in the very striking HTML message format, but recently several business associates have asked you to send e-mail in Plain Text format (they think it's more businesslike, and there's less threat of a script-borne virus arriving in their incoming mail). You want to comply with the requests, but you don't remember how to change your default message format. Or, you've always sent messages in Plain Text format, but your new employer likes to see colorful, highly formatted e-mail.

## Outlook 2000 How to fix it

1. On the Tools menu, click Options, and then click the Mail Format tab.
2. In the Send In This Message Format box, click a default message format—Plain Text, Microsoft Outlook Rich Text, or HTML. ▶
3. Click OK.

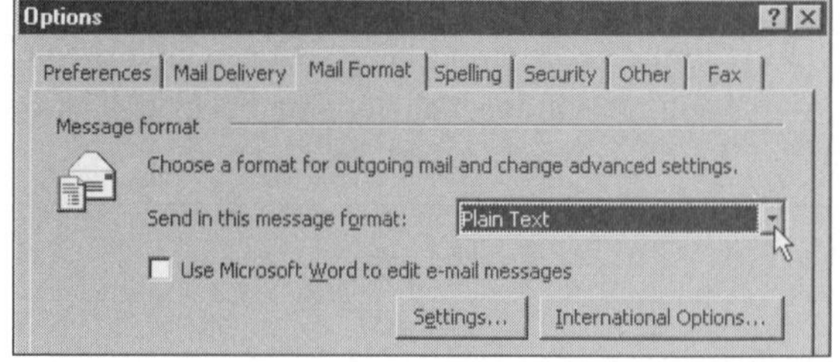

## How to fix it

1. On the Tools menu, click Options, and then click the Send tab.
2. Under Mail Sending Format, click the message format option you want. ▶
3. Click OK.

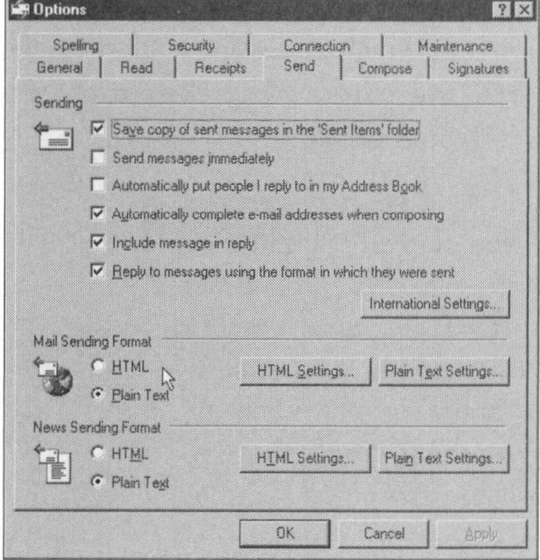


### Tip

If you participate in newsgroups, you can choose a format for posting messages to those newsgroups under News Sending Format. In most cases, you'll want to post messages to newsgroups using Plain Text format, because many of the recipients of your posted messages won't be able to read messages with fancy formatting.

# E-mail, in

**Do you have all your e-mail addresses in a program that's not listed in Outlook's Import Wizard?**

yes

no

Do you need to import your contacts into a new computer?

yes

no

Do you need to use your Outlook Express addresses in Outlook?

yes

no

Are your e-mail addresses all stored in Netscape Messenger?

yes

**Go to...**

**I don't know how to import my e-mail addresses from Netscape Messenger, page 72.**

no

Do you have contact data in WordPerfect that you need to use in Outlook?

yes

no

Are you trying to import a text file into Outlook?

yes

**Go to...**

**I can't import my Comma Separated Values text file into Outlook, page 76.**

**Quick fix**

Follow the procedure in the solution to "I can't import my WordPerfect mail-merge list into Outlook." Use a Comma Separated Values text file (a *.csv* file) as the intermediary file type that you export from your existing program and import into Outlook and Outlook Express.

**Quick fix**

See the solutions "I don't know how to back up my data" on and "I don't know how to move my data to a different computer."

**Go to...**

**I can't use my Outlook Express e-mail addresses in Outlook, page 70.**

**Go to...**

**I can't import my WordPerfect mail-merge list into Outlook, page 74.**

**If your solution isn't here**

Check this related chapter:

Switching e-mail programs, 252

Or see the general troubleshooting tips on page xiii.

# I can't use my Outlook Express e-mail addresses in Outlook

## Source of the problem

You've been using Outlook Express, and now you've added Outlook 2000 to the same machine. Your long list of e-mail addresses is in Outlook Express, and you need to get them into Outlook.

If you're using Outlook in the Internet Mail Only configuration, you can set the Outlook Express Address Book to share all your Contacts folders with Outlook. But if you're using Outlook in the Corporate/Workgroup configuration, you can't share contacts; instead, you must import the Outlook Express addresses into Outlook.

## How to fix it

### In Outlook, Corporate/Workgroup configuration

1. On the File menu, click Import And Export.
2. In the first wizard step, click Import Internet Mail And Addresses, and then click Next. ▶

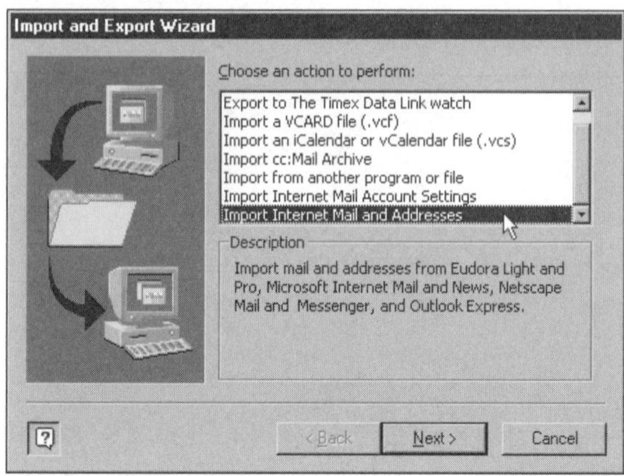

3. In the second wizard step, click Outlook Express. Select the Import Address Book check box to import your e-mail addresses and contact information. ▶

   You can also import existing e-mail in the Outlook Express Inbox, and any Rules you might have created to control mail flow in Outlook Express, by selecting the check boxes for the items you want to import.

4. Click Next and follow the rest of the steps in the wizard to finish importing your addresses.

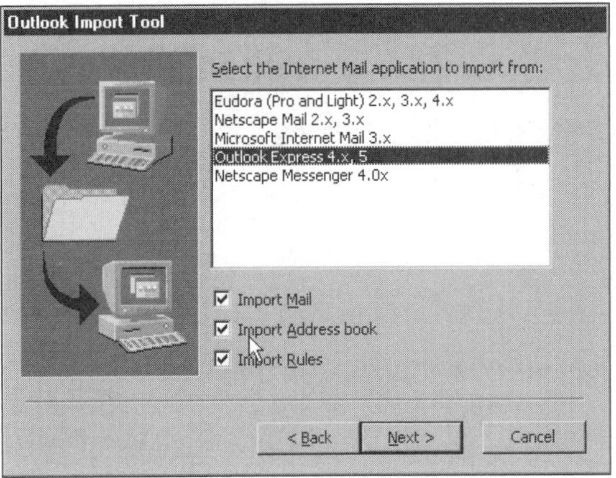


# How to fix it

## In Outlook, Internet Mail Only configuration

To share all addresses between Outlook 2000 (Internet Mail Only configuration) and Outlook Express, see "Outlook and Outlook Express have different address lists" on page 70.

# I don't know how to import my e-mail addresses from Netscape Messenger

## Source of the problem

You've been using Netscape Messenger, and that's where all your contacts and e-mail addresses are stored. Now that you're using Outlook (or Outlook Express), you don't want to reenter all that data—there must be an easier way to get your contacts and e-mail addresses into Outlook (or Outlook Express).

You're in luck—Microsoft anticipated your problem and made it easy to import Netscape Messenger contacts into Outlook or Outlook Express.

## Outlook 2000 How to fix it

1. On the File menu, click Import And Export.
2. In the first wizard step, click Import Internet Mail And Addresses, and then click Next.
3. In the second wizard step, click the appropriate version of Netscape. ▶
4. Select the Import Address Book check box to import your e-mail addresses and contact information.

   You can also import existing e-mail in Netscape by selecting the Import Mail check box.

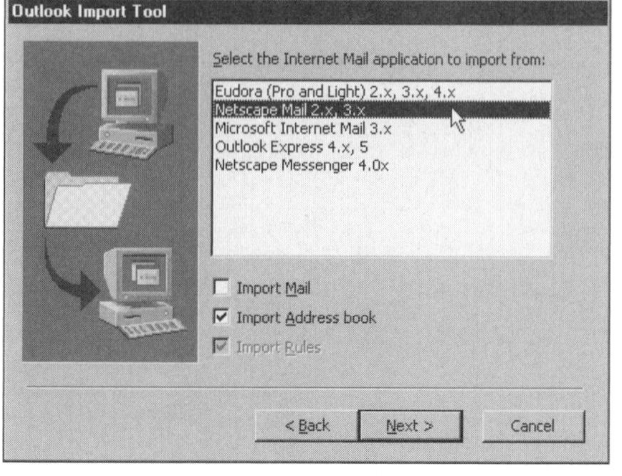


5. Click Next and follow the rest of the steps in the wizard to finish importing your addresses.

## How to fix it

1. On the File menu, point to Import, and click Other Address Book.
2. In the Address Book Import Tool dialog box, click your version of Netscape. ▶
3. Click Import and follow the rest of the wizard steps to finish importing your addresses.

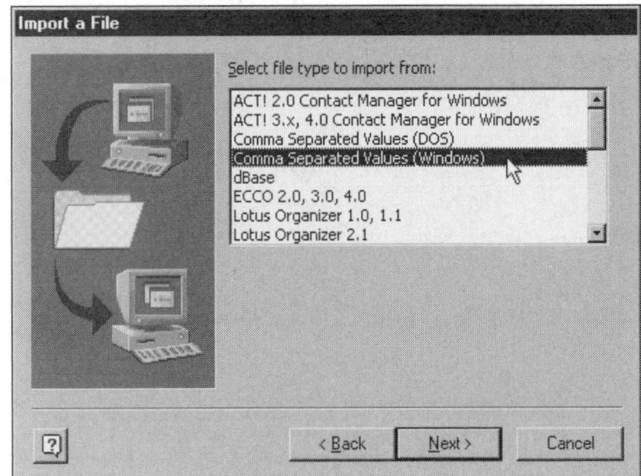

# I can't import my WordPerfect mail-merge list into Outlook

## Source of the problem

You have a sizable list of contacts built up in WordPerfect, and you want to import all this information into Outlook (or Outlook Express). But in Outlook's Import And Export Wizard (and in Outlook Express), there's no provision for importing addresses directly from WordPerfect.

The solution is to use a text file as an intermediary file type between WordPerfect and Outlook (or Outlook Express). First, consult your WordPerfect documentation to save or export your address book as a text file (Comma Separated Values), and then follow the steps in the next sections to import the new text file into Outlook or Outlook Express.

## Outlook 2000 How to fix it

1. On the File menu, click Import And Export.
2. In the first wizard step, click Import From Another Program Or File, and click Next.
3. In the second wizard step, click the text file type into which you saved or exported your WordPerfect addresses, and follow the wizard steps to import the addresses into Outlook. ▶

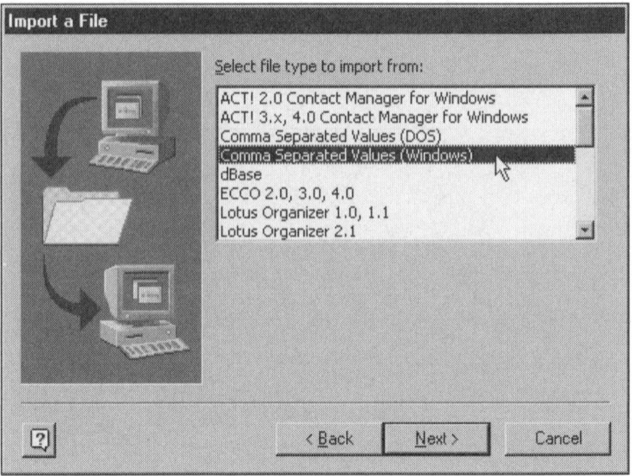

## How to fix it

1. On the File menu, point to Import, and click Other Address Book.
2. In the Address Book Import Tool dialog box, click Text File (Comma Separated Values). ▶
3. Click Import and follow the rest of the wizard steps to finish importing your addresses.

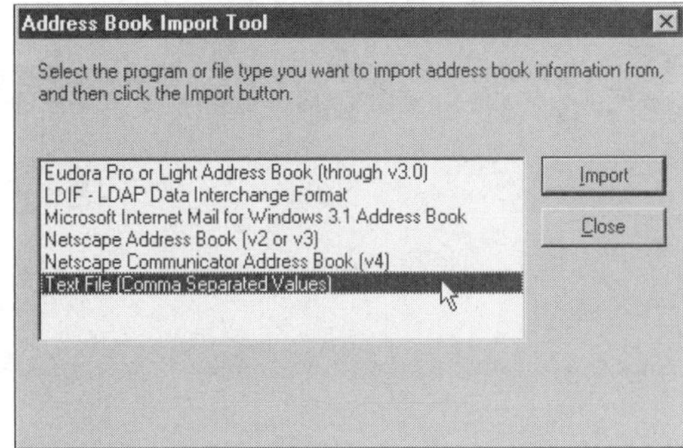

# I can't import my Comma Separated Values text file into Outlook

## Source of the problem

You exported or saved your contacts from another program as a Comma Separated Values (*.csv*) text file, and when you import it into Outlook, you don't see the individual fields listed in the Map Custom Fields dialog box. Instead, all the imported fields are in a single row, separated by small box characters. Even in a text file, formatting can be not quite readable by the importing program, but that's a problem you can fix. If you open the text file in Microsoft Excel, the Text Import Wizard reformats the file so that Outlook can read it. You can then use Excel to save the file, in either Comma Separated Values or Tab Separated Values format, and import that file into Outlook.

## How to fix it

First, open the text file in Microsoft Excel. Next, save the file in Excel as a text file type. Finally, import the resaved file into Outlook.

### Open the text file in Excel

1. In Excel, on the File menu, click Open.
2. Navigate to the text file and click Open. ▶
3. If the Text Import Wizard opens, click Finish.

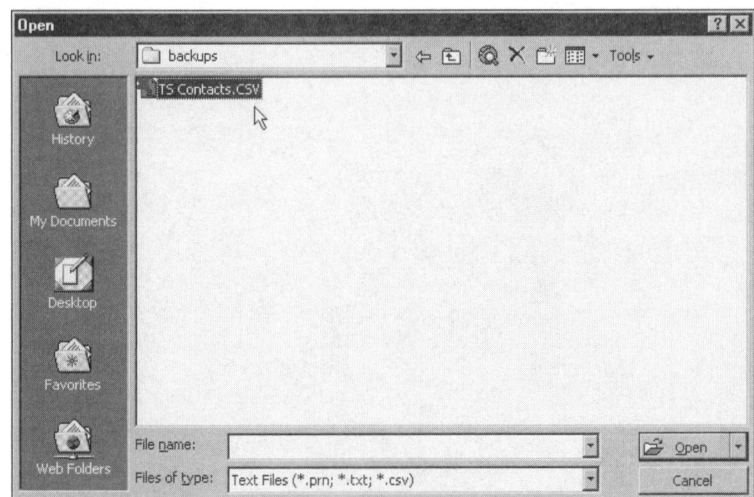

## Resave the file as a text file type

1. In Excel, on the File menu, click Save As.
2. In the Save As Type box, click Text (Tab Delimited) (.txt), and then click Save. ▶

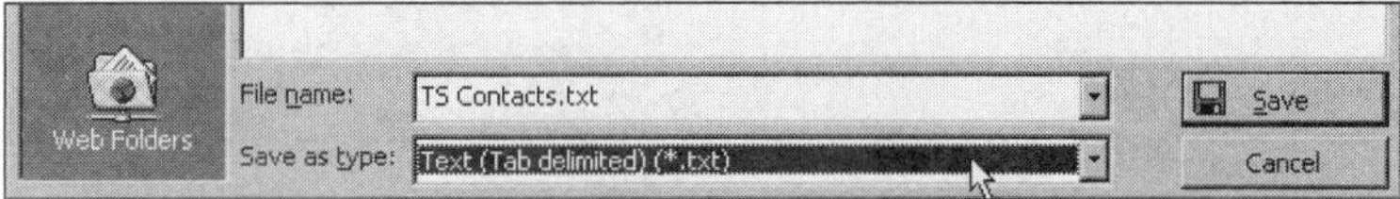


   If you're asked whether you want to keep this format, click Yes.
3. Close the text file and quit Excel.

   Now, import the resaved text file into Outlook.

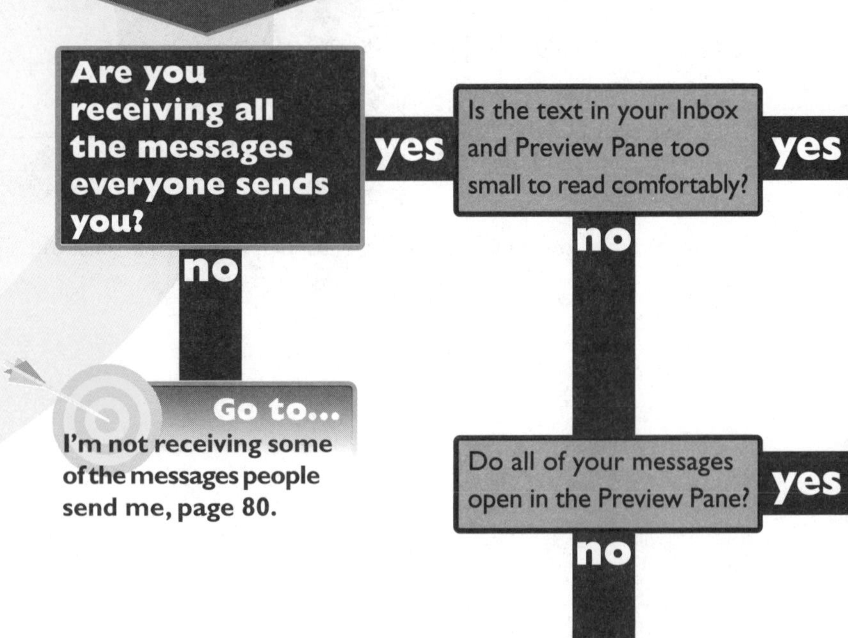
Are you receiving all the messages everyone sends you?
yes
no
Is the text in your Inbox and Preview Pane too small to read comfortably?
yes
no
Go to...
I'm not receiving some of the messages people send me, page 80.
Do all of your messages open in the Preview Pane?
yes
no

**Quick fix**

If a message is encrypted, you can't read it in the Preview Pane. Double-click the message to open it instead of reading it in the Preview Pane.

**Go to...**
The text in my Inbox and Preview Pane is too small to read comfortably, page 84.

Does Outlook download messages that flash through and disappear?

yes

**Quick fix**

In Outlook, you can create a mail rule that permanently deletes an incoming message rather than sending it to the Deleted Items folder (where you can find it before you delete it). Any incoming message that meets the criteria of that rule won't stop in your Inbox long enough for you to see it—it flashes through and gets permanently deleted. If you created this rule, and a message you're expecting inadvertently meets your "permanently delete this message" criteria, you'll never see the message.

If you have this problem with messages from specific contacts, add those contacts to your rule as "exceptions" so that the rule will ignore messages from them.

**If your solution isn't here**

Check these related chapters:

E-mail, sending, page 92

Files, receiving, page 136

Or see the general troubleshooting tips on page xiii.

# I'm not receiving some of the messages people send me

## Source of the problem

You know people are sending you e-mail, but some of the messages people have sent you don't appear in your Inbox.

There are a few reasons why you might not see messages that you receive: a filter in your Inbox, a junk mail filter, or mail rules that are sending your mail to a subfolder.

## How to fix it

### Remove the filter

If you see the words *Filter Applied* in the lower-right corner of your Outlook window or on the right side of the Folder banner, there's a filter applied to your Inbox. The filter might be hiding the new messages you can't find.

To remove the filter:

1. Right-click in the column headings row, and click Customize Current View.
2. In the View Summary dialog box, click the Filter button.
3. In the Filter dialog box, click the Clear All button. ▶
4. Click OK to close each open dialog box.

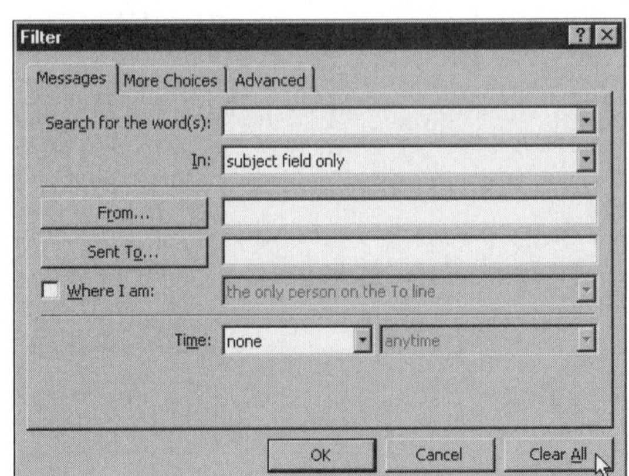


### Turn off the junk mail filter

If you have the junk mail filter turned on, any messages that appear to be junk mail are swept directly to your Deleted Items folder. The built-in junk mail filter looks for specific words and phrases in incoming messages that are likely to be found in junk mail, such as "advertisement," "money back," "over 18," and "100% satisfied." Unfortunately, some legitimate messages can contain junk mail filter criteria, and they, too, get swept into the Deleted Items folder.

To turn the junk mail filter off:

1. In the Inbox, on the Tools menu, click Organize.
2. In the Organize pane, on the left side, click Junk E-Mail. ▶

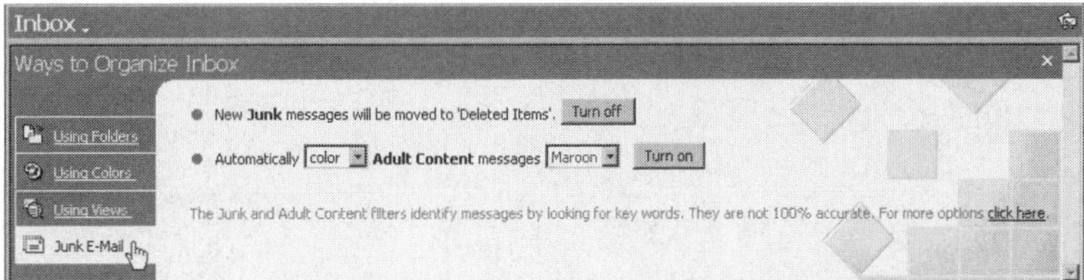


A Turn Off button in either the Junk or the Adult Content option means the filter is turned on.

3. In the Junk option, click the Turn Off button.
4. Click the X button in the upper-right corner of the Organize pane to close it.

**Tip**

To see the list of filter criteria that the junk mail filter uses, open the file *filters.txt* (in the folder where Outlook is installed). You can add or delete words and phrases to personalize your junk mail filter.

## Check your mail rules

If you created a mail rule that delivers incoming mail to a mail subfolder, the messages you're expecting might be in that subfolder (it's easy to forget that you created the rule or that the subfolder exists).

To look at the rules that are currently at work in Outlook:

1. On the Tools menu, click Rules Wizard.
2. In the Rules Wizard dialog box, scan the list of rules in the upper pane. If you want to know what a specific rule does, click the rule and read its description in the lower pane. ▶

   You might discover that mail is being channeled to a forgotten subfolder.

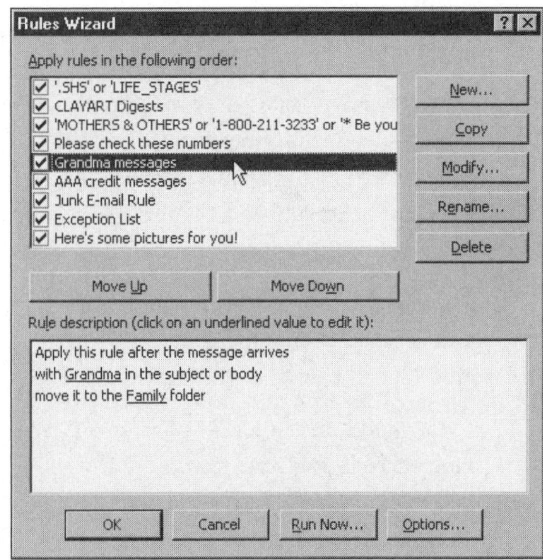


3. If you want to turn a rule off, clear its check box. If you want to delete the rule, click the rule name and then click the Delete button.
4. Click OK to close the dialog box.

***If this solution didn't solve your problem, go to the next page.***

# I'm not receiving some of the messages people send me

*(continued from page 81)*

## How to fix it

### Change the view

1. On the View menu, point to Current View, and then click Show All Messages.

   Any filters in your inbox are removed.

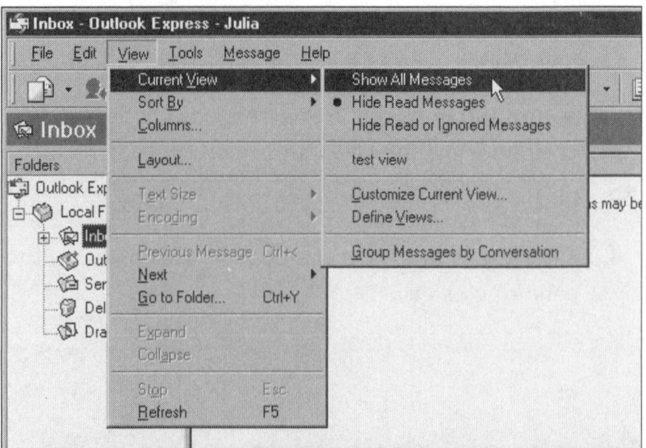


### Check your message rules

1. On the Tools menu, point to Message Rules, and then click Mail.
2. In the Message Rules dialog box, scan the list of rules in the upper pane. If you want to know what a specific rule does, click the rule and read its description in the lower pane.

   You might discover that some of your mail is being channeled to a forgotten subfolder.
3. If you want to turn a rule off, clear its check box. If you want to delete the rule, click the rule name and then click the Remove button.
4. Click OK to close the dialog box.

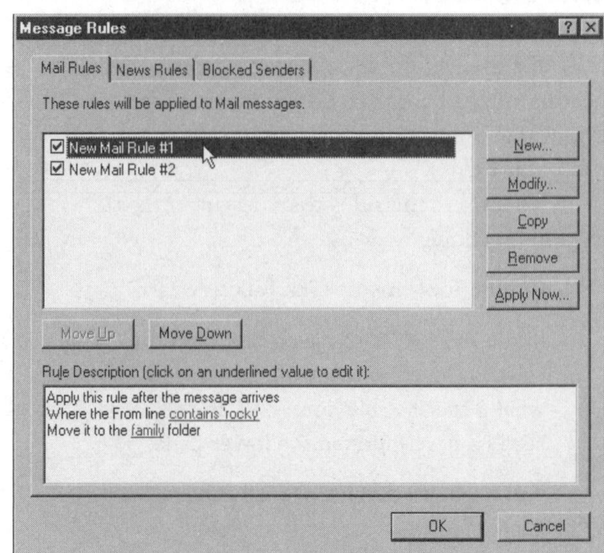


**Tip**

If you have no Rules set up, you'll see the New Mail Rule dialog box instead of the Message Rules dialog box; and, if you don't have any Rules, a forgotten rule isn't a problem.

# The text in my Inbox and Preview Pane is too small to read comfortably

## Source of the problem

You sit in front of that darn computer too many hours a day, and when your eyes are tired, the text in your messages seems to get uncomfortably small. Wouldn't it be great if you could make the text bigger and easier to read? Well, you can.

## Outlook 2000 How to fix it

To change the font size in plain text messages that you create and receive:

1. On the Tools menu, click Options.
2. On the Mail Format tab, under Stationery and Fonts, click the Fonts button.

**Tip**

This procedure changes the text that you see, but your plain text messages still go out without formatting, so your recipients read your messages in whatever font they've chosen in their mail program.

3. Next to the When Composing And Reading Plain Text box, click the Choose Font button. ▶
4. Click a font and font size.
5. Click OK to close each dialog box.

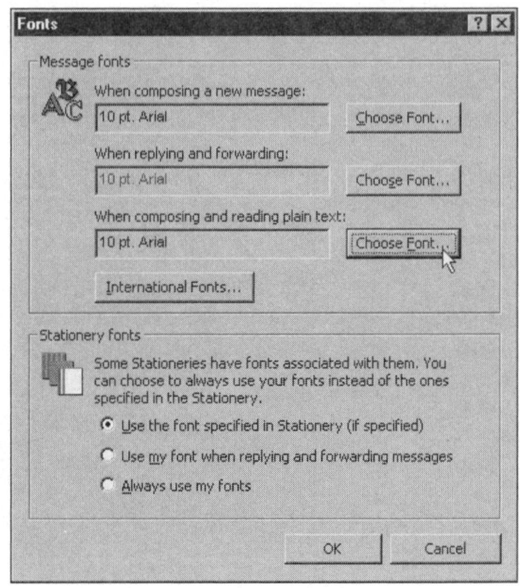

## Change the font in the Preview Pane header

1. With the Preview Pane open, right-click the Preview Pane header.
2. Click Preview Pane Options.
3. In the Preview Pane dialog box, under Preview Header, click the Font button. ▶
4. Click a new font size.
5. Click OK to close each dialog box.

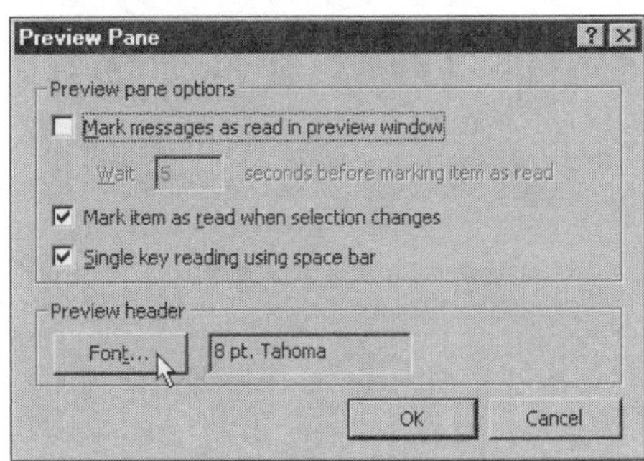


## Change the font in the list of message headers in your Inbox

1. On the View menu, point to Current View, and click Customize Current View.
2. In the View Summary dialog box, click the Other Settings button.
3. In the Other Settings dialog box, under Rows, click the Font button. ▶
4. Make your font changes in the Font dialog box.
5. Click OK to close each dialog box.

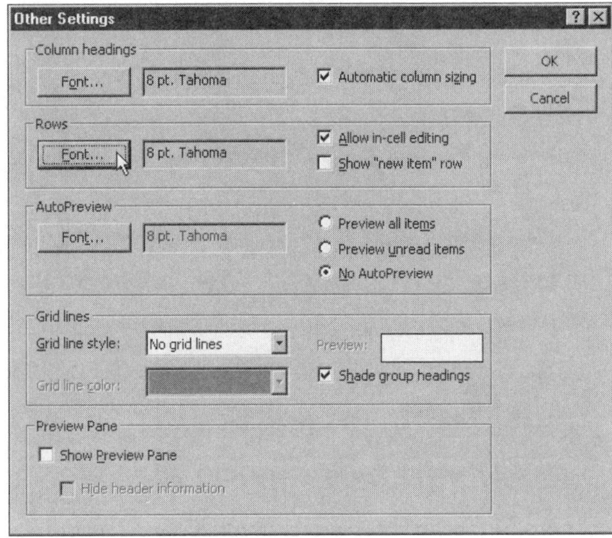


**Tip**

In the Other Settings dialog box, you can also change the font for the three AutoPreview lines and the column headings.

*If this solution didn't solve your problem, go to the next page.*

# The text in my Inbox and Preview Pane is too small to read comfortably

*(continued from page 85)*

## How to fix it

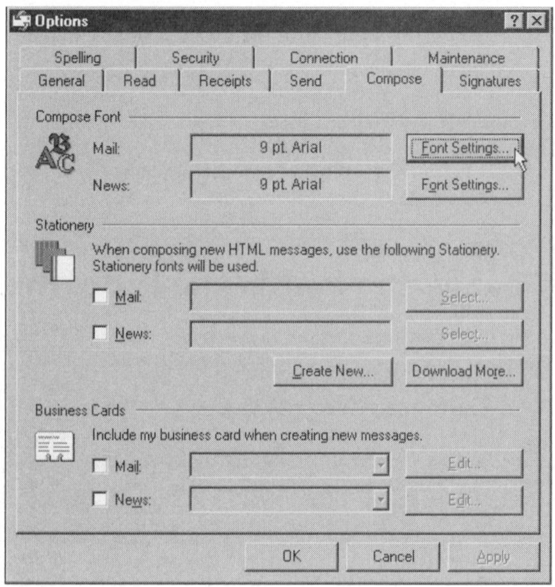


### Change the default size of text in outgoing messages

1. On the Tools menu, click Options, and then click the Compose tab.
2. Under Compose Font, in the Mail row, click the Font Settings button. ▶
3. In the Font dialog box, click the new font size.
4. Click OK to close each dialog box.

### Change the default font and font size in messages you receive

1. On the Tools menu, click Options, and then click the Read tab.
2. Under Fonts, click the Fonts button.
3. In the Proportional Font box, click a font.
4. In the Font Size box, click a font size.
5. Click OK to close each dialog box.

### Change the size of text in a message you're reading

- If you're reading an open message, on the message's View menu, point to Text Size, and then click Larger or Largest. ▶
- If you're reading the message in the Preview Pane, on the View menu, point to Text Size, and then click Larger or Largest.

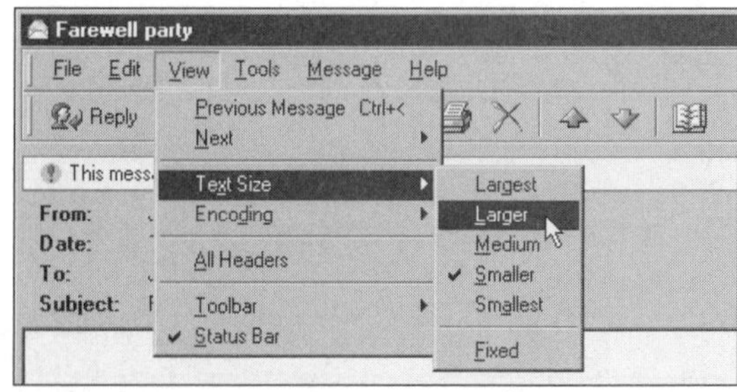

# E-mail, re

**Did your recipient fail to receive your message at all?** yes

no

Did your recipient get your message with a *winmail.dat* attachment? yes

no

Did the message you sent have the last word or two of each line cut off? yes

no

Did your recipient get a message that was all gibberish? yes

no

Did each of your recipients get the names and e-mail addresses of everyone who got a copy of your message? yes

no

Has your colleague asked you to send messages in a different encoding format? yes

no

Does your recipient receive all the message features you send?

no

**Go to...**
**My recipient doesn't receive the message features I send, page 91.**

# cipients' problems

**Quick fix**

Send the message again. Sometimes a mail server is down and messages can be lost permanently.

**Go to...**

**My recipient got my messaage with a *winmail.dat* attachment, page 90.**

**Go to...**

**My message lines wrap and break in the wrong places, page 64.**

**Go to...**

**I don't know how to change my message encoding format, page 62.**

**Go to...**

**I don't know how to hide recipient names, page 156.**

**Go to...**

**I don't know how to change my message encoding format, page 62.**

**If your solution isn't here**

Check these related chapters:

E-mail, sending, page 92
E-mail, receiving, page 78
E-mail, creating, page 56
Hidden names (blind copies), page 154
Or see the general troubleshooting tips on page xiii.

# My recipient got my message with a *winmail.dat* attachment

## Source of the problem

You sent a message to an associate that was in Rich Text format, with indented, bulleted lines of text and a variety of colors that emphasized the important parts of your message. But the message your recipient got had a mysterious attachment named *winmail.dat* (which the recipient couldn't open), and none of your colorful formatting.

The problem lies in your recipient's mail program or in a mail server through which the message must pass to reach your recipient—the program or server either can't or won't read your message. All the accessory coding for colors and bullets and extra features, such as voting buttons, which can't be read by the recipient's mail server or mail program, are contained in the attached file *winmail.dat*. The attachment is useless, but it serves to keep the message clean so that your recipient can read the plain text of your message.

**Tip**

If your recipient gets an attachment with a name that starts with *ATT0000*, it's the same as the *winmail.dat* attachment, but your recipient's mail program doesn't recognize the *winmail.dat* attachment name.

## How to fix it

Always send mail to that recipient in Plain Text so that he or she doesn't get the extra attachments. There are three ways to do this:

- Make Plain Text your default message format so that everyone gets plain text messages (on the Outlook Tools menu, click Options, click the Mail Format tab, and in the Send In This Message Format box, click Plain Text).
- Change the message format for that recipient when you create the message (in the open message, on the Format menu, click Plain Text).
- On that recipient's Contact form, below the E-mail Address box, select the Send Using Plain Text check box. Any message you address to that recipient will be formatted in Plain Text, regardless of your default message format. ▶

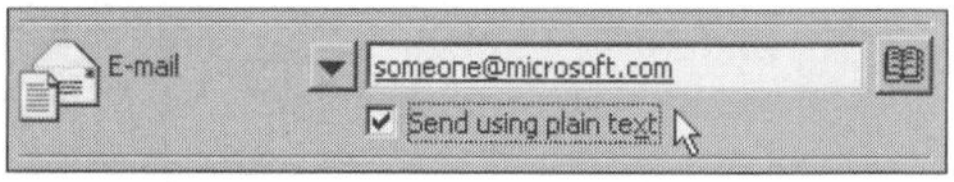

# My recipient doesn't receive the message features I send

## Source of the problem

You sent a message to an associate that was in Rich Text format, with indented, bulleted lines of text and a variety of colors that emphasized the important parts of your message. But when your recipient opened the message, it was in Plain Text, with no colors or indents. So what happened to all your detailed formatting?

Your recipient probably used Outlook Express to receive e-mail (it also happens in some other mail programs). The mail program ignores extra formatting and features. Also, some mail servers (such as Microsoft Exchange Server) have the option to remove the extra coding from Rich Text messages, so those recipients always receive Plain Text messages.

## How to fix it

Send richly formatted messages formatted in HTML (to colleagues who don't mind receiving HTML messages), or limit yourself to Plain Text messages so that you know what your recipient will see (and you don't waste time on useless message formatting).

In the two figures at the right, the upper figure is a message created in Outlook and formatted in Rich Text, and the lower figure is the same message received in Outlook Express. ▶

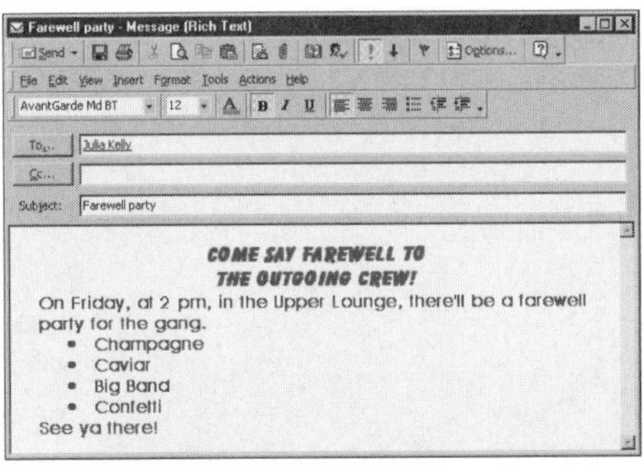


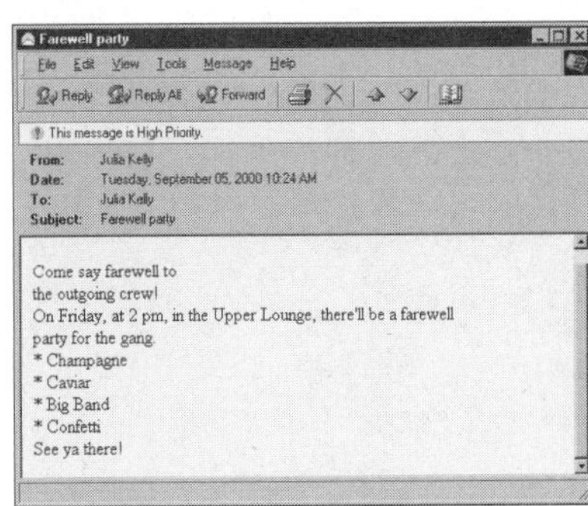


Other special message features, such as voting buttons, are received only by correspondents who run Outlook on the Microsoft Exchange Server. This probably includes everyone on your network (because if you didn't have Microsoft Exchange Server, you couldn't have sent the voting buttons), but correspondents who got your message through Internet mail and don't run Outlook on the Microsoft Exchange Server receive normal messages without voting buttons.

**Tip**

If you send voting buttons off your network, include a line in your message that says **Please respond by using the voting buttons—if you don't see voting buttons in this message, send a reply specifying your choice.**

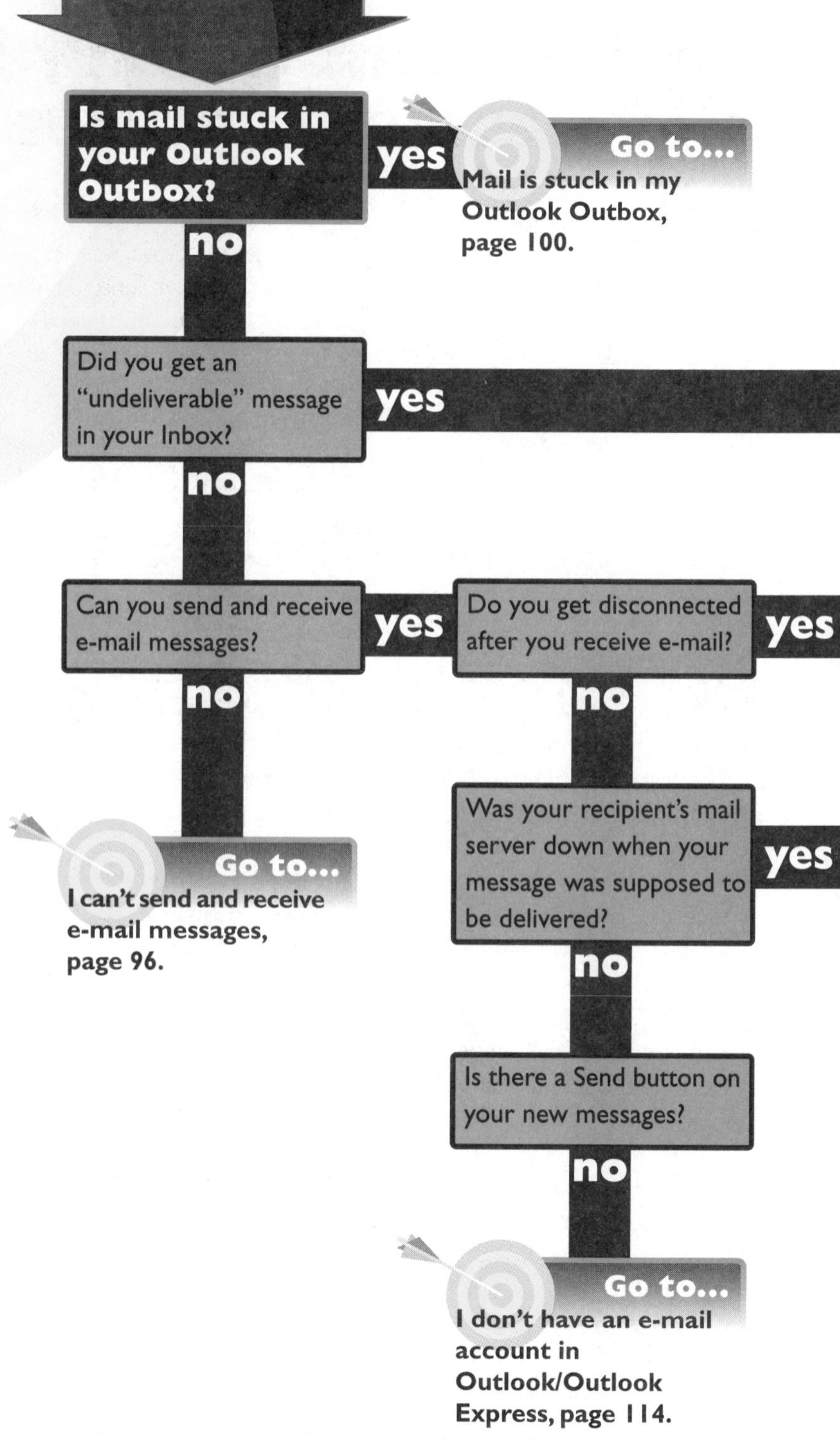
Is mail stuck in your Outlook Outbox?
yes
Go to...
Mail is stuck in my Outlook Outbox, page 100.
no
Did you get an "undeliverable" message in your Inbox?
yes
no
Can you send and receive e-mail messages?
yes
Do you get disconnected after you receive e-mail?
yes
no
no
Go to...
I can't send and receive e-mail messages, page 96.
Was your recipient's mail server down when your message was supposed to be delivered?
yes
no
Is there a Send button on your new messages?
no
Go to...
I don't have an e-mail account in Outlook/Outlook Express, page 114.

**Quick fix**

This can happen if your recipient's e-mail address is incorrect, or if your ISP is busy or out of service. You should first check the recipient's address and make sure it's entered correctly. If it is, resend the message when the ISP is available (either at a different time of day, or after any problems at the ISP have been fixed).

**Go to...**

**After I send or receive e-mail, I get disconnected, page 94.**

**Quick fix**

When your recipient tells you the mail server is up again, resend the original message from the Sent Items folder:

1. In the Sent Items folder, open the message.
2. On the message's Actions menu, click Resend This Message.
3. When the original message appears, click the Send button on the message's toolbar.

**If your solution isn't here**

Check these related chapters:

E-mail account, 108

Error messages, 122

Or see the general troubleshooting tips on page xiii.

# After I send or receive e-mail, I get disconnected

## Source of the problem

If you need to limit your ISP connection time, it's very helpful to have Outlook or Outlook Express disconnect itself when it's finished performing its online tasks. But if connection time is not a problem (for example, if your computer has a dedicated phone line and your e-mail account provides unlimited connection time), automatic disconnection can be very annoying—you spend too much extra time dialing up and reconnecting every time you need to send and receive e-mail or visit a web site. By changing a single check box setting, you can control when you disconnect from your ISP.

## Outlook 2000 How to fix it

### In Internet Mail Only configuration

1. On the Tools menu, click Options.
2. Click the Mail Delivery tab.
3. Clear the Hang Up When Finished Sending, Receiving, Or Updating check box. ▶
4. Click OK to close the dialog box.

When you're ready to disconnect, right-click the connection icon on the right side of the Taskbar, and click Disconnect. ▶ 4:29 PM

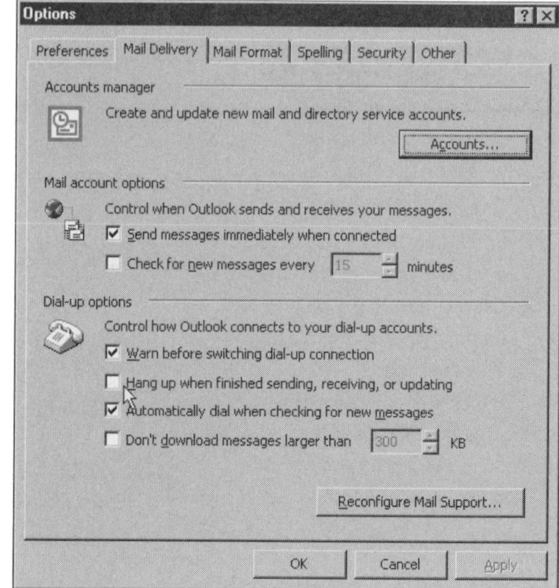

## In Outlook, Corporate/Workgroup configuration

1. On the Tools menu, click Options.
2. Click the Internet E-mail tab.
3. Clear the If Using A Dial-Up Connection Hang Up When Finished Sending And Receiving Mail check box. ▶
4. Click OK to close the dialog box.

   When you're ready to disconnect, right-click the connection icon on the right side of the Taskbar, and click Disconnect. ▶

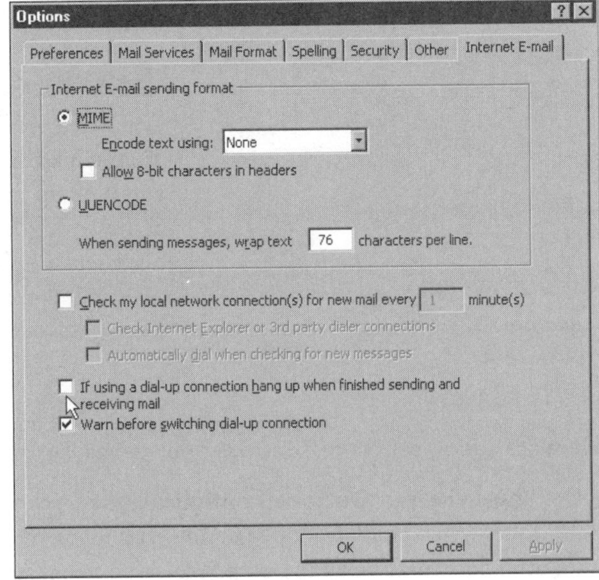


## Outlook Express How to fix it

1. On the Tools menu, click Options.
2. Click the Connection tab.
3. Clear the Hang Up After Sending And Receiving check box. ▶
4. Click OK to close the dialog box.

   When you're ready to disconnect, right-click the connection icon on the right side of the Taskbar, and click Disconnect.

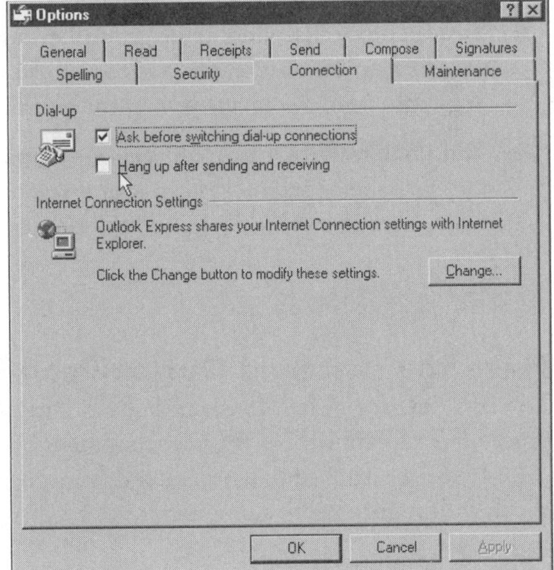

# I can't send and receive e-mail messages

## Source of the problem

You write new messages, send them to the Outbox, and then click the Send/Receive button to send outgoing mail and pick up incoming mail. But nothing happens. You might or might not get connected to your ISP, and if you do get connected, you might or might not get any of several error messages. All you know for sure is that your e-mail does not go out or come in.

Here are a few possible reasons why your e-mail isn't moving:

- **You switched Outlook configurations**—Each Outlook configuration (Corporate/Workgroup and Internet Mail Only) has its own mailbox setup. The first time you switch from one configuration to the other, you need to set up the appropriate mail delivery route and means of connection. After you've set up mail delivery the first time in each configuration, you can switch between configurations quickly without setting up mail delivery again.
- **You recently installed or upgraded an anti-virus program**—In both Outlook and Outlook Express, installation of some anti-virus programs can alter your Internet account settings. You might need to reenter your account information.
- **You uninstalled Outlook Express**—Outlook and Outlook Express share files that are necessary for sending and receiving e-mail. If you uninstalled Outlook Express, Outlook's mail service won't function properly. You need to reinstall Outlook Express.

## How to fix it

### Have you switched Outlook configurations?

The first time you switch configurations in Outlook, you need to make sure that the connection procedure is appropriate in the new configuration.

If you've switched to Corporate/Workgroup configuration and are using a network mailbox, check with your network administrator to be sure that your mailbox and connection are set up correctly.

If you switched to Corporate/Workgroup configuration, and you're connecting directly to the Internet to send and receive e-mail, check these connection settings to be sure your connection is correct:

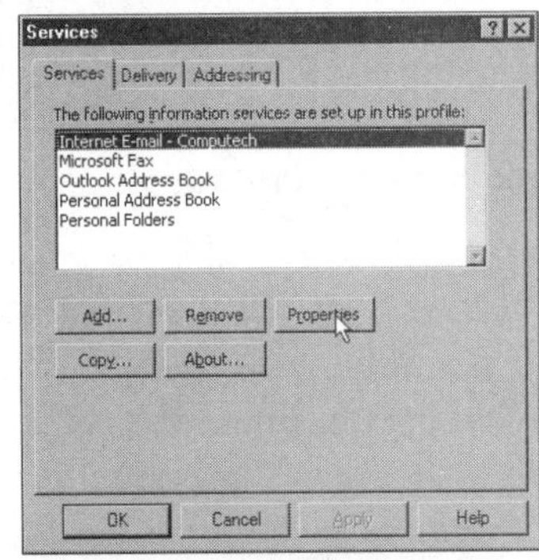


1. On the Tools menu, click Services.
2. On the Services tab, click the account name, and click Properties. ▶
3. In the account Properties dialog box, click the Connection tab.
4. Click the correct connection type. For an Internet e-mail account that you dial into with a modem, click the Connect Using My Phone Line option. ▶
5. Click OK twice to close both dialog boxes.

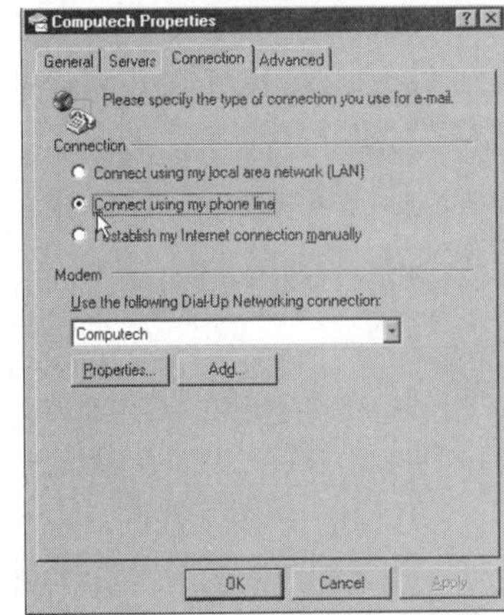


If you switched to Internet Mail Only configuration, check these connection settings to be sure your account information is correct:

1. On the Tools menu, click Accounts.
2. On the Mail tab, click the account name, and click Properties. ▶
3. In the account Properties dialog box, click the Connection tab.
4. Click the correct connection type. For an Internet e-mail account that you dial into with a modem, click the Connect Using My Phone Line option.
5. Click OK and Close to close both dialog boxes.

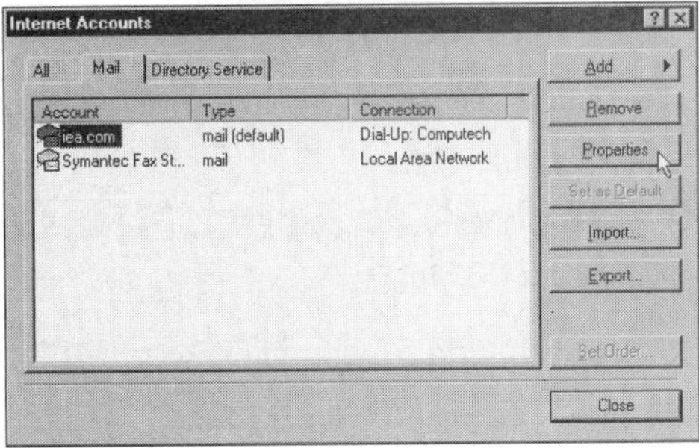


## Have you uninstalled Outlook Express?

Outlook needs to use shared files that are uninstalled if you uninstall Outlook Express.

To reinstall Outlook Express, visit the Microsoft upgrade site (at *http://www.microsoft.com/windows/ie/download/*) and download the most current version of Internet Explorer for your operating system, which installs the most current version of Outlook Express.

***If this solution didn't solve your problem, go to the next page.***

# I can't send and receive e-mail messages

*(continued from page 97)*

## Have you recently installed or upgraded an anti-virus program?

If you recently installed or upgraded an anti-virus program, that new program might have changed some of your Internet account settings. The method you use to change those settings back to what they should be depends on your program (Outlook or Outlook Express) and configuration (Internet Mail Only or Corporate/Workgroup).

### In Outlook, Corporate/Workgroup configuration

1. On the Tools menu, click Services.
2. On the Services tab, click the account name, and then click the Properties button. ▶
3. In the account Properties dialog box, click the Servers tab.
4. On the Servers tab, delete any existing server names and retype the correct server names (if you don't have this information, your ISP can give it to you). ▶
5. Delete and retype your user name and password.
6. Click OK twice to close both dialog boxes.

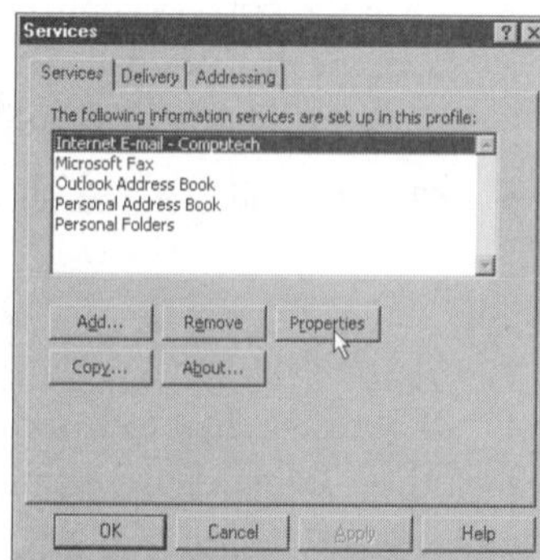


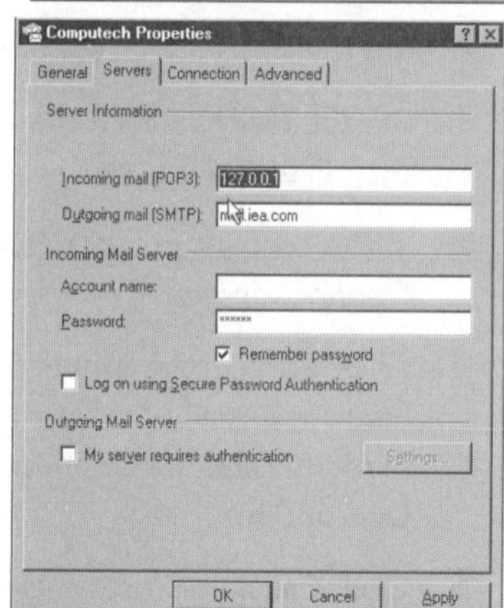


### In Outlook, Internet Mail Only configuration

1. On the Tools menu, click Accounts.
2. On the Mail tab, click your account name.
3. If you have more than one account listed (which is the case after installing some anti-virus programs), click the name of the original account, and click the Set As Default button. ▶
4. Click the original account name, and then click the Properties button.
5. In the account Properties dialog box, click the Servers tab.

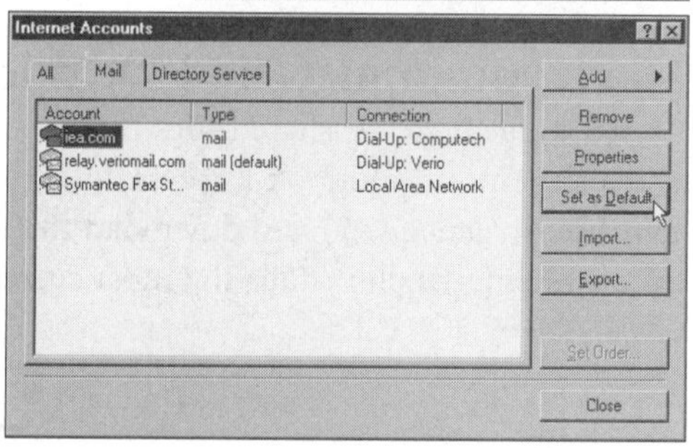

6. On the Servers tab, delete any existing server names and retype the correct server names (if you don't have this information, your ISP can give it to you). ▶

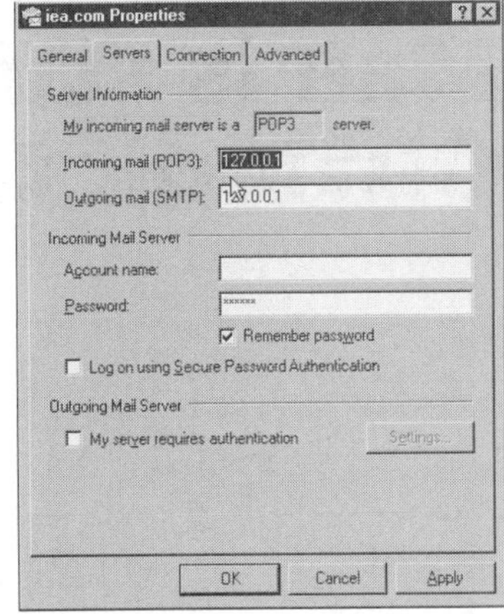


7. Click OK and Close to close the open dialog boxes.

8. Quit Outlook and then start it again.

Outlook Express

## How to fix it

1. On the Tools menu, click Accounts.

2. Click the Mail tab, and then click your account name. ▶

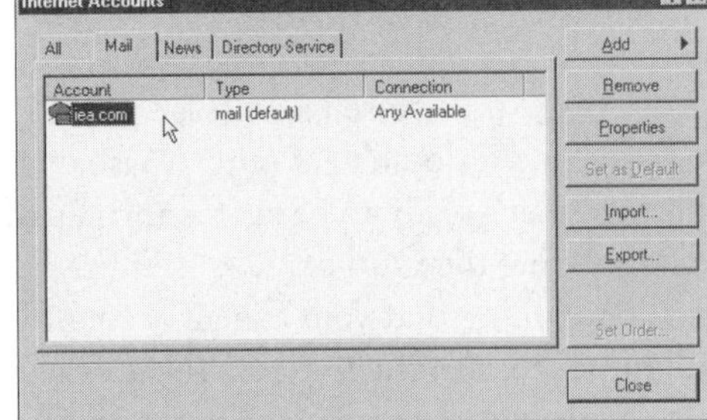


3. If you have more than one account listed (which is the case after installing some anti-virus programs), click the name of the original account, and click the Set As Default button.

4. Click the account name, and then click the Properties button.

5. In the account Properties dialog box, click the Servers tab.

6. Delete any existing server names and retype the correct server names (if you don't have this information, your ISP can give it to you). ▶

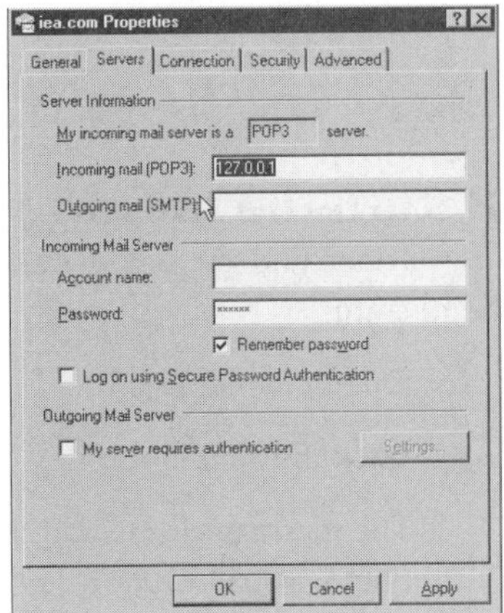


7. Delete and retype your user name and password.

8. Click OK and Close to close the open dialog boxes.

9. Quit Outlook Express and then start it again.

# Mail is stuck in my Outlook Outbox

## Source of the problem

When you send e-mail, the messages in your Outbox don't leave, even though you can connect and download your incoming e-mail. There are several possible reasons (and solutions) for mail stuck in the Outbox, and the reasons (and solutions) might differ depending on your Outlook configuration.

The most common reason why messages don't leave your Outbox, regardless of your configuration, is that you opened and then closed a message while it was still in your Outbox. That changes the status of the message and it doesn't get sent. A visual clue that this is the problem is in the message title—a message that's ready to be sent is formatted in italics, and a message that's not formatted in italics is not leaving the Outbox.

Assuming that your e-mail account is set up correctly, there are other reasons why a message might be stuck in the Outbox: the message is corrupt, you're sending e-mail on an account that's not the default outgoing mail account, you're working offline, or your Personal Folders file is damaged.

Try the short solutions in the next How to fix it section first, and if those don't work, try the short solutions in the section for your configuration. If the message is still stuck, try repairing the Personal Folders file.

## How to fix it in both configurations

### Return the message to Send status

If you open and then close a message while it's in the Outbox, you need to return the message to Send status.

1. Open the message.
2. Click the Send button on the message toolbar.

   The message closes, and the message title is italicized. The next time you connect to send outgoing mail, Outlook sends the message.

### Find out whether the message is corrupt

To find out whether a message is not departing the Outbox because it's corrupt, move the message out of the Outbox and try to send a new message.

1. Move the stuck message into your Deleted Items folder.
2. Create a short new message (send it to yourself or to a colleague who doesn't mind helping you).
3. Send the new message.

If the new message goes out successfully, the stuck message is somehow corrupted—you should delete it and recreate it. If the new message doesn't go out successfully, move the stuck message back into your Outbox and try a different solution.

## Repair a damaged Personal Folders file

Run the Inbox Repair Tool to repair your Personal Folders file.

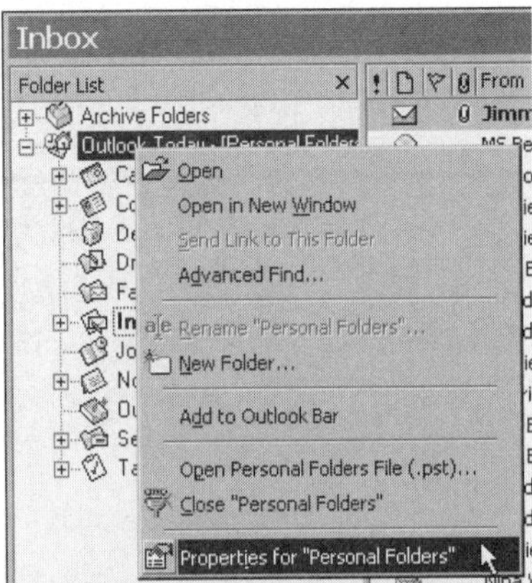


1. Display the Folder list (on the View menu, click Folder List).
2. In the Folder list, right-click the Personal Folders icon (it might be labeled Outlook Today), and click Properties For "Personal Folders". ▶
3. On the General tab, click the Advanced button.
4. In the Personal Folders dialog box, write down (on a piece of paper) the path and name of your *outlook.pst* file. Then click Cancel twice to close both dialog boxes. ▶

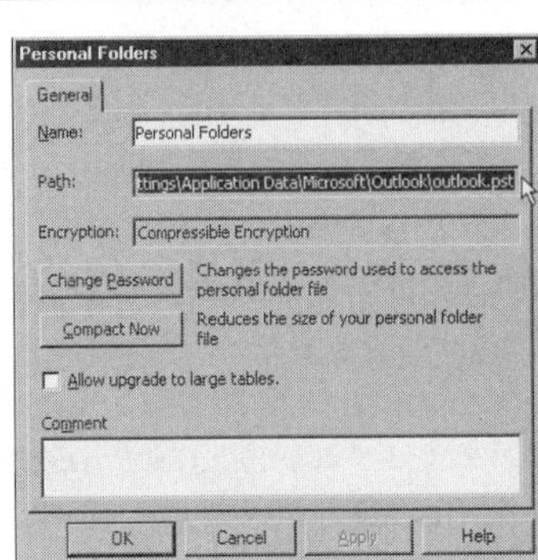


**Tip**

Drag to click the entire path in the Path box, and then press Ctrl+C to copy it. Then you can paste it into the Inbox Repair Tool in step 7.

5. On the File menu, click Exit (to quit Outlook).
6. Click the Windows Start button, point to Programs, point to Accessories, point to System Tools, and then click Inbox Repair Tool.

   If you don't see Inbox Repair Tool on your System Tools menu, click the Start button, point to Find, click Files Or Folders, and search for the file *scanpst.exe*. In the Find Files dialog box, double-click the file *scanpst.exe* to run the Inbox Repair Tool.

***If this solution didn't solve your problem, go to the next page.***

# Mail is stuck in my Outlook Outbox

(continued from page 101)

7. In the Inbox Repair Tool dialog box, click the Browse button, and navigate to the path and name of the *outlook.pst* file you wrote down in step 4. ▶

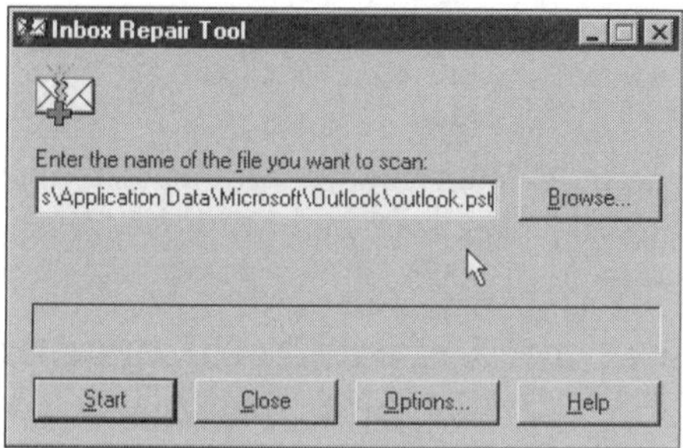


8. In the Inbox Repair Tool, click the Start button. The Inbox Repair Tool begins scanning your files.
9. When the Inbox Repair Tool is finished, restart Outlook.
10. Open the message that's stuck in your Outbox, copy the contents of the message (drag to click the contents of the message and then press Ctrl+C).
11. Create a new message, and paste the copied contents of the stuck message (click in the body of the message and press Ctrl+V).
12. Delete the original stuck message and try sending the new message.

**Tip**
If you copied the path and file name in step 4, you can click in the path box and press Ctrl+V to paste it in the Inbox Repair Tool.

If you still can't send the message, try the solutions in the section for your Outlook configuration.

## How to fix it

### In Corporate/Workgroup

In the Corporate/Workgroup configuration, one possible cause of stuck messages is having multiple Internet service accounts in the same profile and sending your e-mail using an account that is not the default outgoing account. Even though you can have multiple Internet e-mail accounts, you can specify only one of them as the default account for outgoing e-mail.

You can choose your default outgoing account each time you send e-mail, or you can change the default delivery account. If that doesn't work, try repairing your Personal Folders file (see the solution "Repair a damaged Personal Folders file" in the previous How to fix it section covering both configurations).

### Send your outgoing e-mail using the default e-mail account

1. On the Tools menu, point to Send and Receive.
2. Click the account at the bottom of the list of accounts (this is the default account). Your outgoing e-mail will be sent using that account.

## Change your default delivery account

1. On the Tools menu, click Services.
2. On the Delivery tab, click the account you want to set as the default outgoing e-mail account.
3. Click the up arrow on the right to move the clicked account to the top of the list, and click OK. ▶
4. Quit and restart Outlook.

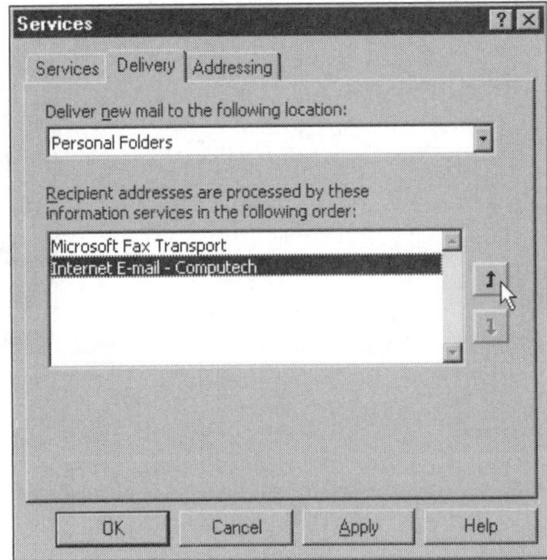


# How to fix it

## In Internet Mail Only

In the Internet Mail Only configuration, you might be working offline or you might have a damaged Personal Folders file.

First, try the easy solution: make sure you're working online. If that doesn't work, try repairing your Personal Folders file (see the solution "Repair a damaged Personal Folders file" in the How to fix it section covering both configurations).

To make sure you're working online:

1. On the File menu, clear the Work Offline check box. ▶
2. Send your messages.

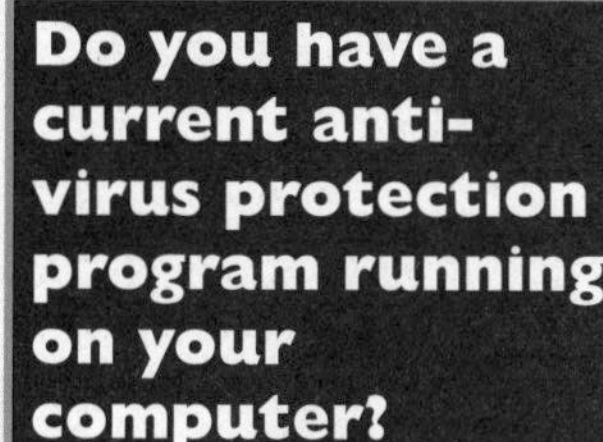

**Do you have a current anti-virus protection program running on your computer?**

yes

Do you always open attachments you receive in e-mail messages?

yes

no

Do you always open every message you receive, even if you don't recognize the sender?

yes

no

Do you want to know more about e-mail–borne viruses and their prevention?

yes

no

**Quick fix**

A good anti-virus program is your first line of defense against any computer virus, regardless of its source, and it's well worth whatever it costs. Norton and McAfee are two prominent and reliable anti-virus programs. But remember that you often need to update your anti-virus program with new virus definitions so that you can stay one step ahead of any new viruses.

**If your solution isn't here**
Check the general troubleshooting tips on page xiii.

**Quick fix**

If you do, you run a risk of infecting your computer with a virus. Most viruses are carried into your computer in attached files, and when you open the file, the virus infects your computer. Although you can get viruses even in presumably safe files sent to you by friends or colleagues who didn't know the file was infected, you can reduce your risk of infection by not opening any kind of attached file you aren't expecting.

**Quick fix**

Opening messages from strangers is risky these days. HTML-formatted messages can carry viruses that infect your computer when the script contained in the HTML code runs, and you can't tell which messages are HTML until you open them.

In Outlook 2000, scripts in an HTML message cannot run when the message is opened in the Preview Pane. In Outlook Express, however, scripts in HTML can run even in the Preview Pane.

**Go to...**

**I don't know how to protect my computer from e-mail viruses, page 106.**

# I don't know how to protect my computer from e-mail viruses

## Source of the problem

As of the publication of this book, e-mail viruses are the latest and most damaging craze in malicious computer viruses. Outlook is an especially promising target for creators of computer viruses because it's widely used and easy to program, and all your contacts, as well as the rest of your hard disk, are within easy reach of any virus-borne programming.

Not so long ago it was easier to avoid e-mail viruses because they always arrived in attached files, and you had to open the attached file for the virus to run. But now some viruses are being sent as scripts hidden in the HTML coding of HTML-formatted messages, and the viruses are released when the HTML message is opened and the scripts it contains are run. In the not-so-distant future, virus creators are likely to find even more insidious ways to use Outlook (and other e-mail programs) to carry and propagate viruses.

## Outlook 2000 How to fix it

Visit Slipstick Systems, at *http://www.slipstick.com*—it's a great source of current Outlook information. While you're there, look up anything related to viruses—you'll find links for downloading lots of security updates and instructions for more ways to protect your computer by making changes in Windows and Internet Explorer.

You can increase your security from HTML viruses by disabling ActiveX controls and scripting within Outlook.

1. On the Tools menu, click Options, and then click the Security tab.
2. Click the Zone Settings button, and then click OK in the warning message.
3. Click the Custom Level button.

**Tip**

When you disable ActiveX controls and scripting, web pages that depend on these will not work. It's a trade-off–more security for less web page functionality. Viruses and information about them change all the time, so check your online virus information sources often to stay up-to-date and as safe as possible.

4. In the Security Settings dialog box, click the Disable option for all the settings under ActiveX Controls And Plug-Ins. ▶

5. Again in the Security Settings dialog box, scroll down and click the Disable option for all the settings under Scripting.

6. Click OK to close each dialog box, and then click Yes to any warning messages.

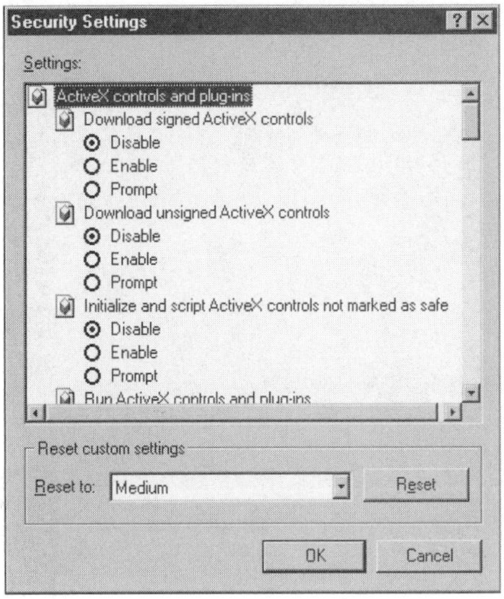

## Outlook Express How to fix it

Outlook Express is vulnerable to viruses in HTML scripts and in attachments. In Outlook Express, an HTML virus can run when you open the message or preview the message in the Preview Pane. In addition, there are viruses that can enter your computer hidden in a signature in a message you receive from someone who uses Outlook Express, and you can innocently pass it on to others if you send messages using Outlook Express. There's no telling what other viruses will exist by the time you read this book.

Go to the Microsoft web site *http://www.microsoft.com/windows/ie/download/* and read about the current patches and security updates. If they're appropriate for your system, download and install them.

And, of course, don't open attachments from senders you don't know, and set up your anti-virus program to scan e-mail attachments when they come in.

**Tip**

Instead of clicking the Disable options, you can click the Prompt options–every time you open a web page that has ActiveX controls or scripting, you are asked whether it's okay to run them.

## If you want to know more about protecting your computer from e-mail viruses

If you use Outlook 2000 in Corporate/Workgroup configuration and are up to programming in Visual Basic for Applications (VBA), you can find sample code that converts incoming HTML messages to Rich Text Format (which removes scripting and active content). Check out this web page for more information—*http://www.slipstick.com/dev/code/zaphtml.htm*—and read the accompanying information carefully before you undertake any reprogramming of Outlook.

Another source of protection against HTML-type viruses can be found at *http://www.slipstick.com/outlook/htmlmail.htm*. Again, read the accompanying information carefully to be sure any patch you download is right for your system.

No doubt the future holds more new e-mail viruses with new techniques for infecting your system. The best ways to protect yourself from viruses, both old and new, are to run an updated anti-virus program regularly and to stay up-to-date with Outlook security patches as they're released by Microsoft.

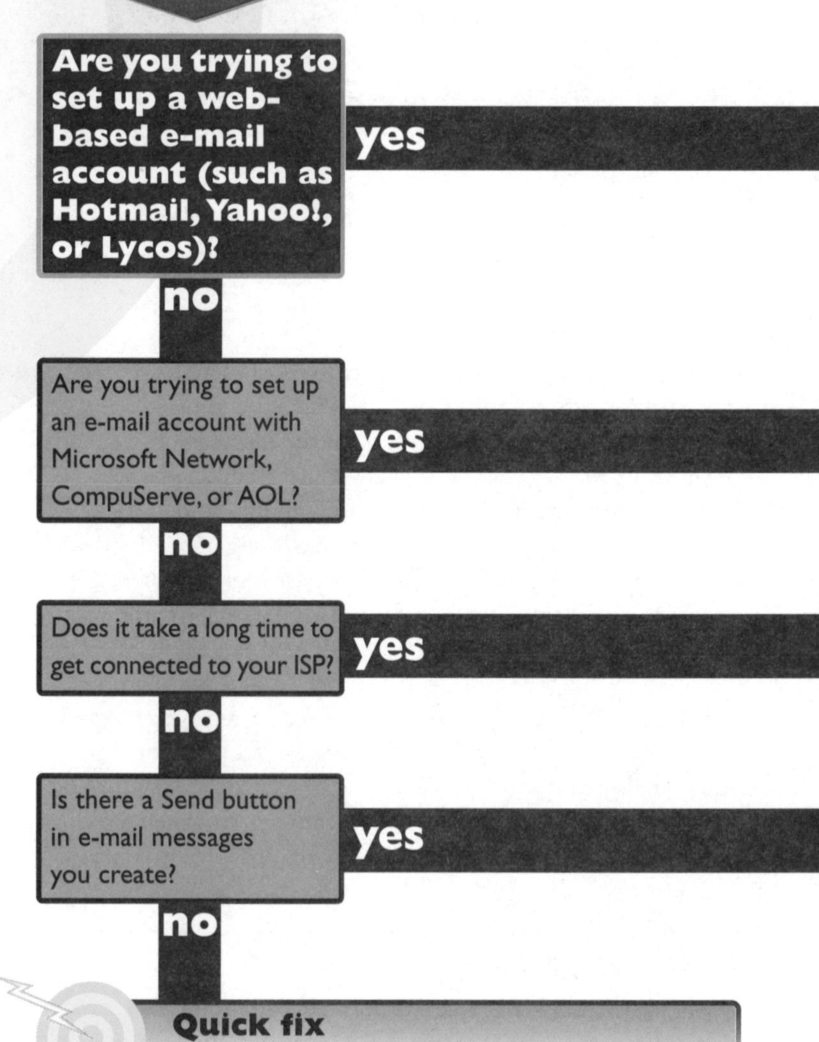

Are you trying to set up a web-based e-mail account (such as Hotmail, Yahoo!, or Lycos)?
yes
no
Are you trying to set up an e-mail account with Microsoft Network, CompuServe, or AOL?
yes
no
Does it take a long time to get connected to your ISP?
yes
no
Is there a Send button in e-mail messages you create?
yes
no

### Quick fix

If there's no Send button in the upper-left corner of a new message, you don't have any accounts set up to which Outlook/Outlook Express can send e-mail.

To set up an e-mail account, find a local Internet Service Provider and set up your Internet account with them. They'll tell you exactly what you need to do to set up Outlook/Outlook Express to send e-mail using the new account (and if they can't tell you how to set up Outlook/Outlook Express, find another ISP).

You can locate Internet Service Providers in the Yellow Pages, but a better way is to get recommendations from local friends, or look at local folks' business cards to see where they have their e-mail accounts.

# E-mail accounts

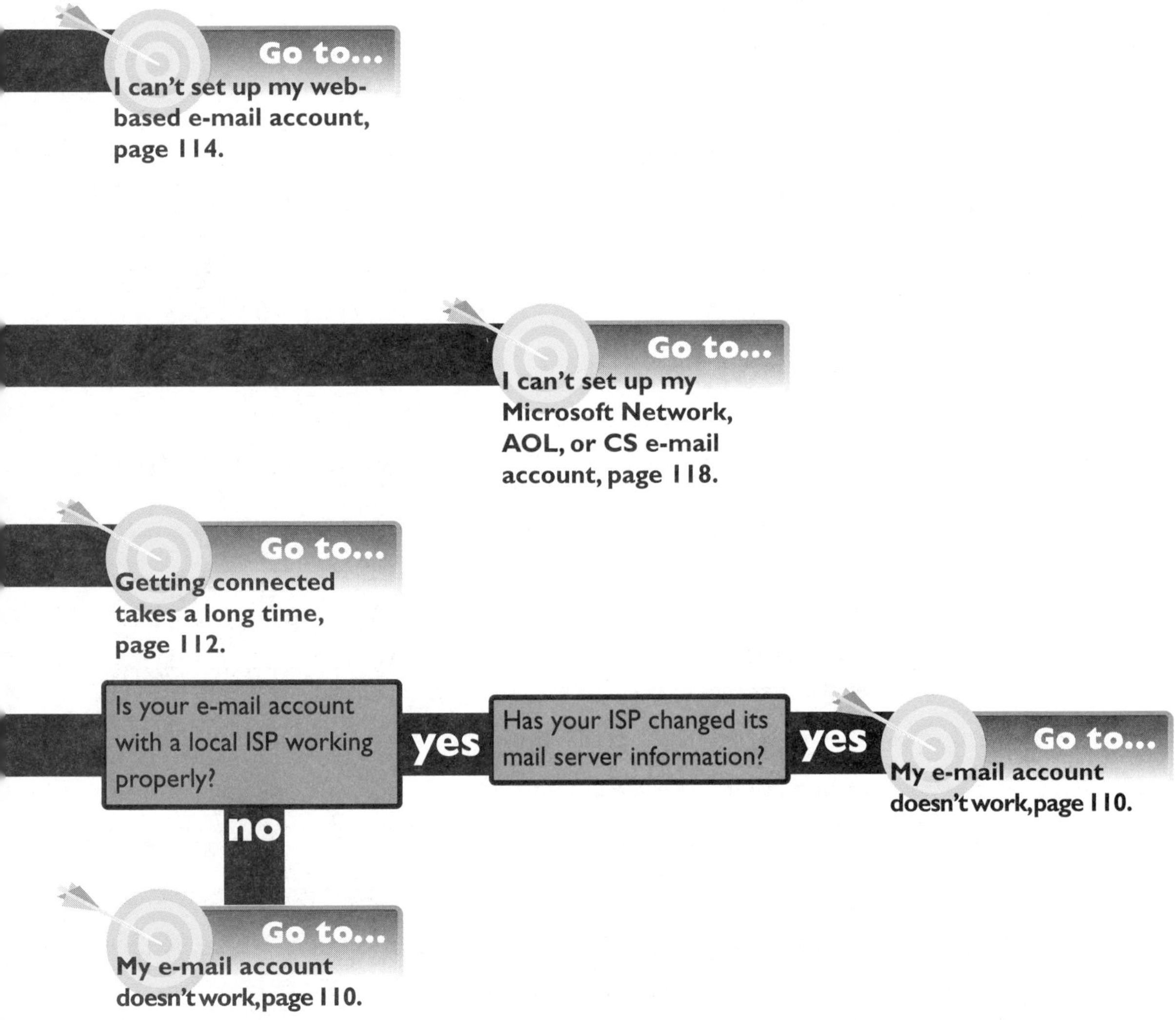

Go to...
I can't set up my web-based e-mail account, page 114.

Go to...
I can't set up my Microsoft Network, AOL, or CS e-mail account, page 118.

Go to...
Getting connected takes a long time, page 112.

Is your e-mail account with a local ISP working properly?

yes

Has your ISP changed its mail server information?

yes

Go to...
My e-mail account doesn't work, page 110.

no

Go to...
My e-mail account doesn't work, page 110.

**If your solution isn't here**
Check these related chapters:

E-mail, sending, page 92
E-mail, importing addresses, page 68
Multiple users, page 182

Or see the general troubleshooting tips on page xiii.

# My e-mail account doesn't work

## Source of the problem

You've set up an e-mail account with a local ISP, and it's given you all the account information that you need to create the account in Outlook or Outlook Express, but for some reason your new e-mail account isn't working.

Or perhaps your ISP changed some of the information for your account, such as the names of the incoming mail server or outgoing mail server, and you don't know where to make those changes.

**Tip**

Record all the account information your ISP gives you in an Outlook note so that you can find it easily when you need it.

## How to fix it

One dialog box stores all your ISP account information, and you can check it and change it if you need to.

To check (or change) your existing account information:

1. On the Tools menu, click Accounts (in Outlook, Corporate/Workgroup configuration, click Services).
2. Click your account name, and then click the Properties button.
3. On the General tab, make sure you have a name and the correct e-mail address entered. ▶

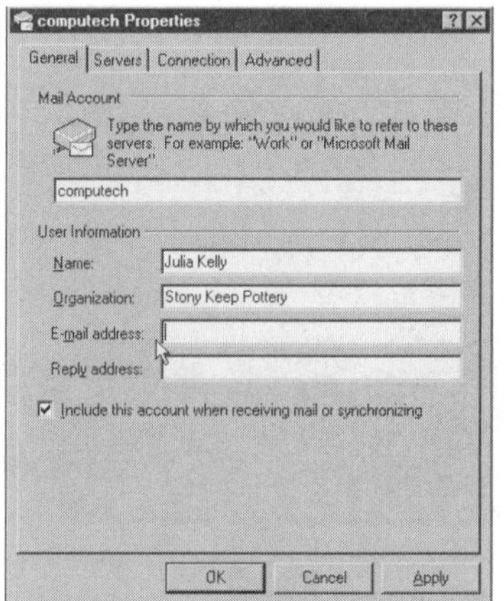


4. On the Servers tab, make sure your Incoming Mail and Outgoing Mail server addresses are correct, with no typing errors. (There are never any spaces in server names.) ▶

   Delete and retype your Account Name and Password. (Some accounts have case-sensitive account names and passwords—if yours does, be sure you type the correct upper- and lowercase letters.)

   If your e-mail account requires that you log on using secure password authentication, be sure the Log On Using Secure Password Authentication check box is selected.

If your ISP told you that you need to log on to your outgoing mail server, select the My Server Requires Authentication check box, and then click the Settings button and check that your Outgoing Mail Server settings are correct.

5. On the Connection tab, be sure you have the correct connection option clicked. If you connect through your computer's modem, click the Connect Using My Phone Line option. ▶

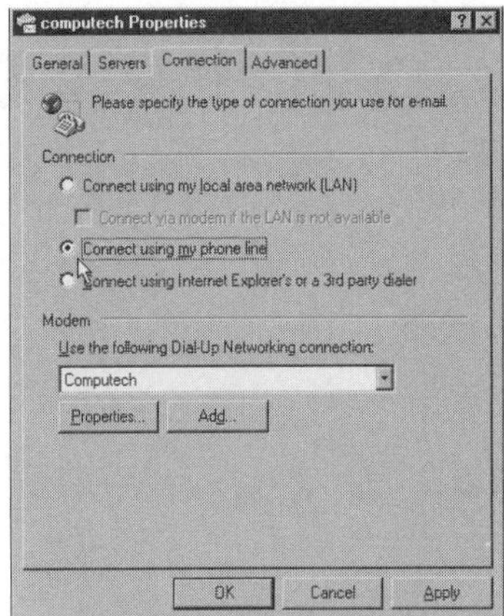


If you use Outlook Express, you normally connect using your default Internet Explorer browser connection. (If you need to use a different dial-up e-mail connection for your Outlook Express account, select the Always Connect To This Account Using check box, and click the connection in the box.)

If you connect using a phone line, under Use The Following Dial-Up Networking Connection, click the Properties button and check the phone number on the General tab. If it's correct, click Cancel; if it's wrong, type the correct phone number and click OK. ▶

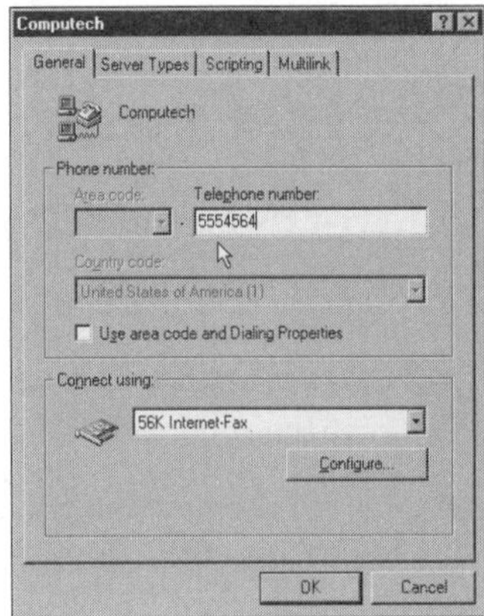


6. On the Advanced tab, don't make any changes unless your ISP or network administrator specifically directs you to do so. The default settings are fine in most cases.

If your account still doesn't work after you've checked and corrected the information in the account's Properties dialog box, telephone your ISP and ask someone to walk you through the Outlook or Outlook Express setup, step by step.

# Getting connected takes a long time

## Source of the problem

Outlook or Outlook Express dials up your Internet Service Provider (ISP), but it seems to take a really long time to get connected. There are a few settings that might be slowing down your connection time. Check (and change, if you need to) these connection settings.

## How to fix it

### In Internet Mail Only configuration

1. On the Tools menu, click Accounts.
2. On the Mail tab, click your account name, and click the Properties button.
3. On the Connection tab, under Modem, click your account name, and click the Properties button.
4. On the Server Types tab: ▶
   - Clear the Log On To Network check box.
   - Clear the NetBEUI check box.
   - Clear the IPX/SPX Compatible check box.
5. Click OK, OK, and Close to close all the dialog boxes.

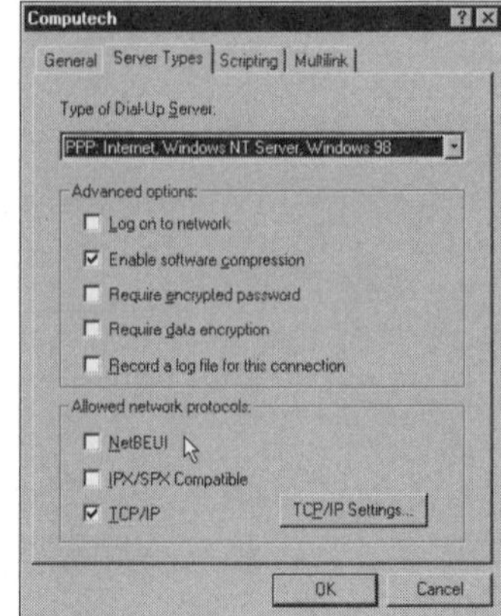

# How to fix it

## In Corporate/Workgroup configuration

1. On the Tools menu, click Services.
2. On the Services tab, click your Internet account name, and click the Properties button ▶

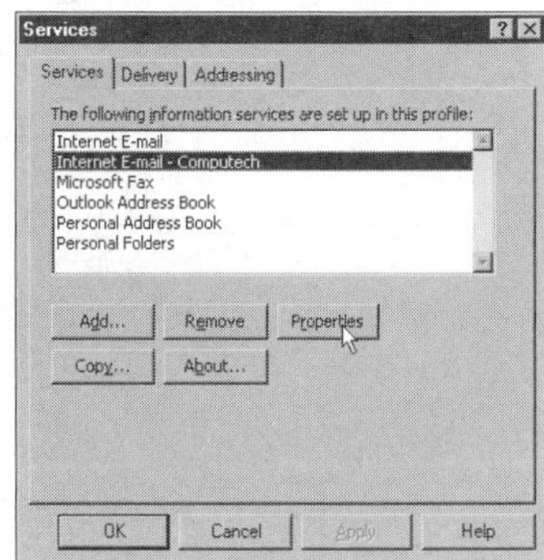

3. On the Connection tab, under Modem, click your account name, and click the Properties button.
4. On the Server Types tab:
   - Clear the Log On To Network check box.
   - Clear the NetBEUI check box.
   - Clear the IPX/SPX Compatible check box.
4. Click OK, OK, and Close to close all the dialog boxes.

# Outlook Express How to fix it

1. On the Tools menu, click Accounts.
2. On the Mail tab, click your account name, and click the Properties button.
3. On the Connection tab, under Modem, select the Always Connect To This Account Using check box.
4. Click your account name, and click the Settings button ▶

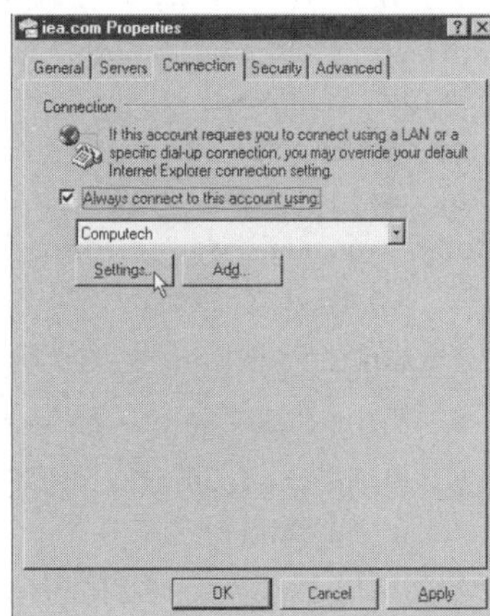

5. On the Server Types tab:
   - Clear the Log On To Network check box.
   - Clear the NetBEUI check box.
   - Clear the IPX/SPX Compatible check box.
6. Click OK, OK, and Close to close all the dialog boxes.

# I can't set up my web-based e-mail account

## Source of the problem

You want to set up a Hotmail, Yahoo!, or other web-based e-mail account (because it's free—what a deal!) or you already have a web-based e-mail account, and you want to use it in Outlook or Outlook Express. But you don't know how to set it up, or you tried to set it up but it didn't work.

Web-based e-mail accounts are different from a normal Internet Service Provider (ISP) e-mail account, because the messages are served through a web page rather than an Internet mail server. Web-based messages aren't integrated with your other Outlook folders the way regular ISP messages are, and they can't be backed up or archived.

> **Tip**
> Although web-based e-mail accounts are free, you must still have a dial-up Internet account to be able to connect to a web-based e-mail program.

## How to fix it

### In Internet Mail Only configuration

A web-based e-mail account isn't as fully functional in Outlook as an Internet server-based e-mail account, because a web-based e-mail account is served through a web page rather than an Internet mail server. But you can access a Hotmail or other web-based e-mail account from Outlook, in the same way that you can open a web page in Outlook. The web-based account must already exist (these are usually set up through the account's home page).

To create easy access to your web-based e-mail account in Outlook:

1. On the View menu, click Folder List.
2. Right-click Outlook Today, and then click New Folder.
3. Name the folder (Hotmail, Yahoo!, or whatever name you want for your web-based account folder), and click OK.
4. Right-click the new folder, and click Properties.

5. In the folder's Properties dialog box, on the Home Page tab, in the Address box, type the URL for the account's web page (for example, if it's a Hotmail account, type **http://www.hotmail.com**).

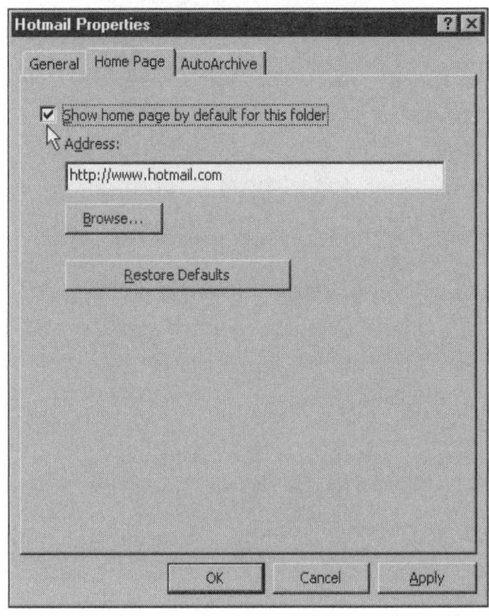


6. Select the Show Home Page By Default For This Folder check box, and click OK.

   To access the account, open the new folder. When you do, Outlook uses your Internet connection to display the account's home page in the Outlook window.

## How to fix it

To set up any web-based e-mail account in Outlook Express, you must already have an Internet dial-up connection set up in Internet Explorer.

## Set up a Hotmail account

To set up a Hotmail account, on the Tools menu, point to New Account Signup, and click Hotmail.

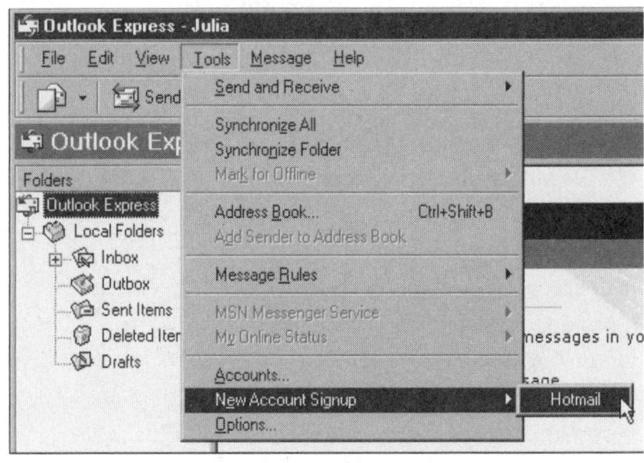


1. Outlook Express will dial up your ISP for Internet access. Follow the setup steps to create your account.

   After you create the Hotmail account, follow the steps in the next section, "Set up another web-based account," to configure Outlook Express to use the new Hotmail account.

**Tip**

If you already have a Hotmail account, and you need to set it up in a new computer, first create the dial-up Internet connection in the new computer. Then, follow the steps in the next section, "Set up another web-based account."

**Tip**

To add a shortcut to the folder to your Outlook bar, open the Folder list, and drag the icon from the Folder list to the Outlook bar.

## Set up another web-based account

To set up a different web-based account in Outlook Express, the account must already exist (these are usually set up through the account's web page).

1. On the Tools menu, click Accounts.
2. Click the Add button, and click Mail. Follow the wizard steps and fill in all the appropriate information.
3. In the third wizard step, click HTTP in the My Incoming Mail Server Is A box. ▶

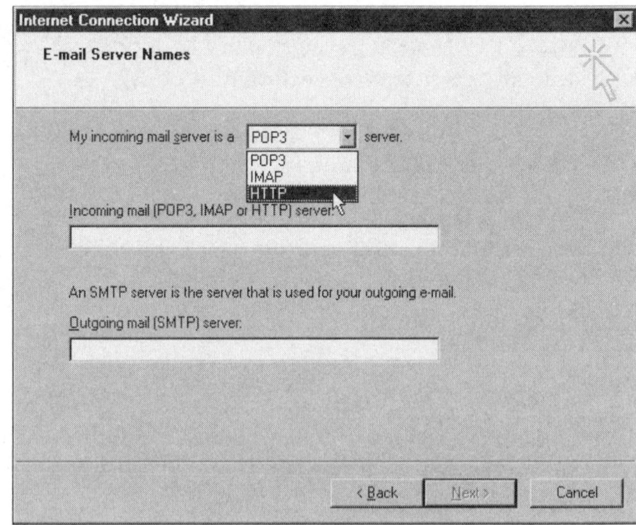


Then follow the remaining wizard steps and fill in the required information about your web-based account.

**Tip**

If you don't see Hotmail on the New Account Signup menu, or HTTP in the My Incoming Mail Server Is A box, the HTTP mail setting is disabled in your Windows Registry. Try reinstalling or upgrading Internet Explorer. If that doesn't make Hotmail and HTTP server types available, you can get help from the Microsoft Knowledge Base article Q24184, at *http://search.support.microsoft.com/kb/*.

# I can't set up my Microsoft Network, AOL, or CompuServe e-mail account

## Source of the problem

You've got an existing America Online (AOL) account, or an account with Microsoft Network or CompuServe, and you're having tremendous difficulty getting Outlook (or Outlook Express) to send and receive e-mail on that account. You might or might not be able to fix the problem, depending on which of these programs you're trying to use.

## How to fix it

### AOL

If your e-mail account is with AOL, there's no way to fix it. As of the writing of this book, AOL uses its own e-mail system, which isn't compatible with the Internet standards supported by independent e-mail programs, such as Outlook, Outlook Express, and others. In other words, you can get your AOL e-mail only through the AOL software.

### CompuServe

You can use only CompuServe 2000 5.0 (or later) with Outlook or Outlook Express. If you have an earlier version of CompuServe, you need to upgrade before you can use Outlook or Outlook Express to send and receive e-mail on your account. Also, in Outlook, you can use your CompuServe 2000 account only in the Internet Mail Only configuration.

To set up your CompuServe 2000 account in Outlook (Internet Mail Only configuration) or Outlook Express, you follow normal account setup procedures, but you need to be sure you set a few specific settings.

1. On the Tools menu, click Accounts.
2. In the Internet Accounts dialog box, click the Add button, and then click Mail to open the Internet Connection Wizard. ▶

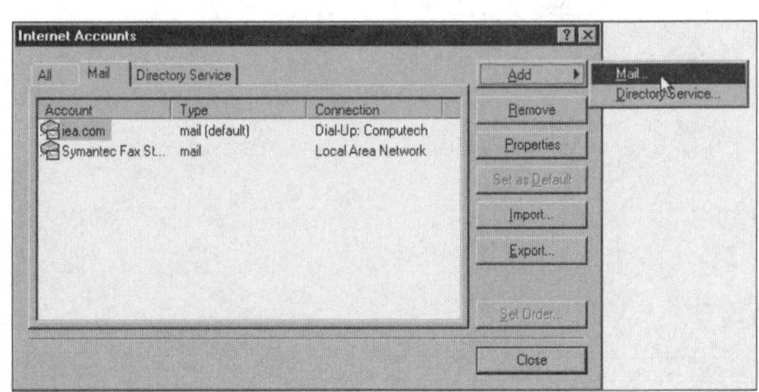

3. Follow the wizard steps to set up your account, and use these settings when the Internet Connection Wizard asks for them:

- In the My Incoming Mail Server Is A box, click IMAP. (The figure shows the Outlook dialog box, and because Outlook can't set up an HTTP (web-based) e-mail account, there's no HTTP choice in the My IncomIng Mail Server Is A box.) ▶
- Type the names in the next two boxes. Your incoming mail server name is **imap.cs.com**, and your outgoing mail server name is **smtp.cs.com** (unless CompuServe tells you otherwise).
- Select the Log On Using Secure Password Authorization (SPA) check box. ▶
- Click the Connect Using My Phone Line option.

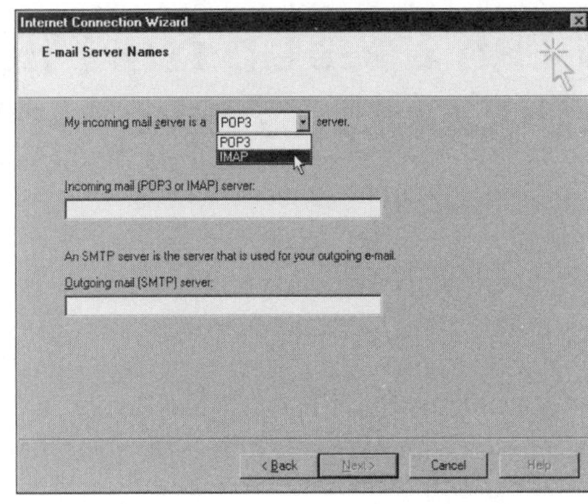


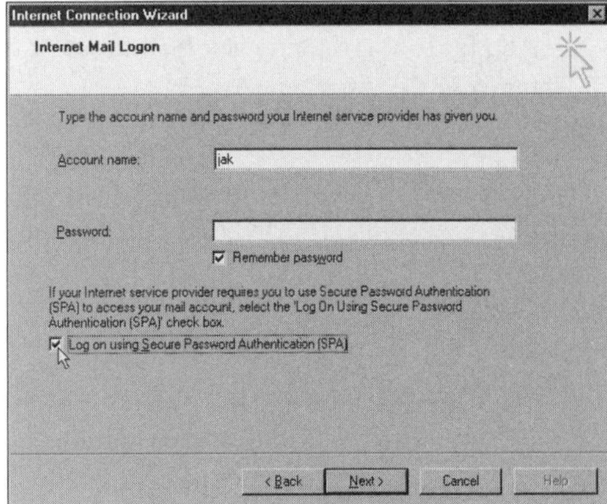


**Tip**
For more questions and answers about your CompuServe 2000 e-mail account, contact CompuServe technical support.

*If this solution didn't solve your problem, go to the next page.*

# I can't set up my Microsoft Network, AOL, or CompuServe e-mail account

*(continued from page 119)*

## Microsoft Network

To use Outlook or Outlook Express with Microsoft Network (MSN), you must be using Microsoft Network 2.5 or later. Also, in Outlook, you can use your Microsoft Network account only in the Internet Mail Only configuration.

To set up your Microsoft Network 2.5 account in Outlook (Internet Mail Only configuration) or Outlook Express, you follow normal account setup procedures, but you need to be sure you set a few specific settings.

1. On the Tools menu, click Accounts.
2. In the Internet Accounts dialog box, click the Add button, and then click Mail to open the Internet Connection Wizard.
3. Follow the wizard steps to set up your account, and use these settings when the Internet Connection Wizard asks for them:
   - In the My Incoming Mail Server Is A box, click POP3. ▶
   - Type the names in the next two boxes. Your incoming mail server name is **pop3.email.msn.com**, and your outgoing mail server name is **secure.smtp.email.msn.com**.
   - Select the Log On Using Secure Password Authorization (SPA) check box..
   - Click the Connect Using My Phone Line option. ▶

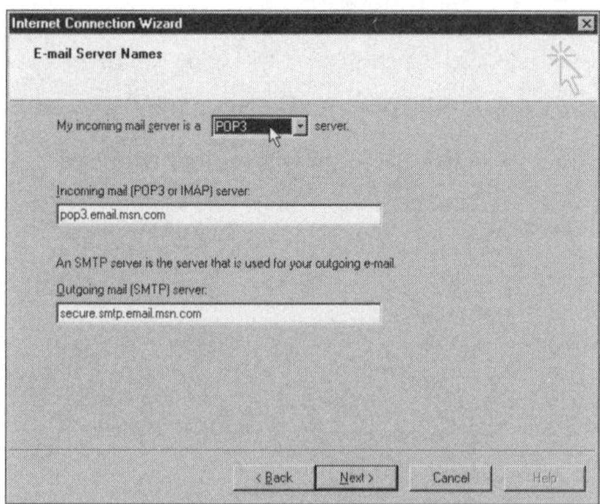


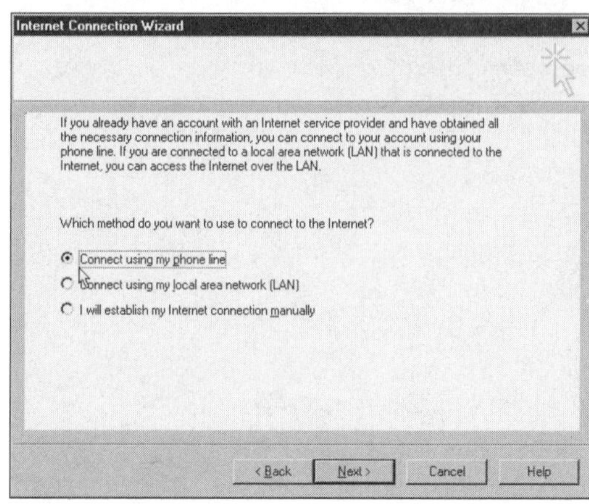


**Tip**

For more questions and answers about your Microsoft Network e-mail account, contact Microsoft Network technical support.

**Are you using Outlook?**

yes

Have you tried repairing Outlook?

yes

no

**Go to...**

**I need to repair Outlook, page 124.**

no

Does your Outlook Express error say "Message could not be displayed"?

yes

**Quick fix**

This can happen if your Internet Service Provider (ISP) account is an Internet Message Access Protocol (IMAP) type account and you lose your connection to the account.

Just reconnect to the account. If this happens often, you might consider using a different ISP or a different account type.

no

Does your Outlook Express error say "No messages can be found" when you try to import old Outlook Express 4. messages?

yes

**Quick fix**

This can happen if you are trying to import Outlook Express 4. messages from a folder that isn't named "Mail".

To solve it, create a folder named Mail, copy your Outlook Express 4. messages into the new Mail folder, and then import the messages from that folder into Outlook Express 5.

no

**Go to...**

**I don't know how to get help from the Microsoft Knowledge Base, page 126.**

# Error messages

Have you tried repairing Office 2000?

yes

Have you updated and run your virus protection program recently?

yes

Have you looked up the error message in the Microsoft Knowledge Base?

no

**Go to...**

**I need to repair Office 2000, page 125.**

no

**Quick fix**

The only way to be sure that your error is not being caused by a virus is to install a good anti-virus program (Norton and MacAfee are two popular and reliable anti-virus programs), update your virus lists at least every two weeks, and run the anti-virus program often.

no

**Go to...**

**I don't know how to get help from the Microsoft Knowledge Base, page 126.**

**If your solution isn't here**

Check this related chapter:

E-mail, viruses, page 104

Or see the general troubleshooting tips on page xiii.

# I don't know how to repair Outlook

## Source of the problem

There are lots of different error messages, some you might see and many you'll never see. There are also many different causes for them, such as outdated or mismatched versions of program files, outdated or damaged driver files, and corrupted files (in other words, it's probably not your fault). There are very few error messages that actually tell you anything worthwhile—most are quite cryptic, which makes them enormously frustrating. Fortunately, there are easy procedures you can do that might banish the error message that's currently pestering you. One of those procedures is to repair Outlook, which instructs Outlook to find and fix its own mismatched or corrupted files.

**Tip**

A single error message that doesn't reappear might be just an "electron cramp"—ignore it, save your current work, and continue working.

## How to fix it

First, quit and restart Outlook. Sometimes closing and restarting the program (or even closing all your open programs and then shutting down and restarting Windows) straightens out whatever's wrong. If that doesn't solve the problem, follow these steps to repair Outlook:

1. On Outlook's Help menu, click Detect And Repair.
2. In the Detect And Repair dialog box, make sure the Restore My Shortcuts While Repairing check box is selected, and then click Start. ▶

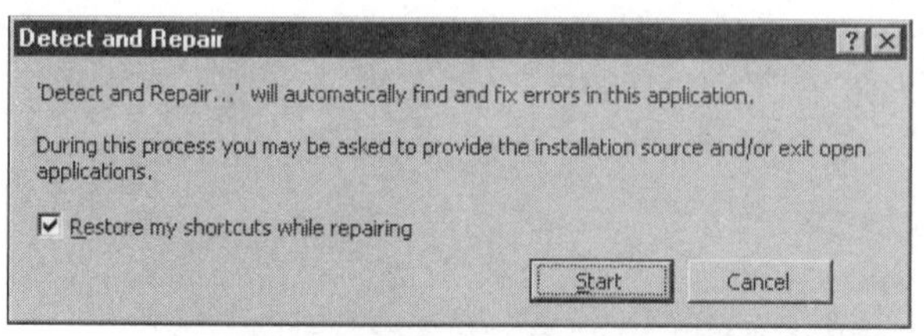


3. Wait several minutes while the program checks your files and makes any needed repairs, and in the last dialog box you'll be asked to restart Windows. ▶

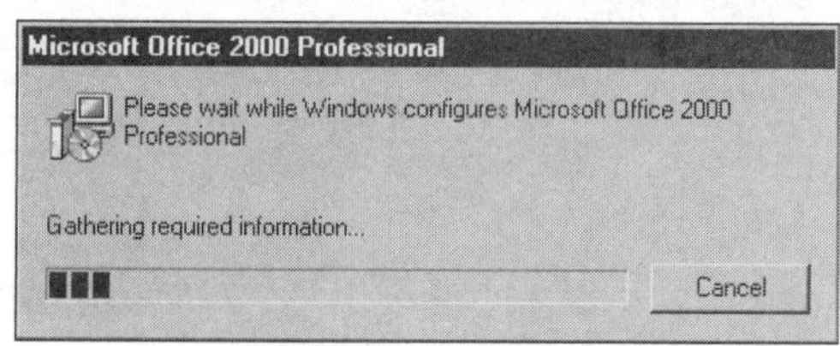


After you restart Windows, your problem might well be solved. If not, try repairing Office 2000 (see "I don't know how to repair Office 2000").

# I don't know how to repair Office 2000

## Source of the problem

Error messages are pretty mysterious, and the same error message can be generated by any number of different, totally unrelated problems. Sometimes the quickest approach to fixing an error message is the shotgun approach: repair the whole program, and probably whatever was wrong will be fixed.

If you've already tried repairing Outlook (see the previous solution, "I don't know how to repair Outlook") and you still get the error message, try repairing Office. This solution instructs Office to make sure all its program files are current and appropriate for your installation.

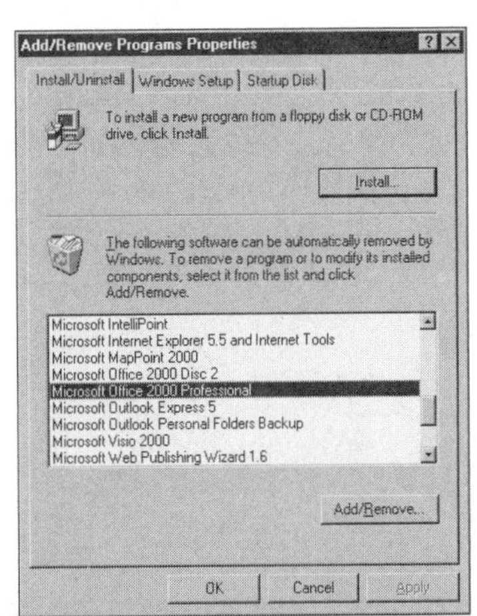


## How to fix it

1. Click the Start button, point to Settings, and then click Control Panel.
2. In the Control Panel, double-click the Add/Remove Programs icon.
3. In the Add/Remove Programs dialog box, double-click Microsoft Office 2000. ▶
4. In the Microsoft Office 2000 Maintenance Mode dialog box, click the Repair Office button.
5. In the Reinstall/Repair Microsoft Office 2000 dialog box, select the Reinstall Office option. ▶
6. Click the Finish button.

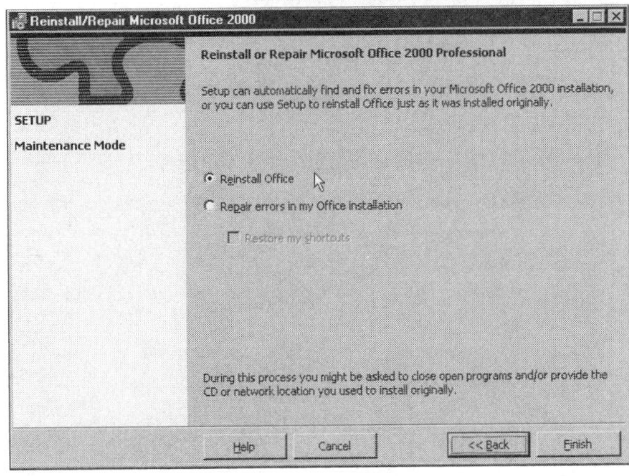


**Tip**

Depending on the particular files that need to be fixed or replaced, you might receive error messages during the reinstallation process. Click the Ignore button in each error message to continue the reinstallation.

# I don't know how to get help from the Microsoft Knowledge Base

## Source of the problem

If repairing Outlook and Office 2000 don't solve the problem of recurring error messages, you might need more in-depth help. You can find lots of in-depth help and fix-it procedures online, in the Microsoft Knowledge Base. The Microsoft Knowledge Base is a storehouse of articles that address specific problems, and there's a search engine to help you locate help for your specific problem.

## How to fix it

1. Write down the entire wording of your error message, including any file names it mentions. You need this information to narrow your Knowledge Base search.

**Tip**

You can receive more information about difficult alerts and error messages with a feature called Customizable Alerts. You can download the file with this feature for Office 2000 programs at *http://officeupdate.Microsoft.com/2000/downloadDetails/alerts.htm*

2. Use your favorite technique to launch your browser, and go to the site *http://search.support.microsoft.com/kb.* ▶

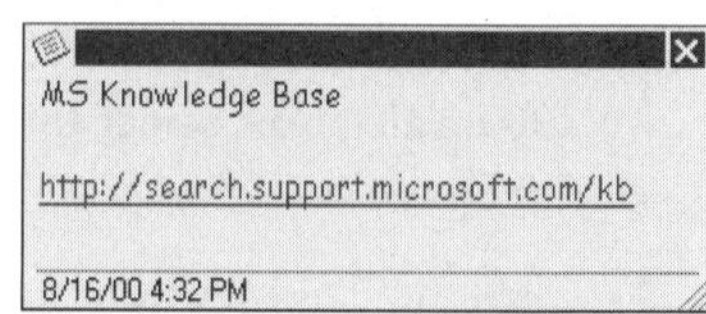

3. On the Microsoft Knowledge Base page, set up your search and click the Go button. ▶

- If you know the specific article ID number you want, select the Specific Article ID Number option, and type the article ID number (beginning with a **Q**), in the My Question Is box.
- If you want to look for articles containing specific words, select the Keyword Search Using option, select All Words or Any Words in the list box, and type the words in the My Question Is box.
- If you don't know a specific article ID number or words to search for, click the Asking A Question Using A Free-Text Query option, and type a question in your own words in the My Question Is box.

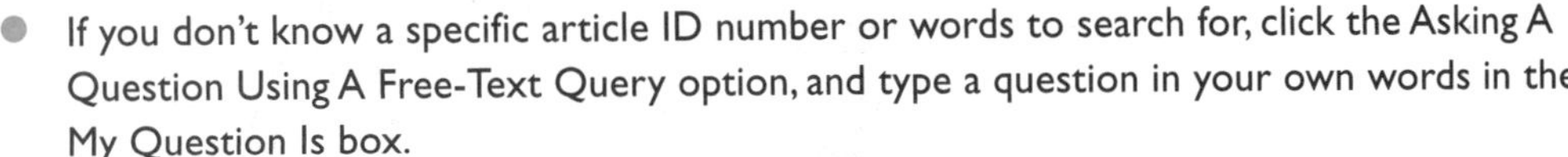

4. Click a prospective article's title to open it. ▶
5. When you find a potentially helpful article, print it so that you can refer to it while you perform whatever procedures it prescribes.

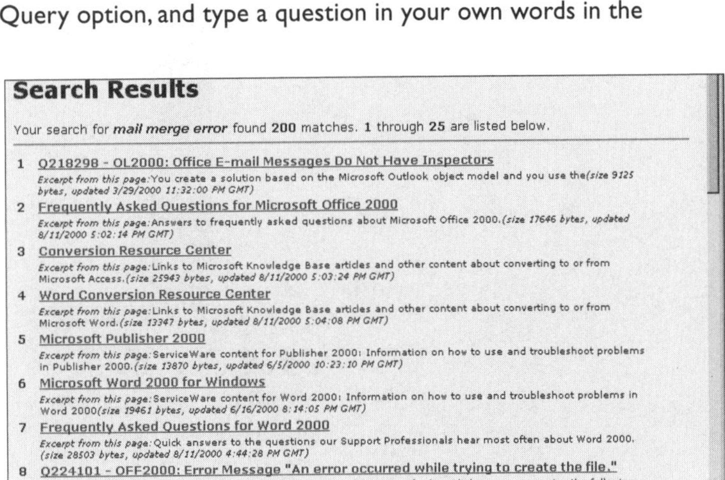

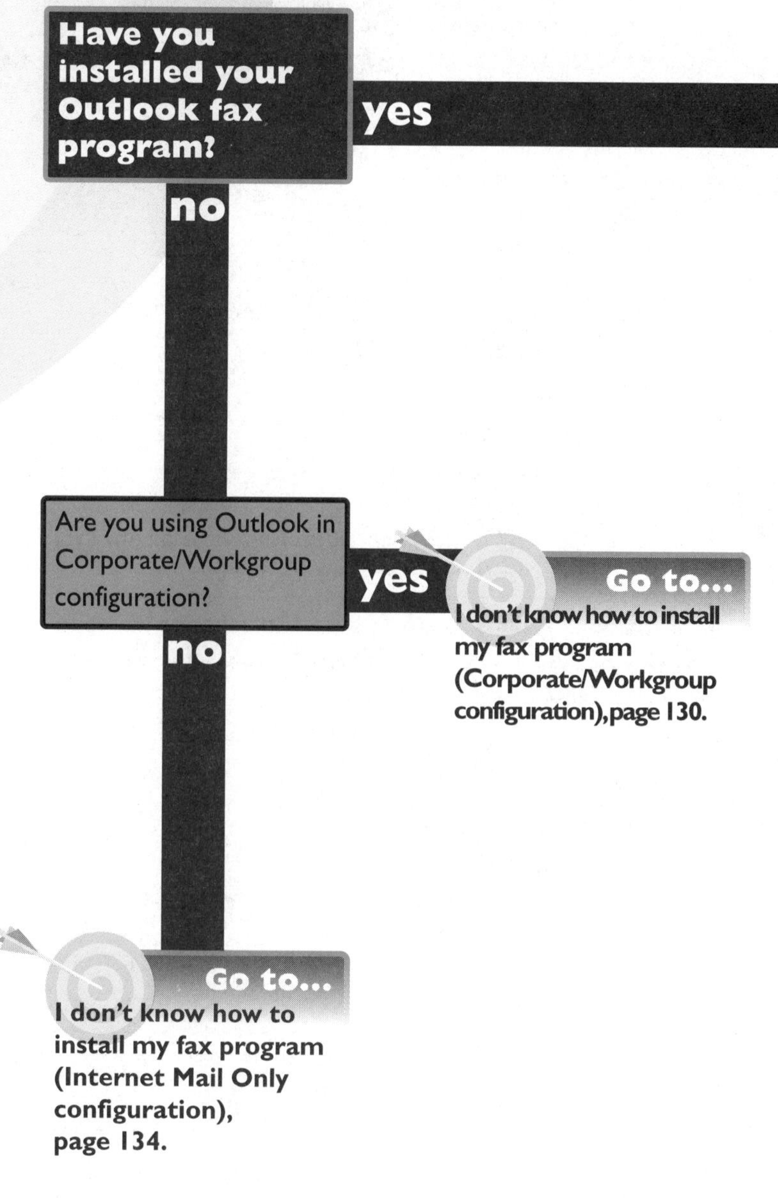
Have you installed your Outlook fax program?
yes
no
Are you using Outlook in Corporate/Workgroup configuration?
yes
Go to...
I don't know how to install my fax program (Corporate/Workgroup configuration), page 130.
no
Go to...
I don't know how to install my fax program (Internet Mail Only configuration), page 134.

Have you switched configurations?

yes

## Quick fix

Each Outlook configuration uses its own fax program—Microsoft Fax in the Corporate/Workgroup configuration, and Symantec Fax in the Internet Mail Only configuration. When you switch configurations, you need to install the appropriate fax program for that configuration. After the fax program is installed, it's available anytime you switch to the corresponding configuration.

no

## Quick fix

If Outlook won't give you a new fax message, or won't send the fax message, try repairing your Outlook files. In Outlook, on the Help menu, click Detect And Repair.

**If your solution isn't here**

Check the general troubleshooting tips on page xiii.

# I don't know how to install my fax program (Corporate/ Workgroup configuration)

## Source of the problem

Sometimes a fax is a quicker and more appropriate way to communicate with someone, and Outlook can dial fax numbers and send faxes for you—but only if the fax program has been set up. If your network administrator hasn't set up the fax program for you, or if you've just switched configurations, you need to install the Microsoft Fax program that's provided with Windows 95 and Windows 98.

If you're on a network, be sure your computer has a modem that's connected to a phone line so you can send faxes directly. If not, see your network administrator about how to send faxes through the network.

## How to fix it

In the Corporate/Workgroup configuration, you need to install the Microsoft Fax program, add it to your mail profile, and finally reinstall Outlook 2000.

Installing Microsoft Fax is different in Windows 95 than in Windows 98. In both cases, have your Windows CD-ROM handy.

### Install Microsoft Fax for Windows 95

1. Close Outlook and any other open programs.
2. Click the Start button, point to Settings, and then click Control Panel.
3. In the Control Panel dialog box, double-click Add/Remove Programs.

**Tip**

After Microsoft Fax has been installed, you can switch configurations as often as you like without having to reinstall the Microsoft Fax program for the Corporate/Workgroup configuration.

4. In the Add/Remove Programs Properties dialog box, on the Windows Setup tab, select the Microsoft Fax check box. (If the Microsoft Fax check box is already selected, Microsoft Fax is already installed—click Cancel to exit the Add/Remove Programs dialog box, and go to step 6.) ▶

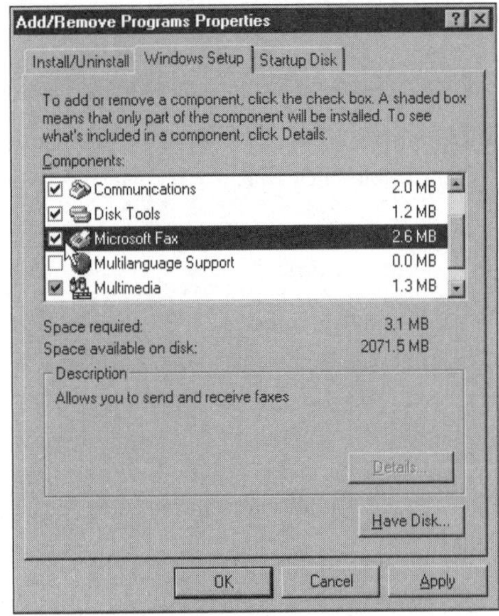


5. Click OK. Windows 95 installs the necessary files. You might be asked to insert your Windows 95 CD-ROM, so have it ready in case you need it.

6. Close the Control Panel dialog box, and go to the section "Add Microsoft Fax to your mail profile" on the next page.

## Install Microsoft Fax for Windows 98

1. Close Outlook and any other open programs.
2. Put your Windows 98 CD-ROM in the CD-ROM drive.
3. In the CD file list, double-click Tools.
4. Double-click the *oldwin95* folder.
5. Double-click the *message* folder.
6. Double-click the *us* folder.
7. Double-click the *awfax.exe* file to install the Microsoft Fax program files. ▲
8. In the License Agreement that appears, click Yes. If you're asked about keeping current versions of your files, click Yes.
9. When a message asks whether you want to restart your computer, click Yes.
10. After Windows restarts, close any open windows, remove the CD-ROM from your CD-ROM drive, and go to the section "Add Microsoft Fax to your mail profile" on the next page.

**Tip**

If the CD-ROM opens a window when you close the drive door, click the Browse This CD button in the window to open the file list. If a CD window doesn't open, double-click the My Computer icon on your desktop to open the My Computer window, and then double-click the CD-ROM drive icon to open the CD file list.

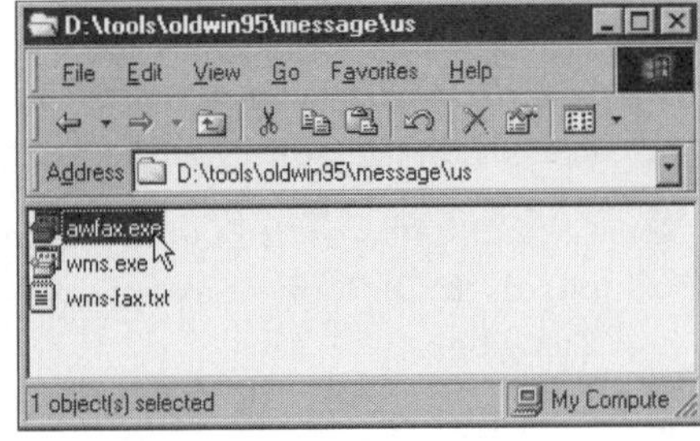

## Add Microsoft Fax to your mail profile

1. Click the Start button, point to Settings, and then click Control Panel.
2. In the Control Panel dialog box, double-click the Mail icon (if you have a Mail And Fax icon, double-click that).
3. In the Microsoft Outlook Internet Settings Properties dialog box, on the Services tab, click the Add button.
4. In the Add Service To Profile dialog box, click Microsoft Fax. ▶

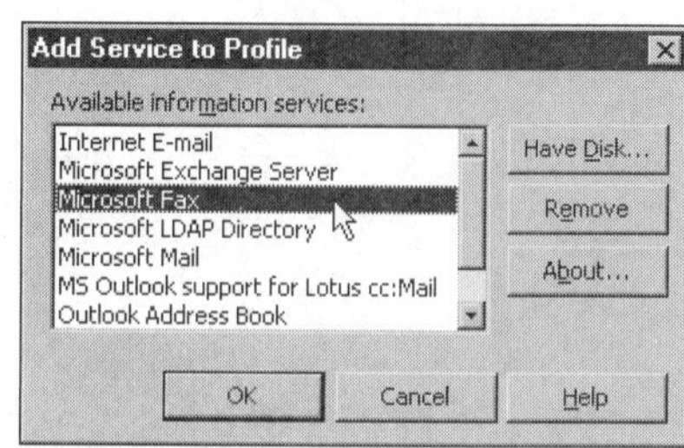


5. Click OK.
6. In the message that asks whether you want to add important fax information now, click Yes.
7. In the Microsoft Fax Properties dialog box, fill in all the information you can in each of the dialog box tabs.

   On the User tab, fill in your fax telephone number and address information.

   On the Modem tab, click the name of the modem you'll use for faxes, and then click the Set As Active Fax Modem button. ▶

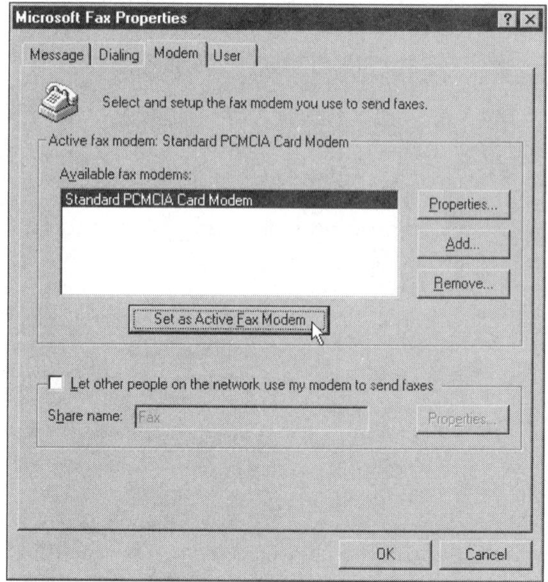


   On the Dialing tab, click the Dialing Properties button and look at the dialing properties for your phone line. If anything is incorrect, make the changes, and then click OK.

   On the Message tab, keep the default settings and choose a cover page. Clear the Send Cover Page check box if you don't use cover pages with your faxes.

8. Click OK. Microsoft Fax appears in your Microsoft Outlook Internet Settings dialog box.
9. Click OK to close the dialog box, and then close the Control Panel window.

## Reinstall Outlook 2000

1. Click the Start button, point to Settings, and then click Control Panel.
2. In the Control Panel dialog box, double-click Add/Remove Programs.
3. In the Add/Remove Programs dialog box, on the Install/Uninstall tab, click Microsoft Office 2000 (or Microsoft Outlook 2000, if you installed it separately). ▶

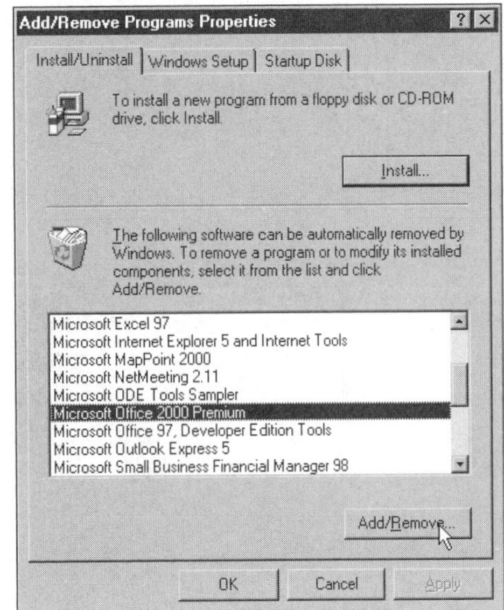


4. Click the Add/Remove button.
5. In the Maintenance Mode dialog box, click the Repair Office button.
6. In the Reinstall/Repair dialog box, click the Reinstall Office option, and then click Finish.
7. When a message tells you that setup has been completed successfully, click OK, and then click Yes in the next dialog box to restart your computer.

After you install Microsoft Fax, a Fax icon appears in your Windows Taskbar tray—it's the icon that looks like a desk telephone. ▶

The fax icon shows you the status of your fax reception, and you can use it to handle incoming faxes.

# I don't know how to install my fax program (Internet Mail Only configuration)

## Source of the problem

Often, a fax is a quicker and more appropriate way to communicate with someone. E-mail can take several hours or even a day to travel through the Internet if you or your recipient is experiencing server problems, but a fax is received as soon as your recipient's fax line answers your call.

Outlook can dial your contacts' fax numbers and send faxes for you—but only if the fax program has been set up. In the Internet Mail Only configuration, Outlook uses the Symantec Fax program. The Symantec Fax Starter Edition Setup Wizard walks you through the steps to set up the program.

## How to fix it

1. Open the Inbox.
2. On the Actions menu, click New Fax Message.
3. In the message that tells you that Symantec Fax Starter Edition is not installed, click Yes to install it now.
4. After the wizard installs several files and then tells you that you must restart Outlook, click OK.
5. Exit Outlook.
6. Restart Outlook.
7. The Symantec Fax Starter Edition Setup Wizard starts. Click Next.
8. Work your way through the wizard, filling in all the information you can. If any option or check box is mysterious, right-click it for an explanation.
9. In the third wizard step, click the Setup Modem button. ▶

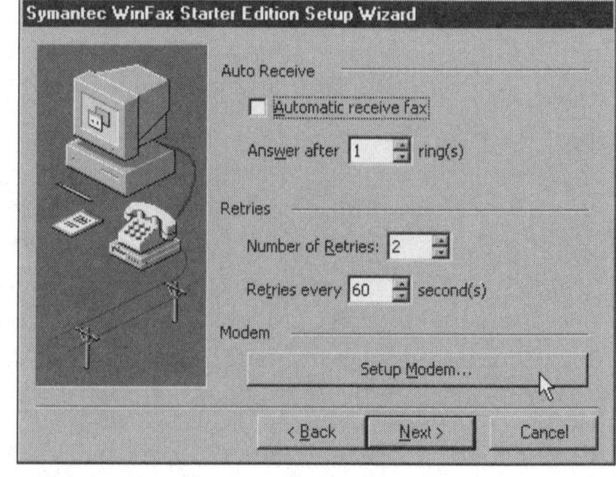

10. In the Modem Properties dialog box, choose the fax/modem you'll use to send faxes, and then click the Properties button.

11. In the Modem Configuration Wizard, read and work your way through the wizard steps. If your fax/modem is external, be sure it's turned on; if your fax/modem is internal, you can assume it's turned on.

**Tip**

Be sure that neither your browser nor Outlook is using the modem (they should not be connected online).

12. In the final Modem Configuration Wizard step, when the wizard tells you that your modem is configured, click Finish.

13. In the Properties dialog box for your modem, click OK.

14. In the Modem Properties dialog box, click OK.

15. In the message that tells you to restart Outlook, click OK.

16. In the Symantec Fax Starter Edition Setup Wizard, click Next.

17. Choose a cover page style (or clear the Send Cover Page check box), click Next, and then click Finish.

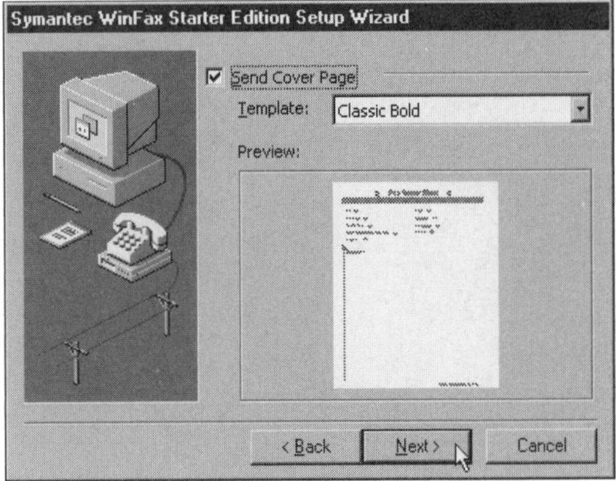


18. Quit and restart Outlook, and send someone a fax to test your setup.

## If you can't start the Symantec Fax Setup Wizard

Sometimes the Symantec Fax Setup Wizard gets derailed. It happened to me when I started the wizard and then quit before the wizard finished setting up the fax program. If you do this, the wizard won't start when you decide to set it up.

To start the wizard, quit Outlook. Click the Start button, point to Find, and then click Files Or Folders.

Search for the file *olfsetup.exe* on the drive where you installed Outlook. In the Search Results list, double-click *olfsetup.exe* to start the wizard. Then follow the steps listed previously to set up your fax program, beginning with step 7.

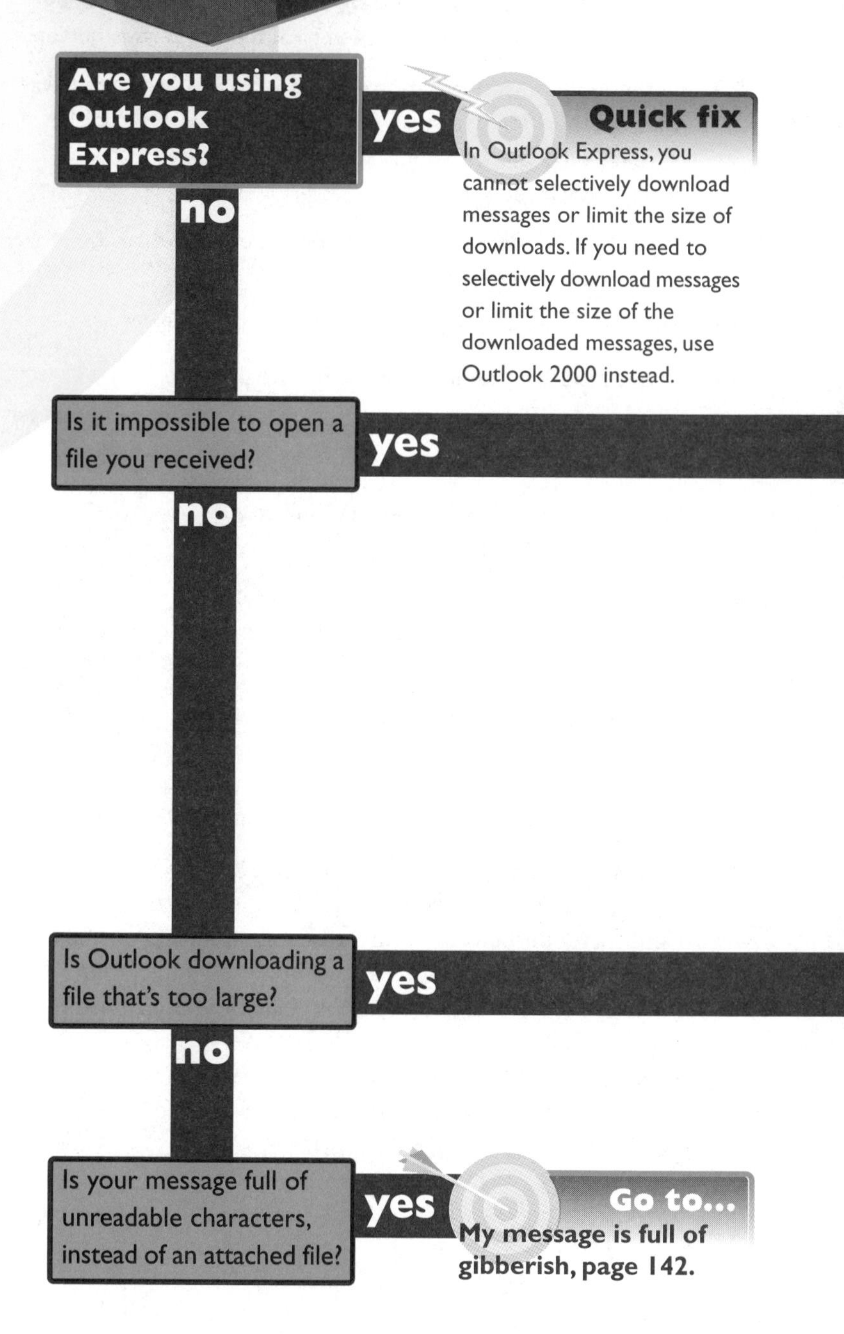
Are you using Outlook Express?
yes
Quick fix
In Outlook Express, you cannot selectively download messages or limit the size of downloads. If you need to selectively download messages or limit the size of the downloaded messages, use Outlook 2000 instead.
no
Is it impossible to open a file you received?
yes
no
Is Outlook downloading a file that's too large?
yes
no
Is your message full of unreadable characters, instead of an attached file?
yes
Go to...
My message is full of gibberish, page 142.

# Files, receiving

Do you have the correct program and version on your computer?

**yes**

Is the file zipped or compressed?

**yes**

**Quick fix**

Ask your correspondent to send you a decompression program or an executable copy of the compressed file (so that you can double-click the file to decompress it and then open it).

**no** (file zipped or compressed?)

**Quick fix**

Ask your correspondent to resend the file. Sometimes a file is corrupted before or while it's being sent.

**no** (correct program and version?)

**Quick fix**

To open any file in your computer, you need the correct program and version for the file. Ask your correspondent to save the file in a format that you can open, and then send it to you again. (Many files can be saved as earlier versions of the program.)

**Go to...**

**I don't want to download messages with very large files, page 138.**

**If your solution isn't here**

Check these related chapters:

Files, sending, page 144

E-mail, receiving, page 78

Or see the general troubleshooting tips on page xiii.

# I don't want to download messages with very large files

## Source of the problem

If you're pressed for time, or on the road and picking up your messages in a hotel room somewhere, downloading a message with a very large attached file is expensive in terms of both time and money. Worse yet, if someone sends you a message with an attached file that exceeds the limitations of your ISP mail server, you probably won't be able to download it at all, even though Outlook might spend hours trying to do just that.

The best way to avoid downloading messages with large files attached is to simply not download them. But how do you know what's waiting to be downloaded, and how can you tell Outlook to download some messages but not others?

There are two solutions: limit the size of your downloads, or use Remote Mail.

## How to fix it

In Outlook, you can limit the size of downloaded messages, or you can choose which messages to download (which is a good idea when you expect an important message with a large attached file, but don't want to download any other large messages).

### Limit the size of download messages

1. On the Tools menu, click Options.
2. On the Mail Delivery tab, select the Don't Download Messages Larger Than check box.
3. In the box to the right, type a maximum number of kilobytes for files you want to download.
4. Click OK.

Outlook will not download any messages larger than this number of kilobytes until you clear the check box. Messages that are larger than your specified limit will remain on the server until you remove the limit and download them.

> **Tip**
>
> You can send and receive files without using e-mail at all. You can send files via File Transfer Protocol (FTP) by using Windows HyperTerminal, Norton pcAnywhere, and other file-transfer software programs.

### Use Remote Mail to selectively download messages

By using remote mail in the Corporate/Workgroup configuration, you can go online and quickly download just message headers. Then you can go back online and download just the messages you select from among the headers. You can leave the messages with large attachments sitting on your mail server until you get back to the office.

If you're not already working in Corporate/Workgroup configuration, see "I don't know how to change my Outlook configuration," on page 20. If you are using Corporate/Workgroup configuration, follow these steps to use Remote Mail to choose which messages to download.

First, you need to create an away-from-office connection; then you select the away-from-office connection before you dial in for remote mail. Finally, you pick up your message headers, choose the headers you want to download, and download the messages you chose.

**Tip**

If the message and its attached file exceed the message size limitation of your ISP mail server, ask your correspondent to compress the attached files and resend the message, or arrange to transfer the files via a different file transfer procedure rather than sending them attached to an e-mail message. You also need to ask your ISP to delete the large message from the mail server so that Outlook will stop trying to download it.

## Create an away-from-office connection (you need to do this only once):

1. On the Tools menu, click Services.
2. In the Services dialog box, on the Services tab, click the name of your e-mail account, and then click the Properties button.
3. In the account Properties dialog box, on the Connection tab, under the Use The Following Dial-Up Networking Connection box, click the Add button. ▶

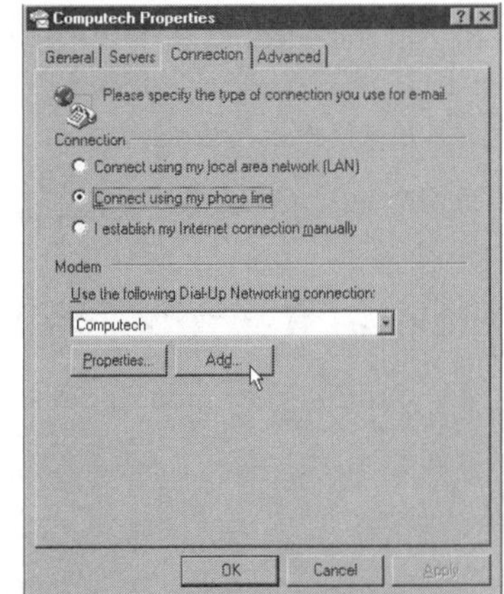


4. In the first dialog box of the Make A New Connection Wizard, type the name for the connection and click Next. ▶

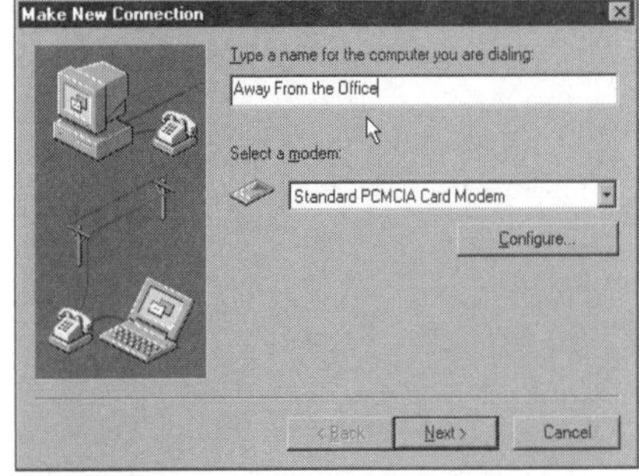


*If this solution didn't solve your problem, go to the next page.*

# I don't want to download messages with very large files

*(continued from page 139)*

5. In the next step, type the telephone number and the area code and country, if necessary. Then click Next.
6. In the last step, click Finish. The new connection is on your list of connections, and you can select it when you dial in for your e-mail from your away-from-office location.

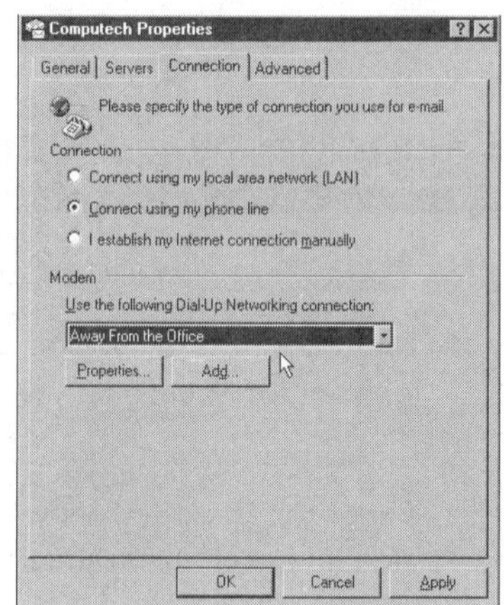


## Select the connection before you dial in

1. On the Tools menu, click Services.
2. In the Services dialog box, on the Services tab, click the name of your e-mail account, and click the Properties button.
3. In the account Properties dialog box, on the Connection tab, in the Use The Following Dial-Up Networking Connection box, select your away-from-office connection.
4. Click OK twice to close the dialog boxes.

## Pick up Remote Mail headers

1. On the Tools menu, point to Remote Mail, and click Connect.
2. In the Remote Connection Wizard, click the mail service you want to connect to, and then click Next.
3. In the next wizard step, click the Do Only The Following option, and be sure the Retrieve New Message Headers check box is selected. Then click Next.

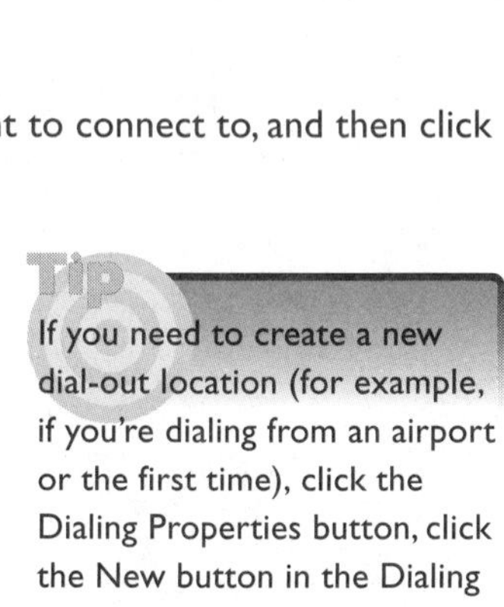


If you need to create a new dial-out location (for example, if you're dialing from an airport or the first time), click the Dialing Properties button, click the New button in the Dialing Properties dialog box, fill in the appropriate information and click OK.

4. In the next step, select the location you're dialing from.
5. When the correct dial-out location is selected, click Finish. Outlook dials up your connection, retrieves the message headers for your waiting messages, and then disconnects.

## Select and download messages

1. Click the message headers for each message you want to download. ▶

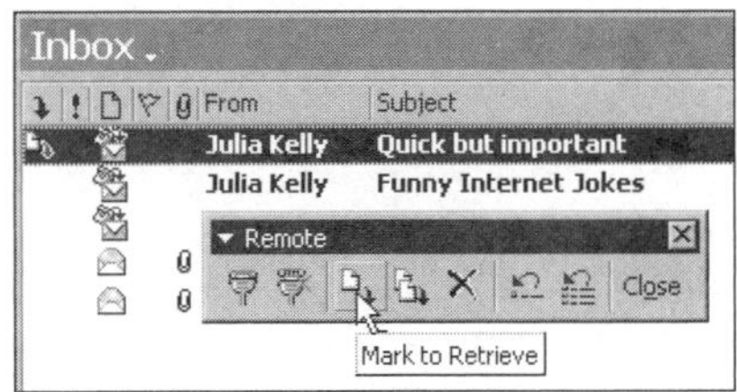


2. On the Tools menu, point to Remote Mail, and click Mark To Retrieve. A Retrieve icon appears next to each message header that Outlook will retrieve. If you mark a message for retrieval and change your mind, click the Unmark command.
3. On the Tools menu, point to Remote Mail, and click Connect. Make sure the correct connection is selected in the first wizard step, and click Next.
4. In each wizard step, check the information to be sure it's correct, and click Next or click Finish.

   Outlook dials your connection, picks up complete messages for each header you selected for downloading, and then disconnects.

**Tip**

At this point, you'll probably find it easier to use the remote mail toolbar instead of your remote mail menu commands.

# My message is full of gibberish

## Source of the problem

E-mail messages can bounce from server to server around the world before they arrive at your address. Sometimes, while bouncing, some mail server in the system fails to pass along your message completely and correctly.

There also are several mail encoding formats in use around the world, and they don't always all work well with every mail system. If someone sends you a message and attached file in an encoding format that your mail server can't read, or that some Internet gateway can't interpret, the attached file might be converted into pages and pages of encoded garbage characters.

## How to fix it

Try these three solutions:

- Ask your correspondent to resend the message in either MIME or UUencode format.
- Ask your correspondent to use a compression program, such as WinZip, to compress the file and then send it to you. Sometimes, compressed attached files are carried through Internet mail gateways more cleanly.
- If the file is fairly short, and you don't need the formatting, ask your correspondent to send it as text in the message rather than attaching it as a file.

### If you want to know more about mail encoding formats

When a binary file is attached to an e-mail message, the file is encoded so that it travels to its destination rapidly and intact. When the file arrives, most e-mail programs decode the file, regardless of the encoding format.

The most common file encoding type is MIME, and an older file type still in use is UUencode. MIME stands for Multipurpose Internet Mail Extensions, and UUencode stands for Unix to Unix Encode. UUencode was the standard for a long time, and was originally designed primarily to support the transfer of text-based files. MIME is newer and supports the transfer of a wider range of file types (such as audio, video, graphics, and e-mail).

There are also other, more obscure encoding types, and these are the ones that are likely to cause you trouble. The encoding type has to be changed by the sender sending the message.

**When you try to send a file as text in an e-mail message, is "Insert As Text" offered as an option?**

yes

When you send a message with an attached file, does the mail service take a long time to send, and then not send the message?

yes

no

Do your recipients receive unreadable attachments?

yes

no

**Quick fix**

In Outlook, if Word is your e-mail editor, Insert As Text is not an option. Either copy and paste the text of the file into your e-mail message, or turn off Word As E-mail Editor: on the Tools menu, click Options, and on the Mail Format tab, clear the Use Microsoft Word To Edit E-mail Messages check box.

In Outlook Express, Insert As Text is not an option. You must copy and paste text from a file into your message.

# Files, sending

**Go to...**

**My message with attached files doesn't get sent, page 146.**

Are you sending the attached files to an AOL address?

**yes**

**Go to...**

**My AOL recipient can't read my message or attached files, page 147.**

**no**

**Quick fix**

If your non-AOL recipients don't have the correct program or version to open the file you sent, they won't be able to read your file. Save and resend file in a format they can open and read.

**If your solution isn't here**

Check these related chapters:

Files, receiving, page 144
E-mail, recipients' problems, page 88
E-mail, sending, page 92
Or see the general troubleshooting tips on page xiii.

# My message with attached file doesn't get sent

## Source of the problem

If a message has a very large attached file (more than 2 MB), many mail servers won't handle it and it doesn't get sent. So, if you've got a huge, complex database to send to your client, how can you get it there electronically?

## How to fix it

First, open your Outbox and look at the size of the outgoing message. If the Size field isn't displayed, display it like this:

1. Right-click in the row of headings, and click Field Chooser.
2. From the Field Chooser, drag the Size field to the headings row and drop it when you see two red arrows. ▶
3. Close the Field Chooser by clicking its X close box.

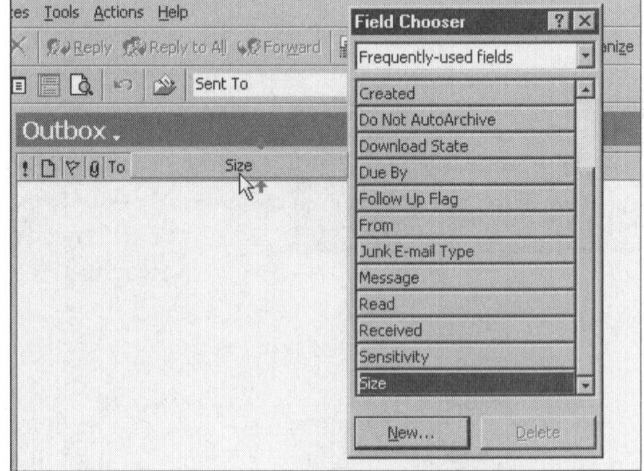


If your message is larger than 2 MB (2000 KB), use WinZip which you can find at *http://www.winzip.com* or another file compression program to reduce the size of the attached file (the compressed file is commonly called a "zipped" file).

If the message is large because it contains multiple attached files, either send the files in separate messages, or zip the multiple files together and attach the single zipped file to your message.

If your message is still too large, send the file directly to your recipient's computer by using a program such as Windows HyperTerminal or Norton pcAnywhere. With these programs, you can contact the other computer directly through the telephone line. Norton pcAnywhere is a commercial program, and Windows HyperTerminal is an optional feature in Windows 95 and Windows 98.

**Tip**

To use HyperTerminal, click the Start button, point to Programs, point to Accessories, point to Communications, click HyperTerminal, and then click *Hypertrm.exe*. To learn how to use HyperTerminal, click the Help menu in HyperTerminal.

# My AOL recipient can't read my message or attached files

## Source of the problem

Whether you use Outlook or Outlook Express, if you send a single message that contains multiple attached files to an America Online (AOL) address, your recipient won't be able to read either the message or the attached files. AOL's mail server combines the message and all its attachments in a single file, and there are no viewers for that type of combined file.

## How to fix it

There are a couple of ways to work around the problem of getting multiple files to a colleague who uses AOL.

- The easiest method is to send multiple separate messages to your recipient and attach a single file to each message.
- Another method is to combine all the attached files into a single compressed file (using a compression program such as WinZip), and attach the zipped (compressed) file to your message. ▶

  If you use this method, you need to tell your recipients that they can open the compressed file using their own copy of WinZip. Recipients can use WinZip 7. or earlier in the Classic mode (the WinZip 7.-and-earlier Wizard won't open the combined-file type), or they can download WinZip 8., in which the WinZip Wizard can extract compressed files from the AOL combined-file type.

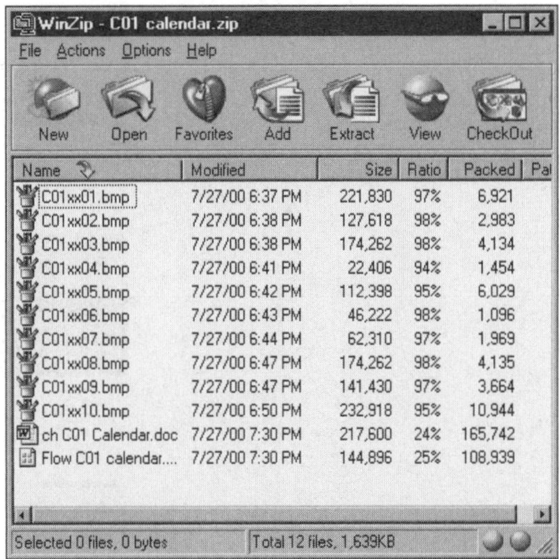


### Tip

WinZip is a popular and widely used file-compression program created by Nico Mac Computing, Inc., and can be found at *http://www.winzip.com*.

Fo

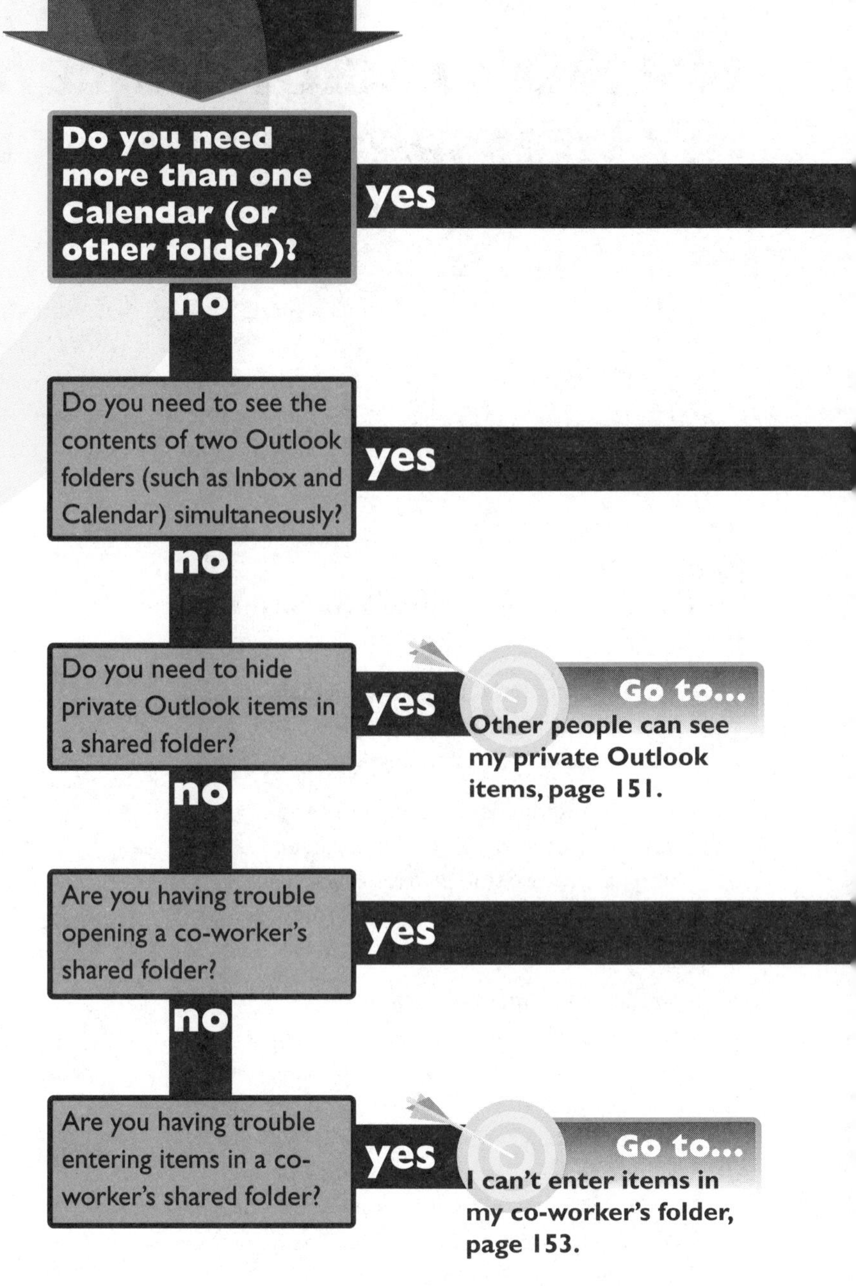

**Do you need more than one Calendar (or other folder)?**

yes

no

Do you need to see the contents of two Outlook folders (such as Inbox and Calendar) simultaneously?

yes

no

Do you need to hide private Outlook items in a shared folder?

yes

Go to...

**Other people can see my private Outlook items, page 151.**

no

Are you having trouble opening a co-worker's shared folder?

yes

no

Are you having trouble entering items in a co-worker's shared folder?

yes

Go to...

**I can't enter items in my co-worker's folder, page 153.**

**Go to...**

**I need more than one Calendar, page 150.**

**Quick fix**

If you want to see the contents of two folders simultaneously (for example, your Inbox and Calendar, or your Inbox and Web page), you can open a separate Outlook window for the second (or third) folder.

1. On the View menu, click Folder List.
2. In the Folder list, right-click the folder you want to see in a second window, and then click Open In New Window.

**Go to...**

**I can't open my co-worker's folder, page 152.**

**If your solution isn't here**

Check these related chapters:

Calendar, page 10
Multiple users, page 182
Outlook bar, page 206
Or see the general troubleshooting tips on page xiii.

# I need more than one Calendar

## Source of the problem

If you have a full load of both work appointments and personal appointments, or you have busy schedules going for multiple separate work projects, your Calendar is both full and confusing.

You can solve the confusion by creating separate Calendar folders.

**Tip**

To create a shortcut in the Outlook bar that opens the new folder, right-click the new folder name in the Folder list, and then click Add To Outlook Bar.

## How to fix it

1. On the View menu, click Folder List (or click the Folder List button on the toolbar).
2. In the Folder list, right-click the Calendar folder, and then click New Folder.
3. In the Create New Folder dialog box, type a name for your new Calendar.
4. Be sure the Folder Contains box reads Appointment Items. ▶

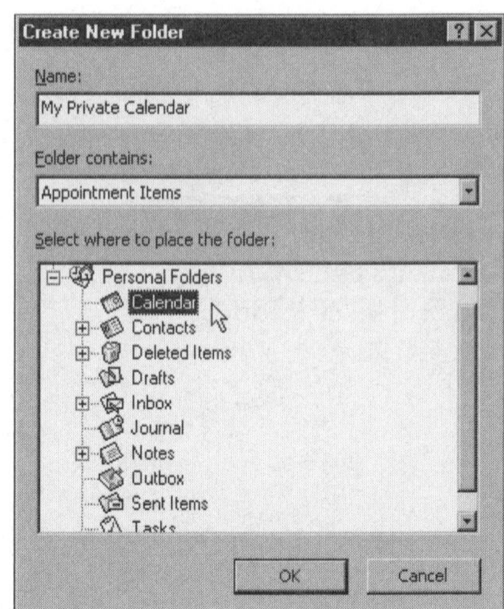


5. In the Select Where To Place The Folder list, click either Personal Folders or Calendar. If you click Personal Folders, the new calendar is a subfolder under Personal Folders, on the same level as the main Calendar folder. If you click Calendar, the new calendar is a subfolder of the main Calendar folder.
6. Click OK.

# Other people can see my private Outlook items

## Source of the problem

Shared Calendar and Contacts folders are very efficient in a work environment, but there are items (appointments, contacts) that you don't need to share with your co-workers. There are two ways to keep items private: keep them in a private folder that's not shared, and mark individual items as private so they don't appear to anyone else who opens the shared folder.

## How to fix it

- To keep all the items in a folder hidden from others, don't make the folder a public folder. (That one was easy.)
- To keep specific items private, even if they're in a public folder, mark the Private check box in the lower-right corner of the open item. Every item in the Contacts, Calendar, Tasks, and Journal folders can be marked private.

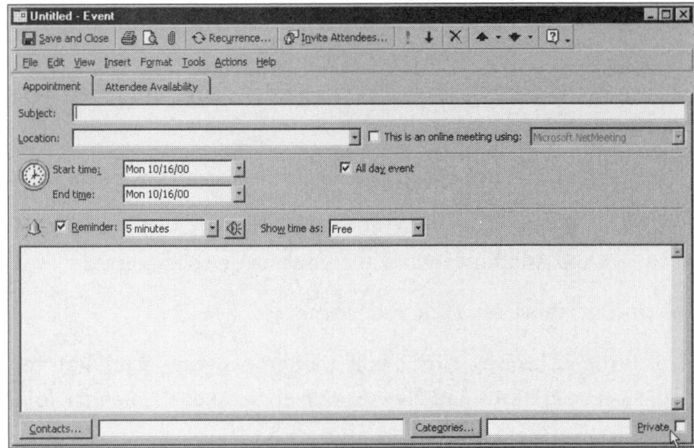


If you don't see the Private check box, drag the lower-right corner of the open item to make the item larger (until you can see the check box).

# I can't open my co-worker's folder

## Source of the problem

If you're using Outlook on a network that uses the Microsoft Exchange Server, you and your co-workers have the capability of sharing Outlook folders, such as the Calendar folder. Now you need to get into your co-worker's shared calendar to find some scheduling details, but you can't open it.

You need to have a chat with your co-worker. Because it's her Calendar folder, she has to give you permission to open it—and you can tell her how to do that.

## How to fix it

1. On the View menu, click Folder List.
2. In the Folder list, right-click the folder name and click Properties.
3. In the Properties dialog box, click the Permissions tab.
4. Be sure your name is listed in the Name list—if it's not there, click the Add button and add your name to the list.
5. In the Name list, click your name.
6. In the Roles box, click a role that grants you permission to at least read items and files in your co-worker's Calendar folder.
7. Below the Roles box is a set of options and check boxes for specific activities you can be granted or denied permission for—be sure that (at least) the Read Items and Folder Visible check boxes are selected.
8. Click OK.

**Tip**

This procedure must be carried out in the computer where the shared folder resides–it can't be done from another computer.

**Tip**

Any role *except* Contributor and None gives you permission to open the folder and read the items.

# I can't enter items in my co-worker's folder

## Source of the problem

You're using Outlook on a network that uses the Microsoft Exchange Server, and you share your supervisor's Calendar folder so that you can schedule appointments for him. Now you need to add some appointments to your supervisor's shared calendar, but Outlook won't let you create new items. Your supervisor forgot to give you the appropriate permission.

If your supervisor is too busy to schedule his own appointments, he's probably too busy to make the permission change. As usual, you have to do it, but it's not difficult.

## How to fix it

1. On the View menu, click Folder List.
2. In the Folder list, right-click the Calendar folder name and click Properties.
3. In the Properties dialog box, click the Permissions tab.
4. In the Name list, click your name.
5. In the Roles box, click a role that grants you permission (at least) to read items and files in your supervisor's Calendar folder.
6. Below the Roles box is a set of options and check boxes for specific activities you can be granted or denied permission for—be sure that (at least) the Create Items and Folder Visible check boxes are selected.
7. Click OK.

**Tip**

This procedure must be carried out in your supervisor's computer, where the shared folder resides.

**Tip**

Any role *except* Reviewer and None gives you permission to open the folder and create new items.

# Hidden na

**Can you find the Bcc field in your message?**

yes

no

Do you use Outlook?

yes

**Quick fix**

If the Bcc field isn't displayed in the message below the Cc field, on the View menu, click Bcc Field.

no

Do you use Outlook Express?

yes

**Quick fix**

If the Bcc field isn't displayed in the message below the Cc field, on the View menu, click All Headers.

When you send a message to several people, do you want recipients to see only their own name?

**yes**

**Go to...**

**Some of my recipients want their identities hidden, page 156.**

**no**

When you send a message to a group, do you want each recipient to see only the group name?

**yes**

**Go to...**

**I don't know how to send a message to a group name, page 157.**

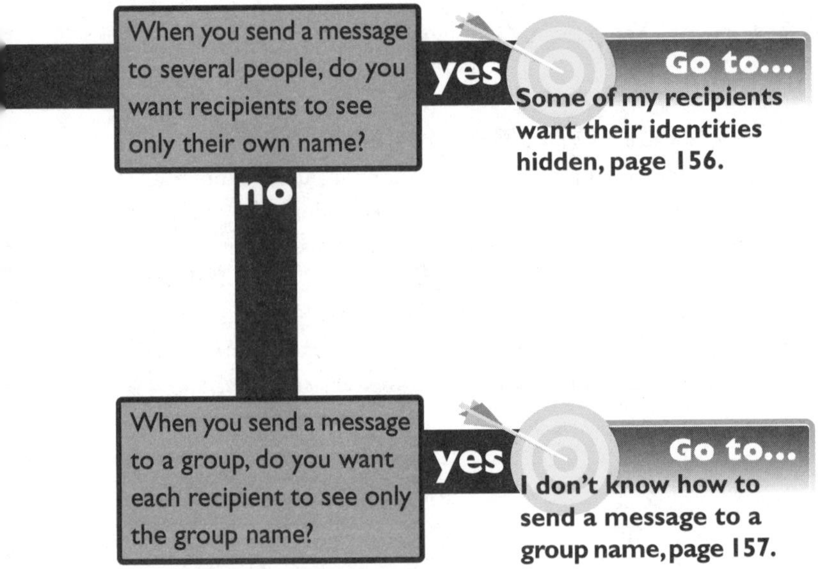

**If your solution isn't here**

Check these related chapters:

E-mail, addressing messages, page 40

E-mail, automatic addresses, page 48

Or see the general troubleshooting tips on page xiii.

# Some of my recipients want their identities hidden

## Source of the problem

When you send a message to a large group of people (or to a distribution list), each recipient sees a long list of all the recipient names in the To or Cc field. The long list of names is often annoying to a recipient, and some of those recipients don't want their names and e-mail addresses broadcast to the whole list. So how can you send a message to the whole group while keeping the list of addressees confidential?

## How to fix it

To hide names and addresses of message recipients, use the Bcc field. Any recipient names in the Bcc field are hidden from all recipients. The procedure is the same in both Outlook and Outlook Express, although an Outlook Express message looks a little different than the Outlook message pictured in the first figure.

In some e-mail systems, recipients see your name in the From field and their own name in the To field. In other e-mail systems, recipients see only your name in both the From and the To fields.

**Tip**

*Bcc* means *blind copy*. Addressees in the Bcc field are hidden from everyone who receives the message, so the message recipients are *blind* to the Bcc recipients.

**Tip**

Any names in the To and Cc fields are visible to all recipients.

1. Open a new message.
2. If you don't see the Bcc field below the Cc field, on the View menu, click Bcc Field. (If you use Outlook Express, on the View menu, click All Headers.)
3. Enter all your hidden names and distribution lists in the Bcc field. You don't need to enter any name in the To field—if you leave the To field empty, some recipients will see *your* name there and some will see *their* name there, depending on their mail system.
4. Finish and send your message.

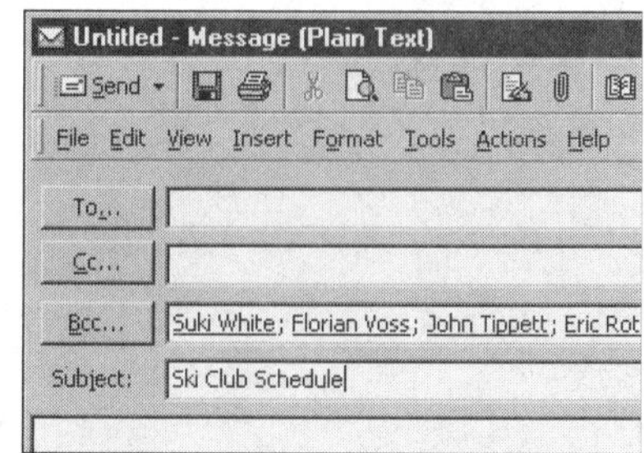

# I don't know how to send a message to a group name

## Source of the problem

You need to send a message to all the members of your ski club (The Mogul Maniacs), and you want each recipient to know that this is a message to the entire Mogul Maniacs club. But if you send blind copies to the members, the message appears to be addressed to each individual instead of the whole club. How can you send a message that's addressed to The Mogul Maniacs?

## How to fix it

Send the message to a group name (that has your own e-mail address), and put all the recipient names in the Bcc field.

Everyone will receive the message addressed from you to the group name.

**Tip**

Although the following figures are from Outlook, the procedure is the same in both Outlook and Outlook Express.

1. Create a new contact.
2. Put the group name in the Company field and your e-mail address in the E-mail field.

   Don't put any other information in the new contact.

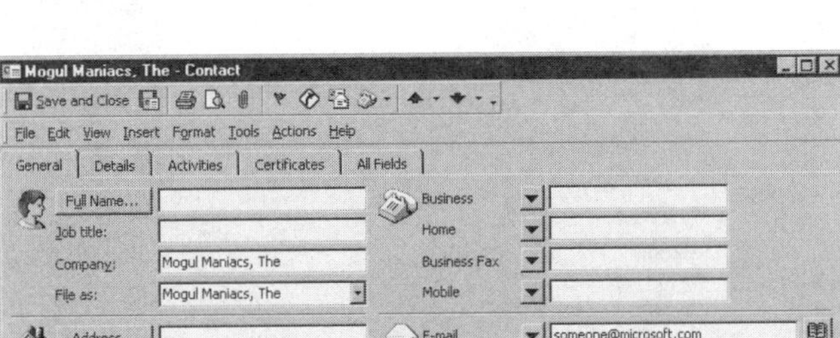


3. Save and close the new contact.
4. Create a new message and address it to the new contact (with the name from the Company field).
5. Place all the recipient and/or distribution list names in the Bcc field.
6. Finish and send the message.

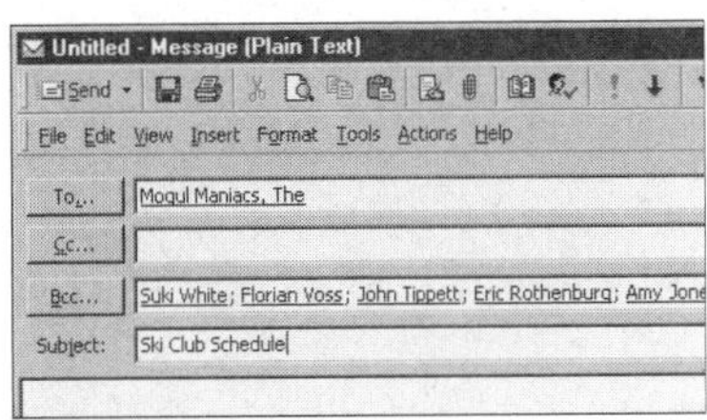

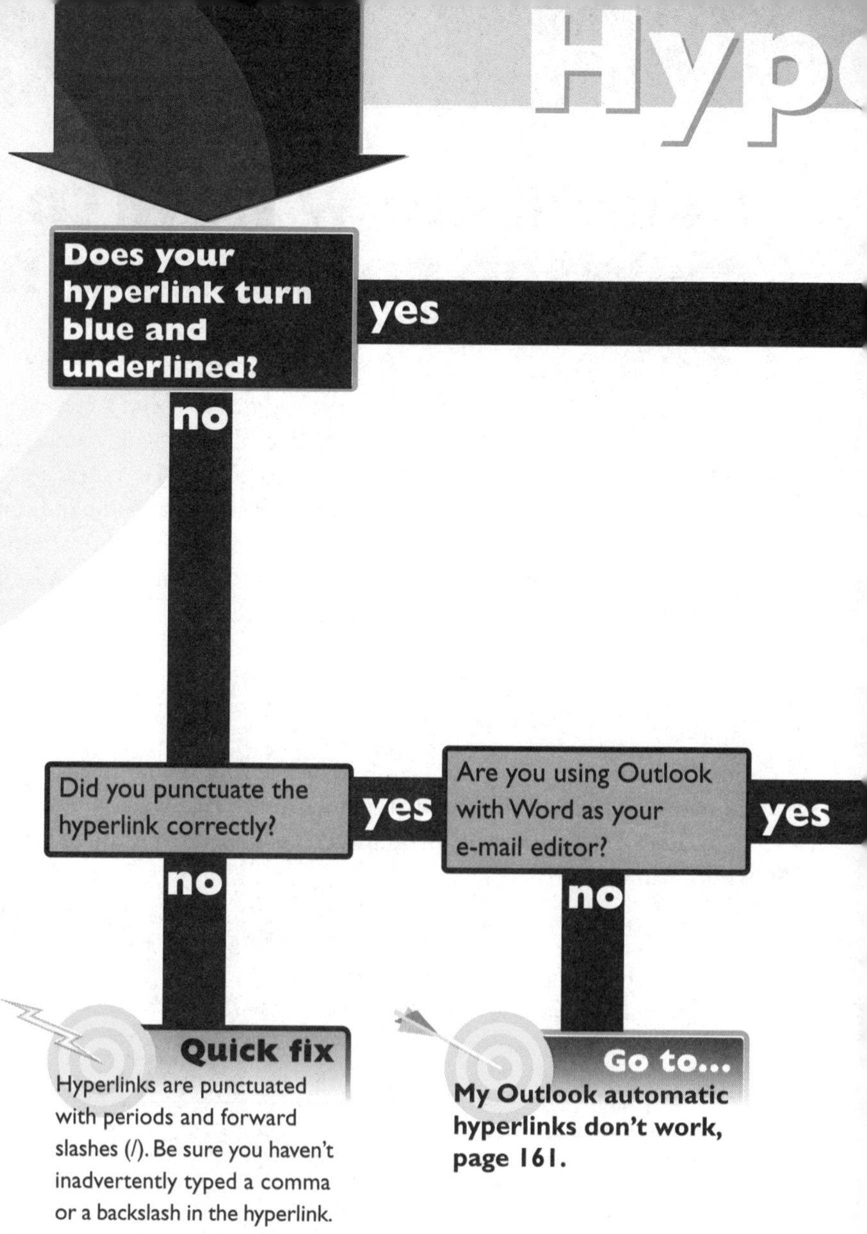

# Hyp

**Does your hyperlink turn blue and underlined?**

yes

no

Did you punctuate the hyperlink correctly?

yes

Are you using Outlook with Word as your e-mail editor?

yes

no

no

**Quick fix**

Hyperlinks are punctuated with periods and forward slashes (/). Be sure you haven't inadvertently typed a comma or a backslash in the hyperlink.

**Go to...**

**My Outlook automatic hyperlinks don't work, page 161.**

Did your recipient receive your hyperlink as an active link?

yes

Does your recipient's browser launch?

yes

**Quick fix**

If your recipient has active scripts disabled in his computer as a security measure, web pages that depend on active scripting to function will open mostly or entirely blank.

See the chapter, "E-mail, viruses," to learn more about disabling and enabling active scripting (and tell your recipient about it, too).

no

**Quick fix**

Your recipient's browser might not support the hyperlink protocol. Recipients of your message must have an Internet browser installed on their computer that supports the hyperlink protocol (such as Microsoft Internet Explorer).

no

**Quick fix**

Your recipient's mail program might not support hyperlinks. If not, he can still copy and paste the inactive link into his browser's address box.

Does your hyperlink start with *www*?

no

**Go to...**

**My hyperlink doesn't start with *www*, page 160.**

**If your solution isn't here**

Check these related chapters:

E-mail, creating, page 56

E-mail, recipients' problems, page 88

Or see the general troubleshooting tips on page xiii.

# My hyperlink doesn't start with www

## Source of the problem

If you type a URL (universal resource locator, or web site address) that begins with *www.* in an Outlook or Outlook Express message, and you're not using Word as your Outlook e-mail editor, the URL is formatted as a live hyperlink. More and more web sites have URLs that don't begin with *www.*, however, and lots of Internet addresses are not web sites, which means they don't have *www.* prefixes, either.

## How to fix it

You need to know, and type, the entire Internet address in the message. Technically, all sites on the World Wide Web begin with the prefix *http://www.*, but Outlook and Outlook Express add a hidden *http://* prefix when you type the *www.* part. If the URL is for a web site and there's no *www.* prefix, you need to type the URL beginning with *http://* so that Outlook or Outlook Express recognizes and formats the URL.

If the URL is not a web site (for example, if the URL is a gopher, news, or ftp site), you need to type the entire URL, including the *gopher://*, *news:*, or *ftp://* prefix and punctuation.

If you're creating a message in HTML formatting (in either Outlook or Outlook Express), you can insert a hyperlink and choose from a list of prefixes:

> **Tip**
> After you finish the hyperlink, you can switch the message format back to Plain Text or Rich Text without losing the hyperlink formatting.

1. Make sure the message is in HTML format, and click the body of the message where you want to place the URL.
2. In the message, on the Insert Menu, click Hyperlink.
3. In the Hyperlink dialog box, in the Type box, click a prefix for the URL. ▶
4. Click in the URL box, on the right side of the prefix, and type the remainder of the URL.
5. Click OK to insert the hyperlink in the message.

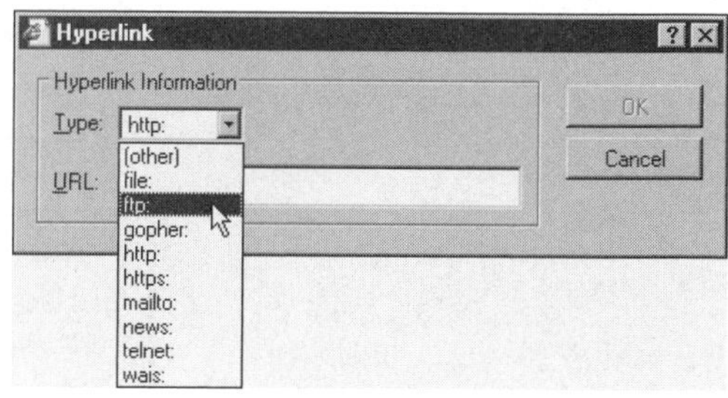

# My Outlook automatic hyperlinks don't work

## Source of the problem

If you're using Outlook with Word as your e-mail editor (so your messages can be formatted with bullets and other Word formatting), and your automatic hyperlink formatting isn't working, it's probably been turned off. When you use Word as your Outlook e-mail editor, you can turn the automatic hyperlink formatting on or off; but if you don't use Word as an e-mail editor, hyperlinks are always formatted as live links (blue and underlined). If you use Outlook Express, hyperlinks are always formatted as live links.

## How to fix it

One way is to turn off Word as your Outlook e-mail editor. In Outlook, on the Tools menu, click Options. On the Mail Format tab, clear the Use Microsoft Word To Edit E-Mail Messages check box, and then click OK.

If you want to continue using the Word e-mail editor, you can turn the automatic hyperlink formatting back on.

1. Open a message.
2. Click in the body of the message to place the insertion point there.
3. On the Tools menu, click AutoCorrect.
4. On the AutoFormat As You Type tab, select the Internet And Network Paths With Hyperlinks check box. ▶
5. Click OK.

**Tip**

Only recipients who have Word 2000 see the formatting in your Word-formatted e-mail messages, so you might not be losing very much by turning off the Word e-mail editor.

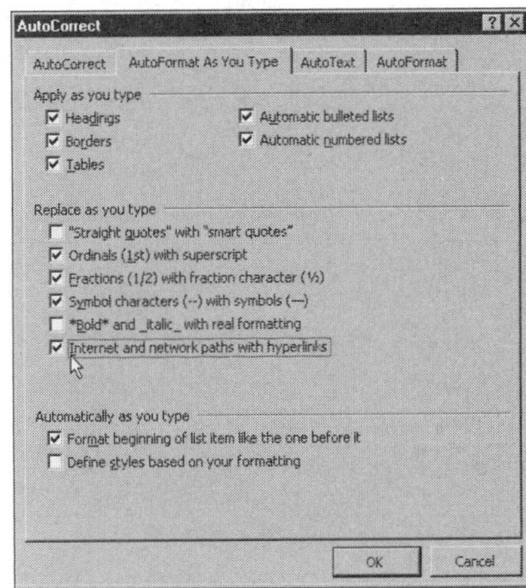

# Impor

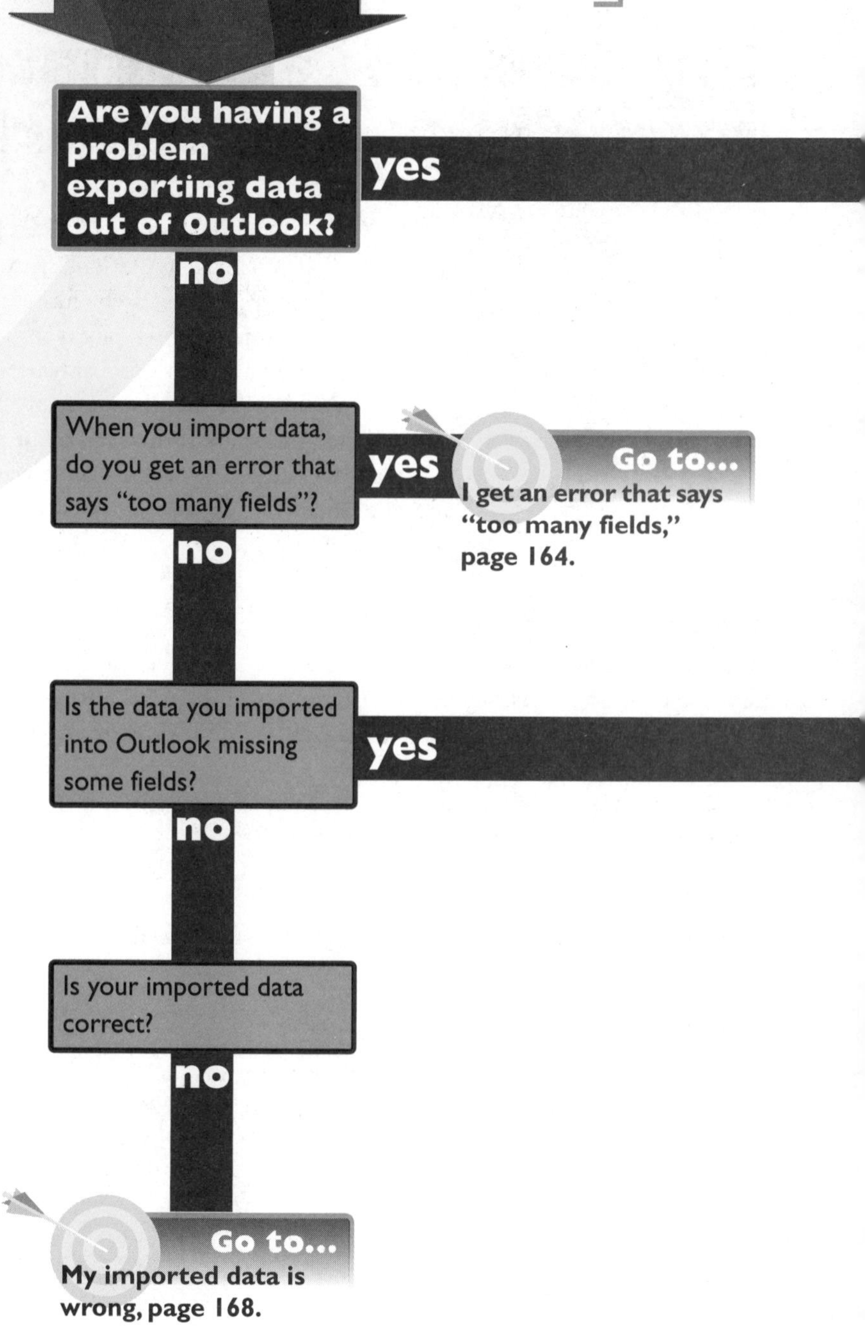

**Are you having a problem exporting data out of Outlook?**

yes

no

When you import data, do you get an error that says "too many fields"?

yes

**Go to...**

**I get an error that says "too many fields," page 164.**

no

Is the data you imported into Outlook missing some fields?

yes

no

Is your imported data correct?

no

**Go to...**

**My imported data is wrong, page 168.**

Are you trying to export custom fields in Outlook to Access or Excel?

yes

**Go to...**

**I can't export custom fields to an Access database, page 166.**

**Quick fix**

If you imported data from another program and some of the fields didn't get imported, you need to "map" your imported fields to match Outlook's field names:

1. In the last step of the Import Wizard, click the Map Custom Fields button. In the Map Custom Fields dialog box, the existing field names are in the list on the left and the Outlook field names are listed on the right.
2. Click the small plus symbols in the list on the right to expand the Name group, the Home Address group, and so forth.
3. Drag each existing field name from the left and drop it on the corresponding Outlook field name on the right.

**If your solution isn't here**

Check these related chapters:

E-mail, importing addresses, page 68

Contacts, custom data, page 22

Or see the general troubleshooting tips on page xiii.

# I get an error that says "too many fields"

## Source of the problem

You're trying to import an Excel table into Outlook, but you keep getting an error that says "ODBC" and "too many fields." Outlook can't determine the range of the list you're trying to import.

## How to fix it

You need to name the table range (the range of cells that compose your list in Excel), or Outlook will try to import the entire worksheet.

**Tip**

A *table* is just a list, a rectangular range of rows and columns, with no totally blank rows and no totally blank columns.

1. Drag from the cell in one corner of the table to the cell in the diagonally opposite corner of the table. Be sure you include the column names (headers) in your table. All the cells in your rectangular table range will be highlighted.
2. With the whole table—and only the table—selected, click in the Name box (on the left end of the Formula bar). Type a name for the selected range—one word, no punctuation, and not the same as any column header. ▶

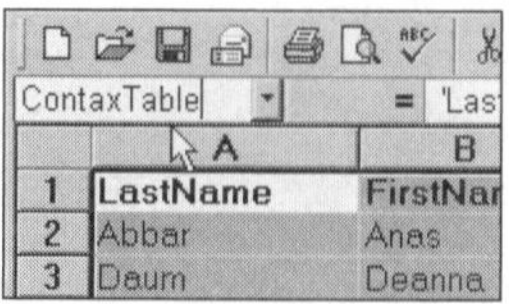


3. After you type the name, press Enter. Don't click or do anything else; just press Enter.
4. Test the name. Click a cell away from the table, and then click the arrow on the right side of the Name box. On the list that drops, click the range name, and your table is selected. That's the table range that Outlook will recognize, with its column headers, to import. ▶

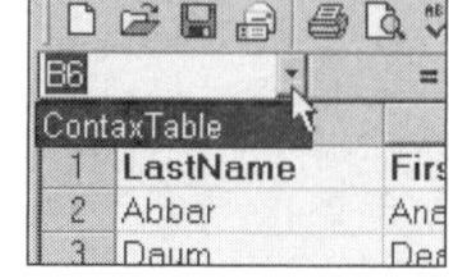


4. Save and close the Excel workbook.
5. In Outlook, import the Excel file.

**Tip**

When you get to the last step of the Import Wizard (the dialog box where you click Finish), you need to click the Map Custom Fields button and "map" your Excel column headers to match Outlook's field names.

# I can't export custom fields to an Access database

## Source of the problem

You've created custom fields in the Tasks folder (or any Outlook folder), and you want to export all the fields in that folder, including the custom fields, to a Microsoft Access database. But when you export Outlook items, the Export Wizard exports only Outlook's built-in fields.

## How to fix it

You can use Excel as an intermediate translator between Outlook and Access. There's a trick to exporting your custom fields from Outlook to Excel without using the Export Wizard, and all your fields, including the custom fields, will be exported.

1. Switch the Outlook folder (in this example, Tasks) to a table view, and display all the fields you want to send to the Access table (which would include your custom fields).
2. Start Excel, and resize both the Excel and Outlook windows so that they sit side-by-side or overlapped. ▶
3. In Outlook, select all the records you want to send to Access (drag down the left side of the table to select them all, or use the Ctrl or Shift key to select specific records).

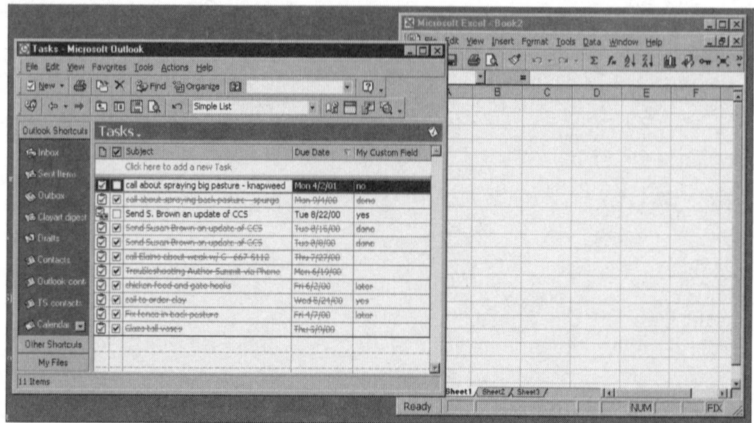

**4.** In Outlook, point to the *border* of the selected records, and drag the selection into the Excel window (you'll see a "move" mouse pointer icon when the mouse moves into the Excel window). ▶

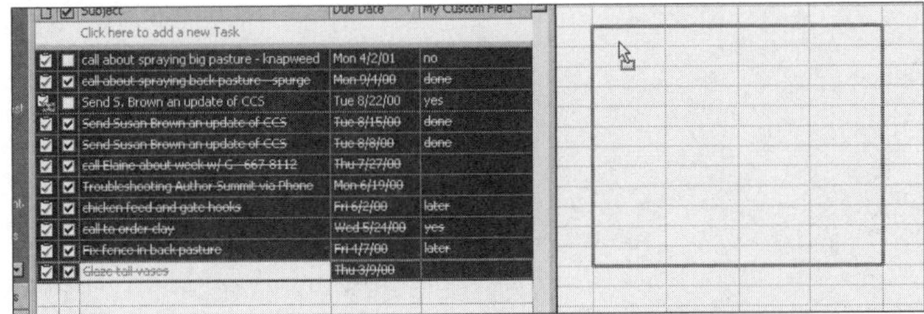


**5.** Before you drop the selected records in Excel, press and hold down the Ctrl key while you release the mouse button. This drops a copy of the records. ▶

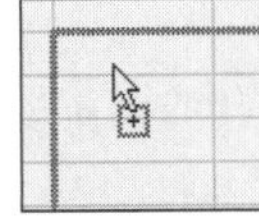

**6.** Now the records are in a table in Excel, including your custom fields. Use any Access import procedure to import the Excel table into Access. (I like to drag the selected Excel table into an Access database, Table pane, to create a fast Access table.) ▶

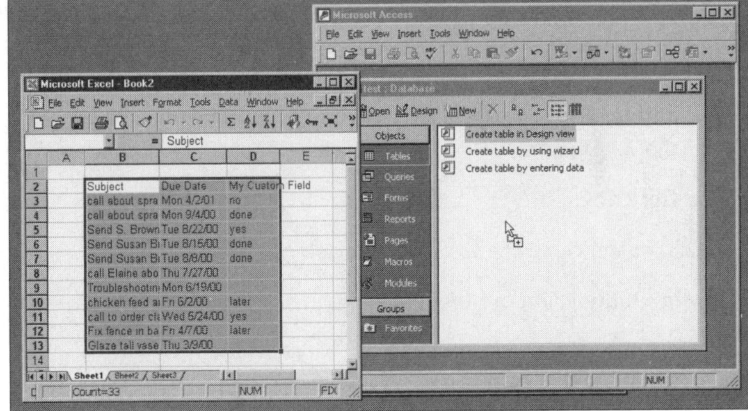

# My imported data is wrong

## Source of the problem

You imported a contacts list from Excel, and some of the phone numbers were imported incorrectly (appearing in Outlook with extra characters in them). It's a long list, with lots of phone numbers, and you shouldn't have to go through and correct them one by one. How can you get an Excel list imported into Outlook with all its data intact and correct?

## How to fix it

The most important part of importing Excel data correctly is setting up the Excel worksheet properly before you begin the import process. You need to format all the phone number and zip code columns as Text.

1. In the Excel worksheet, click the column heading(s) to select entire columns.
2. On the Format menu, click Cells.
3. In the Format Cells dialog box, on the Number tab, select the Text format. ▶
4. Click OK.
5. Save and close the Excel Workbook.
6. In Outlook, import the Excel file.

### If you want to know more about pre-import formatting in Excel

The correct formatting for any Excel data that's not going to be used in calculations is Text (for example, zip codes and phone numbers). Excel has special formats to make data entry in worksheets more efficient, but those special formats might not translate properly when you export the Excel data to another program. Before you export Excel data to any other program (including Outlook), it's a good idea to go through the worksheet and reformat the columns to either Text or Number so the data is exported with the simplest possible formatting.

Although I've written specifically about Excel in this solution, proper pre-import formatting is important in any program from which you import data into Outlook.

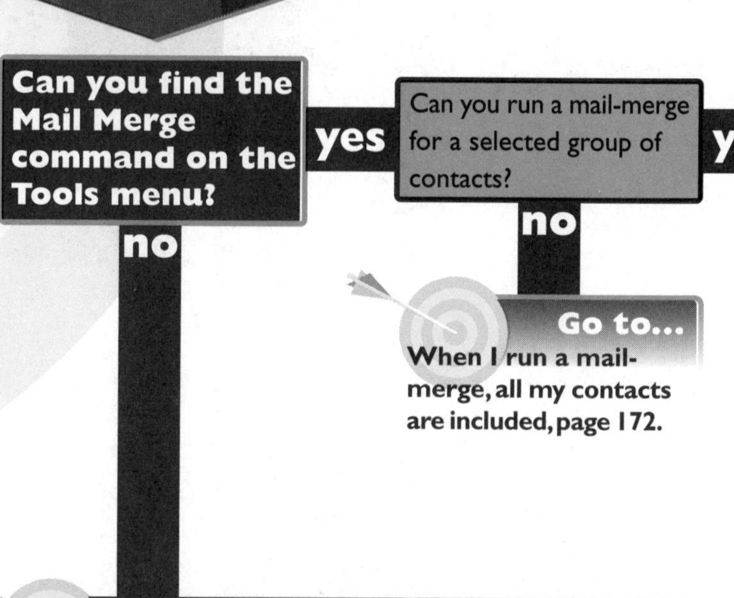
Can you find the Mail Merge command on the Tools menu?
yes
Can you run a mail-merge for a selected group of contacts?
yes
no
no
Go to...

**When I run a mail-merge, all my contacts are included, page 172.**

## Quick fix

You won't see the Mail Merge command on the Tools menu unless you have Contacts or a Contacts subfolder displayed in Outlook.

Also, if your menus are set to hide seldom-used commands, the Mail Merge command might be hidden until you display the full menu. If there's a down-pointing chevron at the bottom of your menu, click the chevron to display all the commands on the menu.

# Mail merge

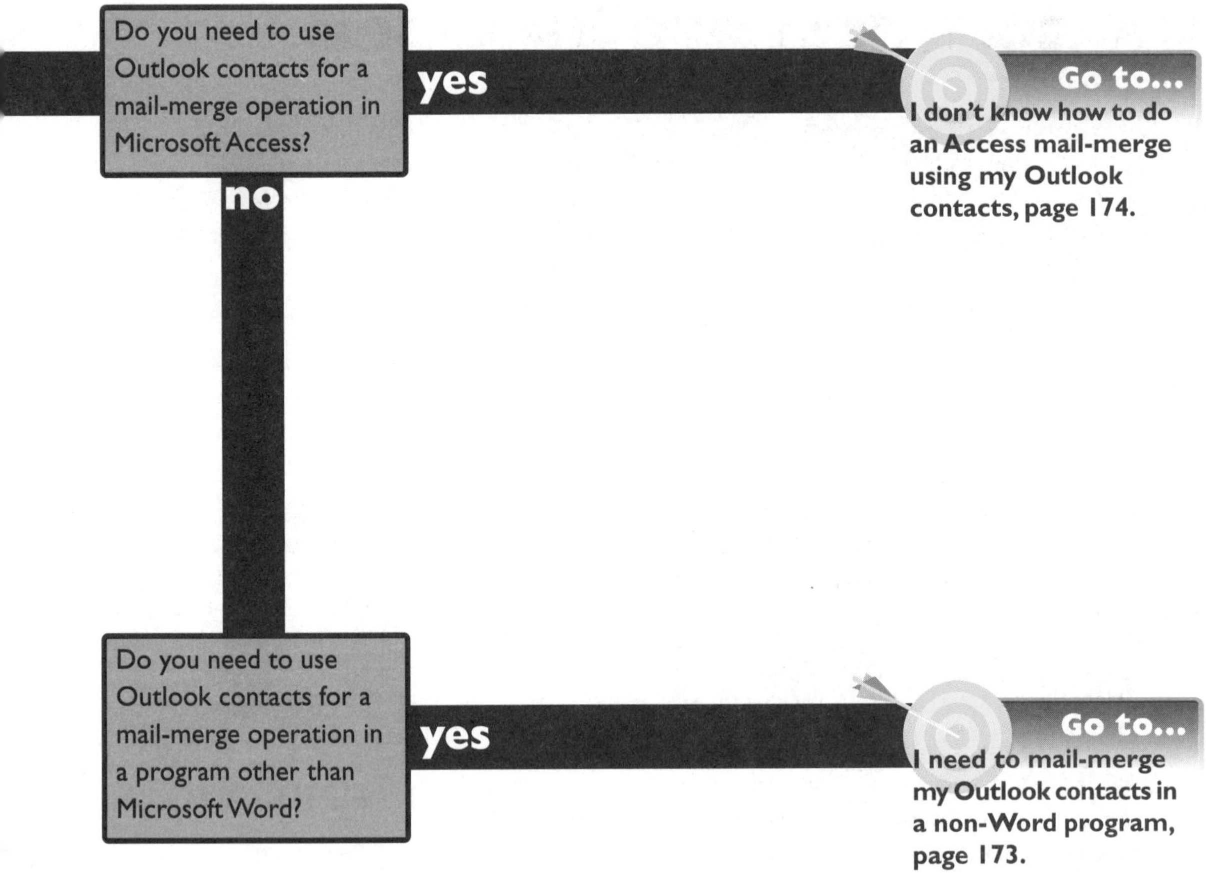

Do you need to use Outlook contacts for a mail-merge operation in Microsoft Access?

yes

Go to...

**I don't know how to do an Access mail-merge using my Outlook contacts, page 174.**

no

Do you need to use Outlook contacts for a mail-merge operation in a program other than Microsoft Word?

yes

Go to...

**I need to mail-merge my Outlook contacts in a non-Word program, page 173.**

**If your solution isn't here**

Check this related chapter:

Importing and exporting, page 162

Or see the general troubleshooting tips on page xiii.

# When I run a mail merge, all my contacts are included

## Source of the problem

You need to send a form letter to a select group of your contacts, but when you run a mail-merge, all your contacts are included. You need to tell Outlook which contacts you want included in the merge.

## How to fix it

You can mail-merge to a select group of contacts by filtering the list before you run the merge, if there's a common criterion among your select group of contacts; or you can select the specific contacts manually (click the first contact, and then click the rest while you hold down the Ctrl key).

1. Select the contacts, either by clicking or with a filter. ▶

   If you filter your contacts view, only the contacts displayed in the filtered view are included in the mail-merge. If you manually select the contacts you want, whether the view is filtered or not, only the selected contacts are included in the mail-merge.

2. On the Tools menu, click Mail Merge.
3. In the Mail Merge Contacts dialog box: ▶

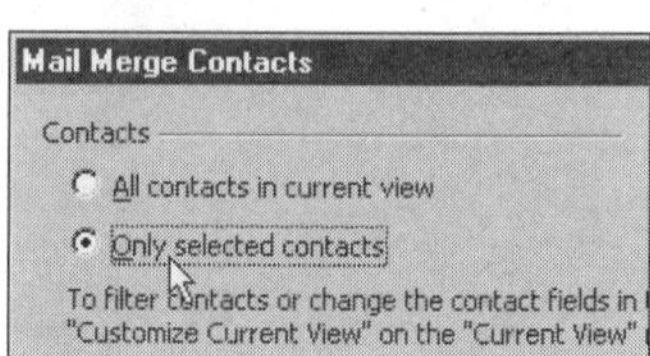


   - If you used a filter to display the contacts you want, click the All Contacts In Current View option.
   - If you manually selected the contacts you want, click the Only Selected Contacts option.

4. Continue with your mail-merge task.

**Tip**

To learn what each option in the dialog box does, right-click the option label to see a brief explanation.

# I need to mail merge my Outlook contacts in a non-Word program

## Source of the problem

You keep all your contacts in Outlook, but you don't have Microsoft Word installed on your computer. How can you run a mail-merge in another word processing program, using your Outlook contacts as a data source?

## How to fix it

You can use an intermediary data file that can be opened and used by both Outlook and your word-processing program.

1. Check your word-processing program to see what file types it can open or use as a data source (most programs can read a comma separated values text file).
2. Export your Outlook Contacts folder to a text file of that type. For example, if your word-processing program can use a comma separated values text file, click Comma Separated Values (Windows) in the second Export Wizard dialog box. ▶

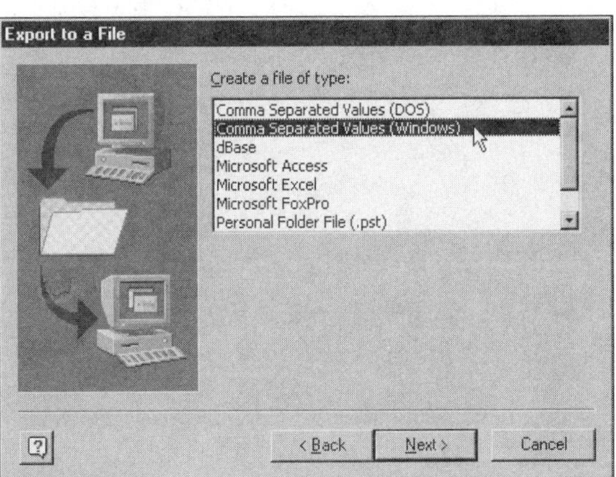


3. Run your mail-merge procedure in the word-processing program, and for a data source, use the text file you created from your Outlook Contacts folder.

**Tip**

If you need only a selected group of contacts for your mail-merge operation, make the process easier by exporting only those contacts to the intermediary text file. Create a new Contacts subfolder, and copy the contacts you want to export into the subfolder. Then, export that subfolder to the text file.

# I don't know how to do an Access mail merge using my Outlook contacts

## Source of the problem

You use Microsoft Access to create mailing labels, and you need to create mailing labels from your Outlook contacts. But you don't know how to get Access to use Outlook's contacts as a data source for your mailing labels report. Not a problem—Access can use current contacts data directly from Outlook, if you set up the Outlook Contacts folder or subfolder as a table in the Access database.

## How to fix it

1. In your Access database, on the Tables tab, click the New button.
2. In the New Table dialog box, double-click Link Table. ▶

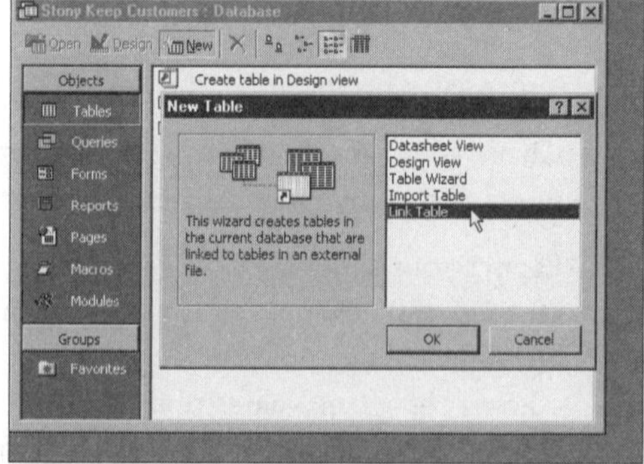


3. In the Link dialog box, in the Files Of Type box, click Outlook. ▶

   The Link Exchange/Outlook Wizard opens.

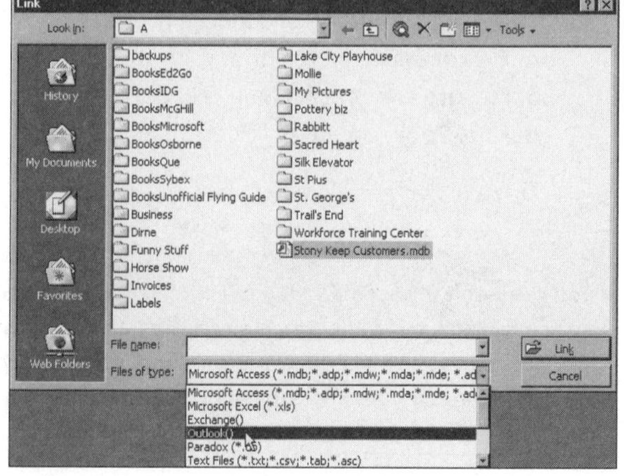

4. In the Link Exchange/Outlook Wizard dialog box, click the small plus symbol next to Personal Folders. ▶

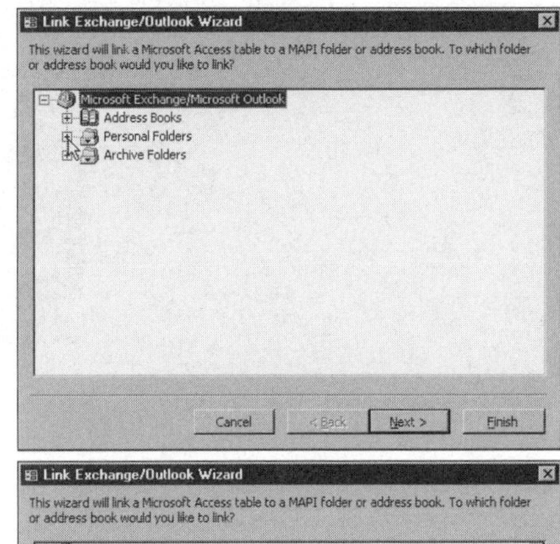


5. Click the small plus symbol next to Contacts to open a list of your Contacts subfolders.

6. Click the Contacts subfolder you want to use for a linked Access table, and then click Next. ◀

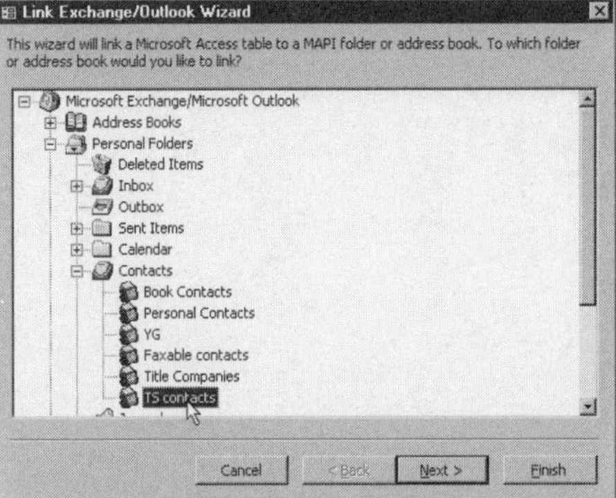


7. Click Finish, and when the wizard tells you it's finished, click OK.

   A new linked table is created in your Access database.

8. In the database, on the Reports tab, click the New button.

9. In the New Report dialog box, click Label Wizard, and then click the linked table name in the Choose The Table Or Query Where The Object's Data Comes From box. ▶

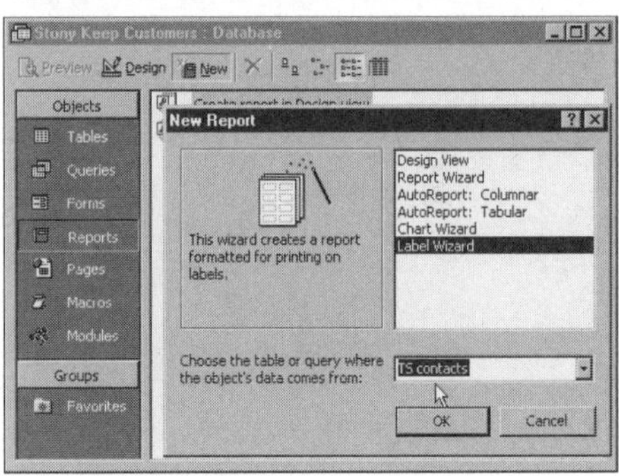


10. Click OK, and then follow the steps in the Label Wizard to create your Access mailing labels report.

## If you want to know more about using Outlook data in an Access database

You can import or link to your Outlook Contacts folder to create a new Access table. Linking the Access table to the Outlook source is a better idea if the Outlook data is likely to change (which contacts tend to do), because the data for your Access labels will always be current. The alternative, importing the Outlook data, creates a static table in Access that doesn't change when your Outlook contacts data changes. This means you must run a fresh import every time you want to print current mailing labels.

When you link to your Outlook data, not only does the linked Access table always have current data, but also your Access mailing labels are always ready to print. If you save the Mailing Labels report in your Access database, the finished report uses linked, current data. To print a current mailing labels report in Access—anytime—right-click the name of the report and click Print.

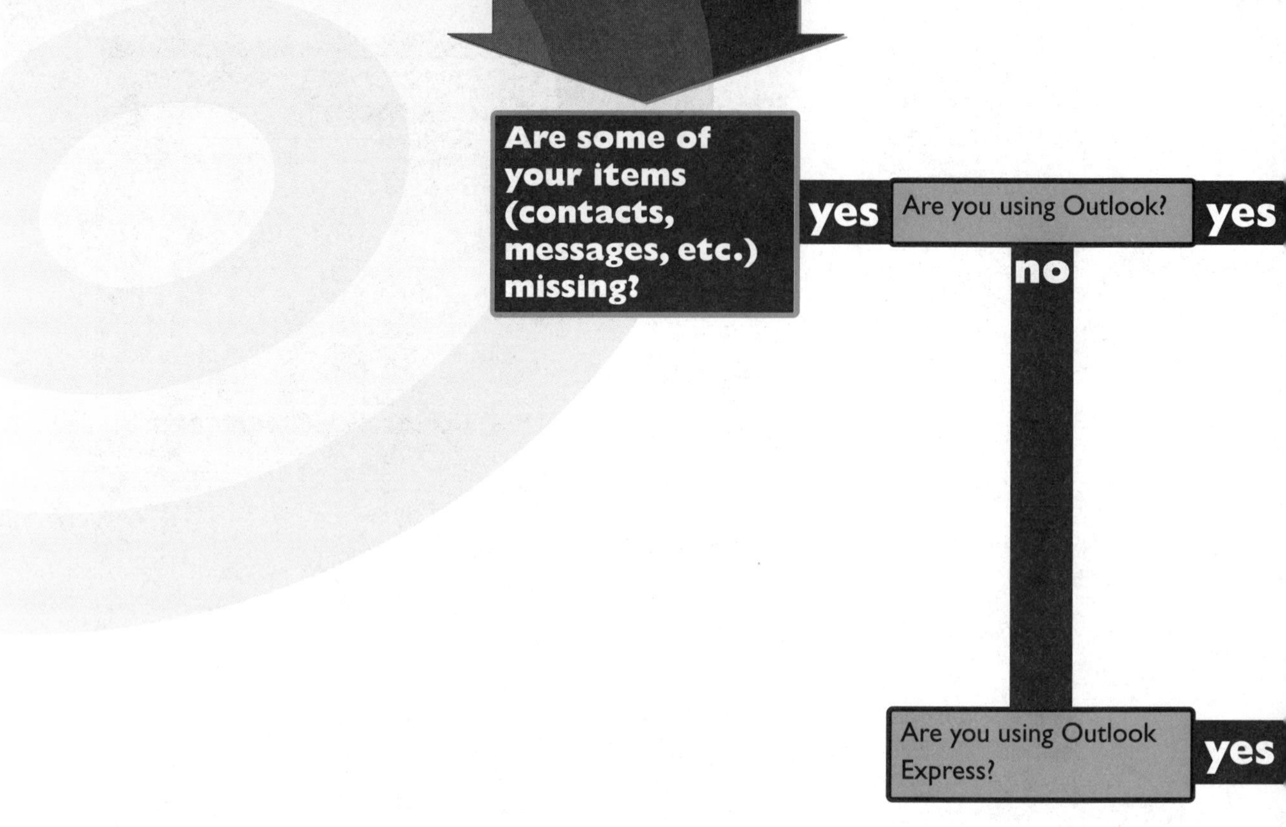
Are some of your items (contacts, messages, etc.) missing?
yes
Are you using Outlook?
yes
no
Are you using Outlook Express?
yes

# Missing items

Is AutoArchive turned on? **yes**

**no**

### Go to...

**Some of my Outlook items are missing, page 178.**

### Quick fix

If AutoArchive is turned on, you may have archived the item you're looking for. If that's the case, you can use the procedure "Search your archive files" in the solution, "Some of my Outlook items are missing."

To check whether AutoArchive is turned on (and to turn it off, if you want to):

1. On the Tools menu, click Options.
2. On the Other tab, click the AutoArchive button.
3. In the AutoArchive dialog box, if the AutoArchive Every check box is selected, AutoArchive is turned on (and the Days box tells you how often your items are AutoArchived).

To see whether AutoArchive is turned on in a specific folder:

1. Right-click the folder icon in either the Outlook bar or the Folder list.
2. Click Properties.
3. On the AutoArchive tab, if the Clean Out Items Older Than check box is selected, AutoArchive is turned on in that folder.

### Go to...

**Some of my Outlook Express items are missing, page 180.**

**If your solution isn't here**
Check this related chapter:
Backing up and moving data, page 2
Or see the general troubleshooting tips on page xiii.

# Some of my Outlook items are missing

## Source of the problem

You've opened your Contacts folder to look up an associate's telephone number, and the contact you're looking for isn't there. Or perhaps you're looking for an e-mail message you received some months ago, and you can't find it. You're sure the item exists and you never deleted it, but there might be another reason why it's hidden—perhaps you're looking in the wrong folder, maybe the view you're searching in has a filter applied, or maybe the item was archived.

## How to fix it

First, make sure you're looking in the correct folder. If you've created subfolders, you might have moved the item you need into a subfolder. Next, make sure you're looking at a view that's not filtered. Finally, if you still haven't found the item, search your archive files.

### Check all your subfolders

1. On the View menu, click Folder List.
2. If any folders in the Folder list have small plus symbols next to them, click the small plus symbol to display subfolders. ▶
3. Search each of the subfolders that contain the type of item you're looking for (for example, if you're looking for a contact, search every contact subfolder).

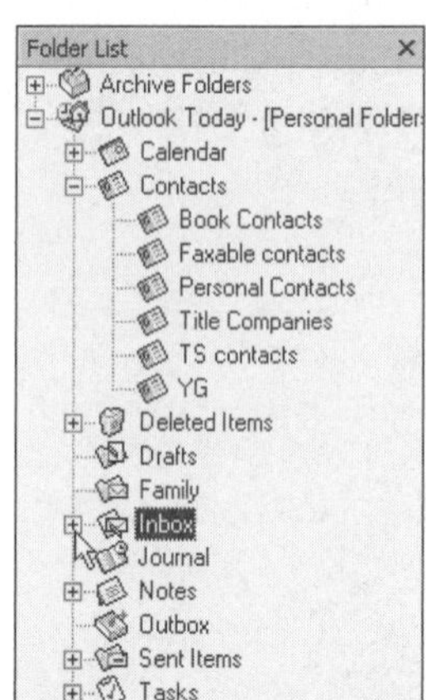


### Check your view for filters

1. Look at the lower-left corner of the Outlook window. If you see the message "Filter applied," there's a filter applied to the current view, which might be hiding the item you're looking for.
2. To switch views, on the View menu, point to Current View, and click a different (unfiltered) view name.

**Tip**

To make an Outlook bar shortcut to the subfolder so you won't forget about it again, drag the subfolder icon from the Folder list and drop it in the Outlook bar.

3. To remove any filters from the current view, on the View menu, point to Current View, and then click Customize Current View.
4. In the View Summary dialog box, look at the label next to the Filter button. The label tells you whether there's a filter applied. ▶
5. If there's a filter applied, click the Filter button.
6. In the lower-right corner of the Filter dialog box, click the Clear All button.
7. Click OK to close each dialog box.

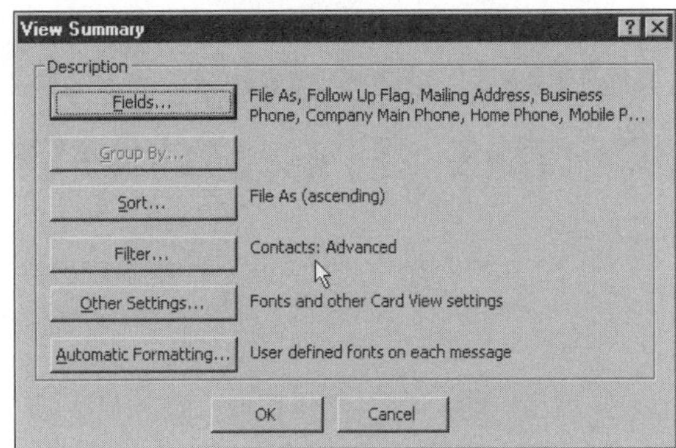


**Tip**

If you still can't find the item, search your backup files—even if it's been deleted, you might have backed it up.

## Search your archive files

1. On the File menu, click Import And Export.
2. In the first wizard step, click Import From Another Program Or File, and click Next.
3. In the second wizard step, click Personal Folder File (.pst), and then click Next.
4. In the third wizard step, look at the path in the File To Import box. If it's not the correct path to your archive file, click the Browse button, locate your archive file, and click Open to return to the Import Personal Folders wizard.
5. Select a duplicates option (you're searching for an item that doesn't exist in your folders, so it doesn't matter which option you select), and then click Next.
6. In the fourth wizard step, select the folder category for the item you're searching for (for example, if you're searching for a message you received, click Inbox), and select the Include Subfolders check box.
7. Click the Filter button.
8. In the Filter dialog box, set criteria that identifies the item you're searching for. For example, if you're searching for a message you received from a specific person, on the Messages tab, click the From button. Then double-click the name of the person who sent you the message, and click OK to return to the Filter dialog box.
9. Click OK in the Filter dialog box.
10. Select an option for the folder where Outlook should copy any found items, and click Finish. Your archive file is searched for items that meet your criteria, and copies of any items found appear in the folder you selected in this step.

# Some of my Outlook Express items are missing

## Source of the problem

You've opened your Outlook Express Inbox to find a message from a colleague, and the message you're looking for isn't there. In fact, it seems as if your list of messages is much shorter than it ought to be. You're sure the message exists and you never deleted it, so there might be another reason why it's hidden—perhaps you're looking in the wrong folder, or maybe the view you're searching in has a filter applied.

## How to fix it

First, check all your message subfolders. If you still can't find the message, check your views in each folder or subfolder to make sure that no filters are applied.

### Check your subfolders

1. On the View menu, click Layout.
2. In the Window Layout Properties dialog box, select the Folder List check box.
3. Click OK.

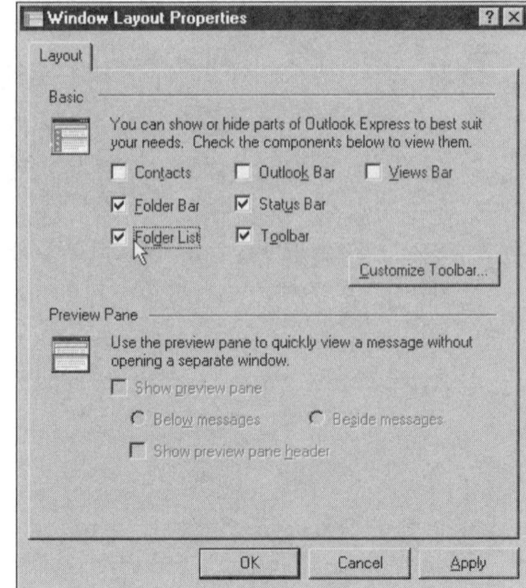

4. If there are any subfolders in the current Outlook Express identity, they are listed in the Folder list. If you see any small plus symbols, click the symbols to display hidden subfolders. ▶

5. Look through all possible subfolders for the missing item.

## Check your view for filters

In each subfolder where the message might be hidden, on the View menu, point to Current View, and click Show All Messages. ▶

Any filters are removed, and all the messages in that folder are displayed.

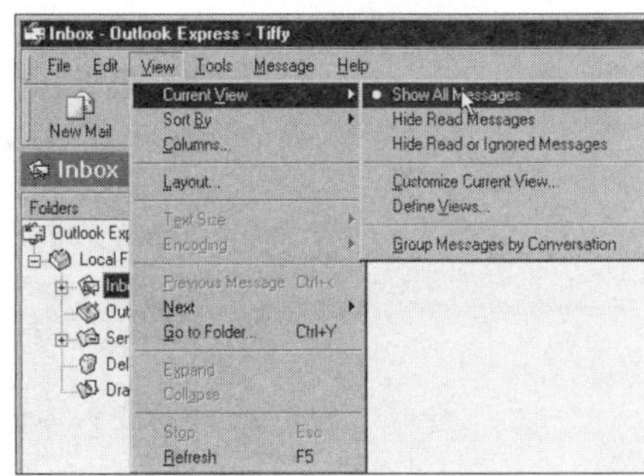


**Tip**

Remember, if you're looking for an item you *sent out*, it'll be in a Sent Items folder or subfolder, not in the Inbox. Or, it might be in the Deleted Items folder if you deleted it, or gone completely if you deleted it and then emptied the Deleted Items folder.

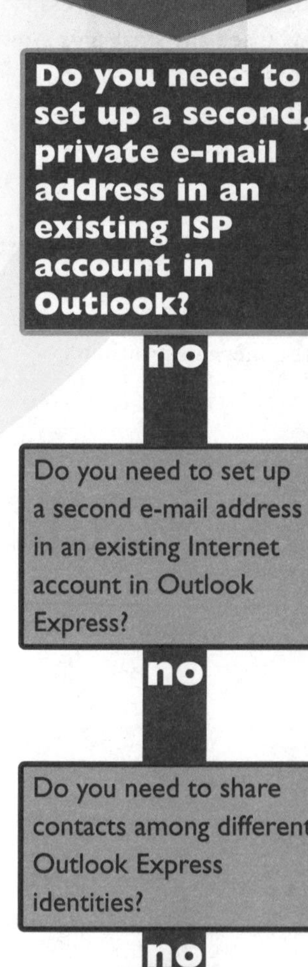

Do you need to set up a second, private e-mail address in an existing ISP account in Outlook?
yes
no
Do you need to set up a second e-mail address in an existing Internet account in Outlook Express?
yes
no
Do you need to share contacts among different Outlook Express identities?
yes
no
Does Outlook Express start up your identity when someone else opens it?
yes

**If your solution isn't here**

Check this related chapter:

E-mail accounts, page 108

Or see the general troubleshooting tips on page xiii.

# Multiple users

**Go to...**
**I don't know how to set up a second, private Outlook e-mail address in my Internet account, page 186.**

**Go to...**
**I need separate Outlook Express e-mail addresses for the same Internet account, page 184.**

**Go to...**
**I don't know how to share my Outlook Express contacts with other Outlook Express identities, page 185.**

**Quick fix**

To keep others out of your identity, be sure you either log off your identity or shut down Windows when you quit Outlook Express. In both cases, the next time Outlook Express is started, the user is prompted for the identity (and password, if one is required).

To log off your Outlook Express identity, on the File menu, click Exit and Log Off Identity.

If you quit Outlook Express by clicking the X box in its upper-right corner, you won't log off your identity, and the next time Outlook Express is opened (unless Windows has been shut down in the meantime), Outlook Express opens in the previous identity.

# I need separate Outlook Express e-mail addresses for the same Internet account

## Source of the problem

You use Outlook Express for e-mail, and you've got only one computer. Now you've got teenagers, or a spouse or a grandfather, who want their own e-mail address (and a bit of privacy). You want to accommodate them (and keep them out of *your* e-mail account). But how?

You can set up separate identities in Outlook Express, with separate e-mail accounts, and passwords for admission to the identity. Creating a new Outlook Express identity is quick.

## How to fix it

1. On the File menu, point to Identities, and click Add New Identity.
2. In the New Identity dialog box, type a name for the identity. ▶
3. To keep the identity private, select the Require A Password check box.

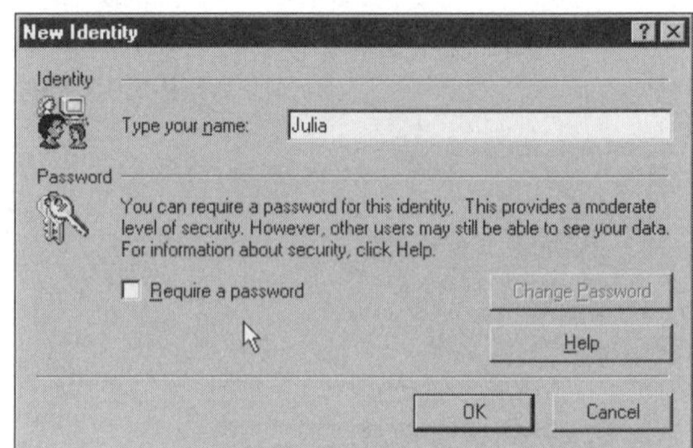


4. In the Enter Password dialog box, type your password (carefully) twice, and click OK. ▶
5. In the New Identity dialog box, click OK.
6. When asked whether you want to switch to the new identity now, click Yes.

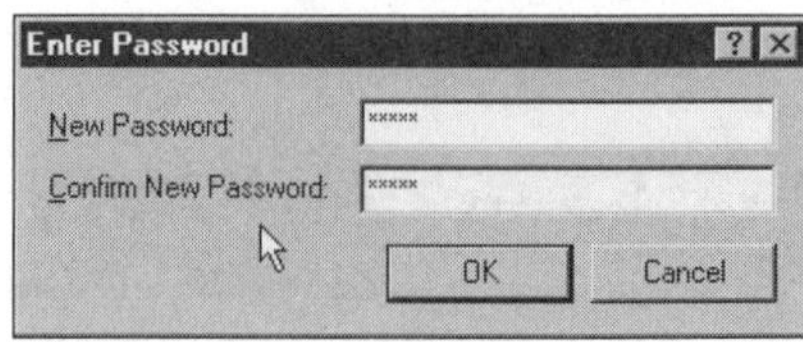


The Internet Connection Wizard opens, and you can enter all the information for the e-mail account that this particular identity will use. This account information is specific to this identity and won't be available in the other identities.

# I don't know how to share my Outlook Express contacts with other Outlook Express identities

## Source of the problem

You've set up separate Outlook Express identities and e-mail accounts for three people on your computer, and all is well except that the other two users keep asking you for your contacts' e-mail addresses. Wouldn't it be simpler if you could just share those particular contacts?

You can share specific contacts, and keep other contacts private in your own identity's folder.

**Tip**

If you have Outlook Express set up to share contacts with Outlook, you won't be able to keep Outlook Express Address Books private among Outlook Express identities. Instead, all identities have full access to Outlook's Contacts folders.

## How to fix it

1. On the Tools menu, click Address Book.
2. On the Address Book's View menu, click Folders And Groups. There are two Contacts folders: Shared Contacts, and the identity's Contacts.
3. To share a contact, open the identity's Contacts folder and drag the contact to the Shared Contacts icon. ▶
4. The contact is moved into the Shared Contacts folder and is available to all the identities in Outlook Express.

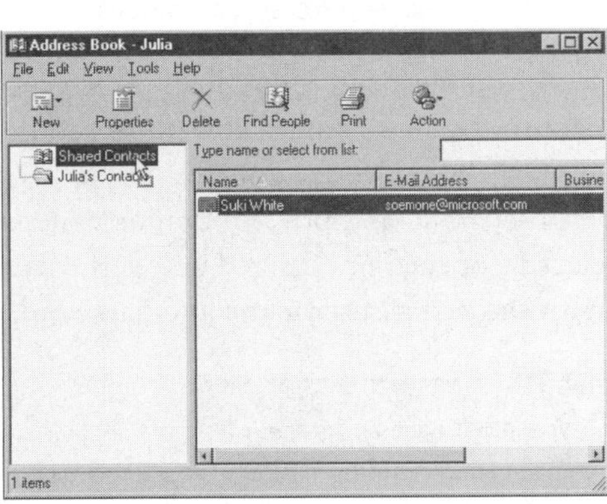


The contacts are in separate Address Book folders, but if you display the Outlook Express Contacts list, all the contacts available to this identity (shared and private) are listed.

To show the Outlook Express Contacts list, on the View menu, click Layout. Select the Contacts check box, and click OK.

# I don't know how to set up a second, private Outlook e-mail address in my Internet account

## Source of the problem

Your family members all use the same computer, and you need separate e-mail accounts (with passwords for privacy). Your Internet Service Provider (ISP) allows multiple e-mail accounts, or addresses, in a single Internet account on a single computer, which is exactly what you need, but how do you set that up?

## How to fix it

There are three procedures to follow for each separate e-mail account you want to set up in the same Internet account:

- Create a new user profile.
- Set up an additional e-mail account.
- Create a new Personal Folders file.

You must run through all three procedures for each separate, private e-mail account you want to set up in the same Internet account. When you're done, you'll have separate user profiles, each with separate (and private) Outlook files and e-mail accounts that can't be opened or changed unless the user logs on to Windows with the correct user name and password.

**Tip**

If you don't have an Internet e-mail account set up in Outlook, start Outlook and set up the account using the information provided by your ISP. After you have the first e-mail account set up, quit Outlook and continue with the procedures that follow.

**Tip**

This procedure is only for Outlook in the Internet Mail Only configuration. If you use Outlook in the Corporate/Workgroup configuration and want to set up a second e-mail account in your existing Internet account, check with your network administrator first. The procedures are different and might interfere with your network e-mail setup.

## Set passwords options

First, set Windows for multiple user profiles (you need to do this only one time):

1. Click the Windows Start button, point to Settings, and click Control Panel.
2. Double-click the Passwords icon.
3. On the User Profiles tab, click Users Can Customize Their Preferences And Desktop Settings, and click OK. ▶
4. Close the Control Panel.

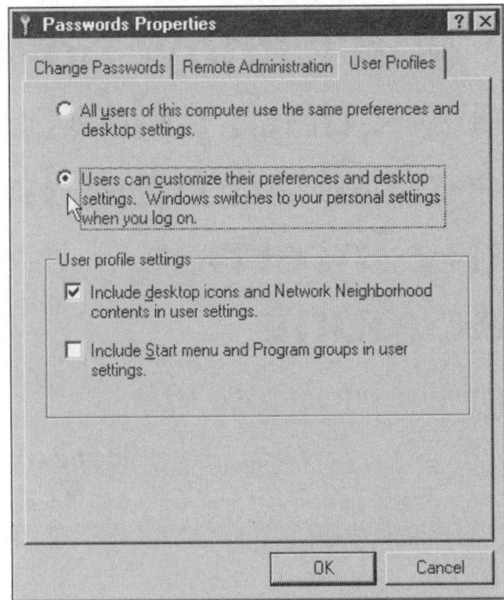


## Create a new user profile

1. Click the Windows Start button, point to Settings, and click Control Panel.
2. Double-click the Users icon.
3. In the User Settings dialog box, click the New User button. ▶
4. In the Add User dialog box, click Next.

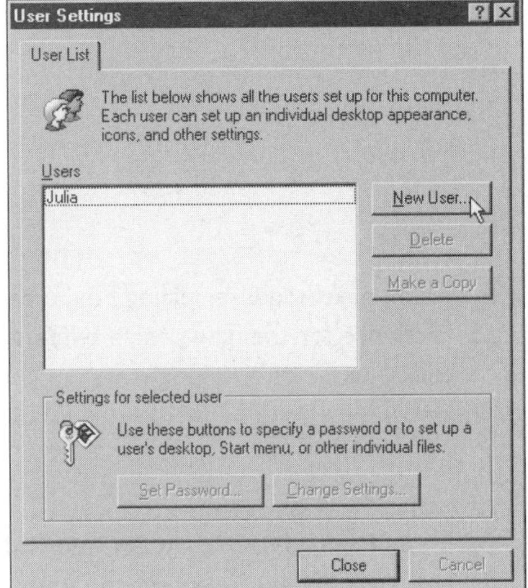


*If this solution didn't solve your problem, go to the next page.*

# I don't know how to set up a second, private Outlook e-mail address in my Internet account

*(continued from page 187)*

5. In the next Add User dialog box, type the User Name for the new profile, and click Next. ▶

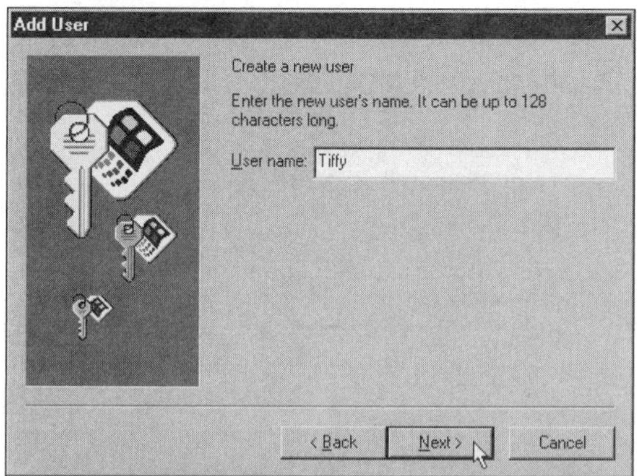


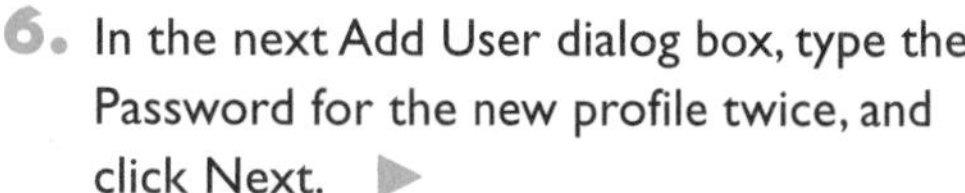

6. In the next Add User dialog box, type the Password for the new profile twice, and click Next. ▶

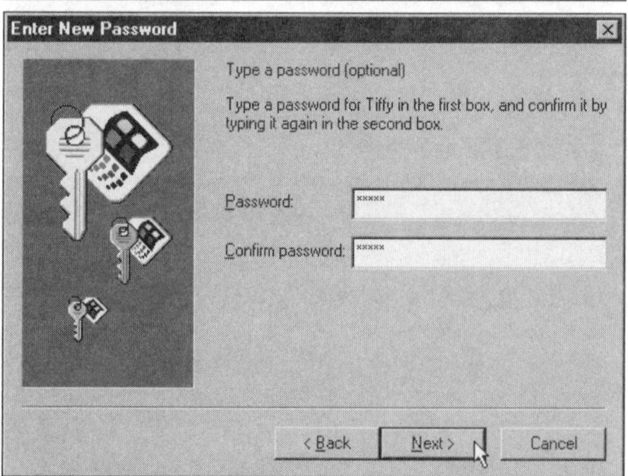


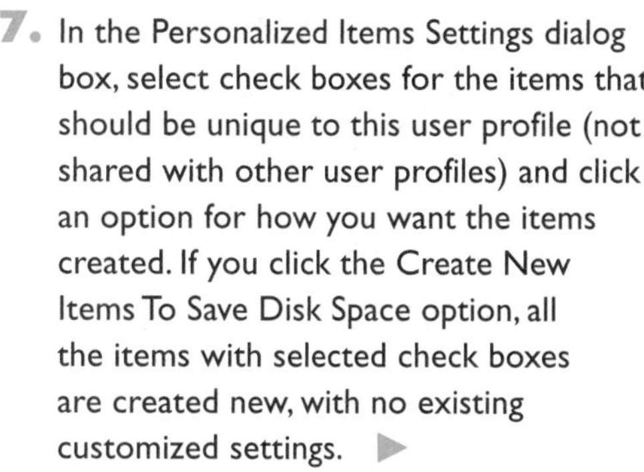

7. In the Personalized Items Settings dialog box, select check boxes for the items that should be unique to this user profile (not shared with other user profiles) and click an option for how you want the items created. If you click the Create New Items To Save Disk Space option, all the items with selected check boxes are created new, with no existing customized settings. ▶

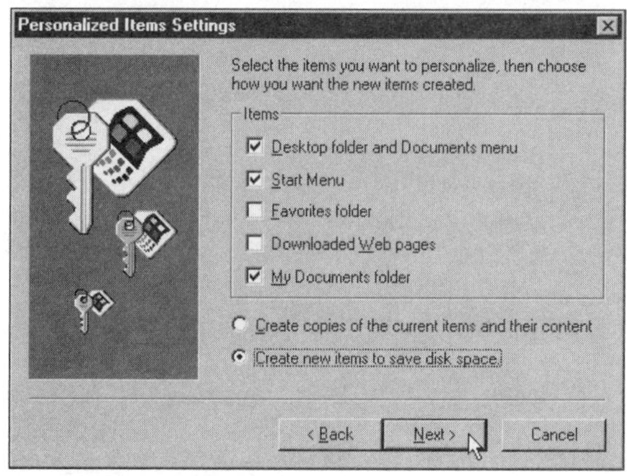

8. Click Next.

9. Click Finish.

The new user name appears in the Users List in the User Settings dialog box that you opened from the Control Panel. If, in the future, you need to make changes to the user settings or password, or if you decide to delete this user, open the User Settings dialog box again, click the user name, and click the appropriate buttons. ▶

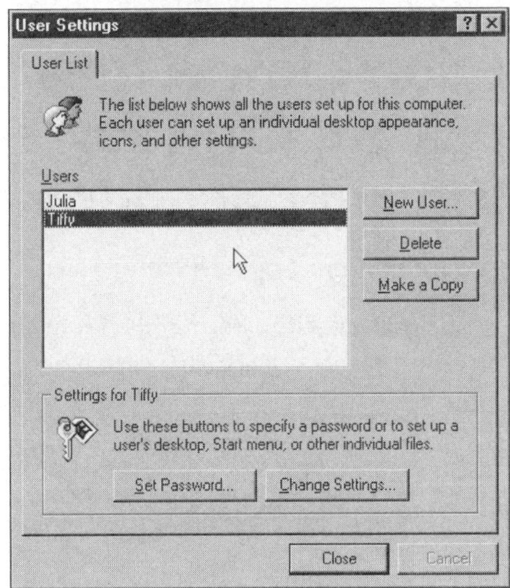


10. Click Close to close the User Settings dialog box, and then close the Control Panel.

## Set up a new e-mail account

1. Quit any open programs, and log off Windows:
   - Click the Windows Start button, and then click Log Off <username>.
   - If you don't see the command Log Off <username>, click Shut Down. In the Shut Down Windows dialog box, click Close All Programs And Log On As A Different User.
2. When Windows starts again, log on with the new user name. In the Enter Network Password dialog box, type the new user's name and password, and click OK.
3. Start Outlook.
4. On the Tools menu, click Accounts.
5. In the Internet Accounts dialog box, click Add, and then click Mail. The Internet Connection Wizard opens. ▶

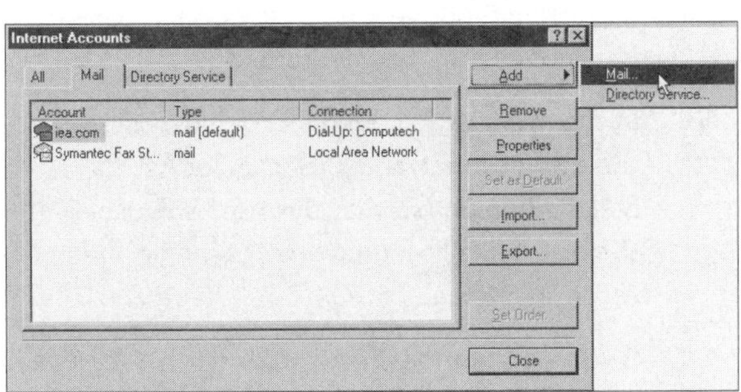


*If this solution didn't solve your problem, go to the next page.*

# I don't know how to set up a second, private Outlook e-mail address in my Internet account

*(continued from page 189)*

6. Type the display name (the From line that recipients will see) and click Next. ▶

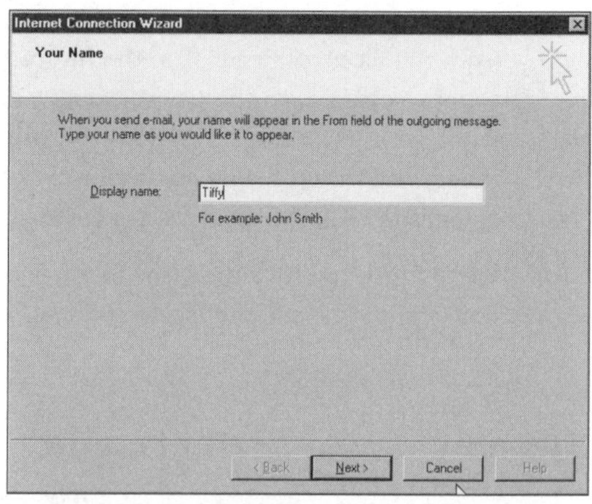


7. Type the e-mail address, and then click Next.
8. Enter the mail server names that your ISP gives you, and click Next.
9. Type the e-mail account name and password. If the e-mail account requires secure password authentication, select the Log On Using Secure Password Authentication (SPA) check box. Then click Next. ▶

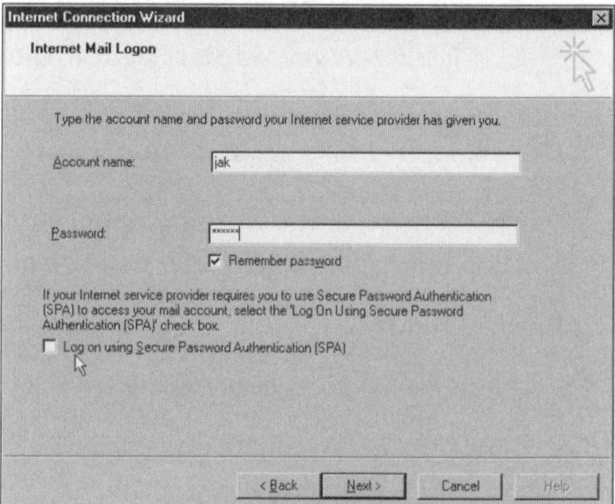


10. Click the connection type (if you're using a modem and phone line, click Connect Using My Phone Line), and click Next.
11. In the Internet Accounts dialog box, click the new account, and click the Set As Default button (so that this user will use the new e-mail account when sending and receiving e-mail).

    If you want a more recognizable name for the new account, click Properties. On the General tab, replace the generic Mail Account server name with one that you prefer, and then click OK. ▶

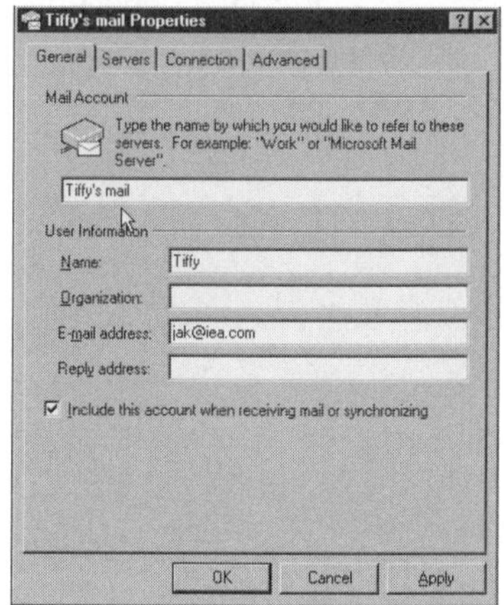

On the Tools menu, when you point to Send/Receive, you'll see this name listed. ▶

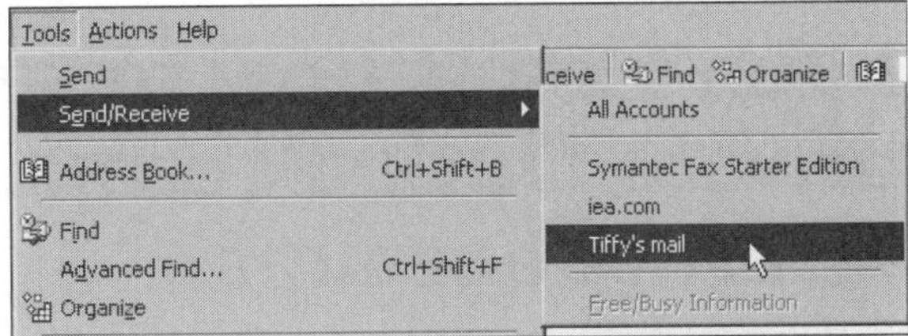


12. Click the Use An Existing Dial-Up Connection option, click Next, and click Finish.
13. Click Close to close the Internet Accounts dialog box.

**Tip**

To prevent future frustration, keep all your e-mail account information (such as server names, user names, and passwords) in a convenient and safe place. I keep a paper copy in my files, and an electronic copy in an Outlook note.

## Create a new Personal Folders file in Outlook

1. On the File menu, point to New, and click Personal Folders File (.pst).
2. In the File Name box, type the name of the new Personal Folders file, and click Create. ▶

3. In the Create Microsoft Personal Folders dialog box, enter a password (twice), and click OK.

   The password keeps other users from changing your Personal Folders file. Write your password someplace safe, in case you need to make changes to this Personal Folders file someday.
4. If the Folder list is not in view, on the View menu, click Folder List.

**Warning**

*Don't* use the name **mailbox**; it's better to call the folder by the user's name. The name *mailbox* has a specific meaning to Outlook, and using it as a Personal Folders file name will cause confusion.

***If this solution didn't solve your problem, go to the next page.***

# I don't know how to set up a second, private Outlook e-mail address in my Internet account

(continued from page 191)

5. Right-click the new Personal Folders file and click Properties.

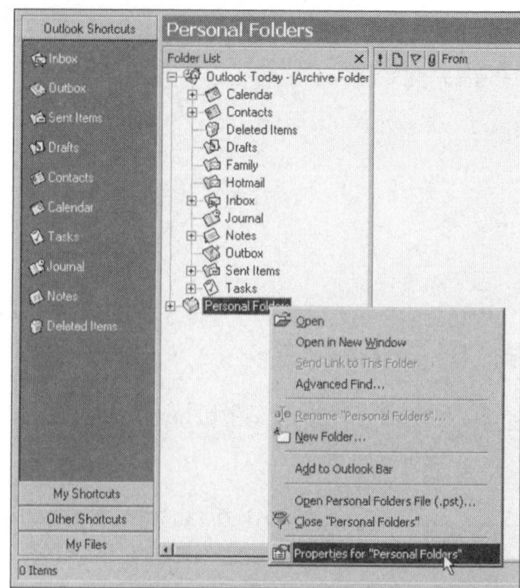

**Tip**

If you're not sure whether this is the *new* Personal Folders file you just created, click the Advanced button and look at the Path box—you should see the profile name in the path to the new Personal Folders file.

6. Click Deliver POP Mail To This Personal Folders File.

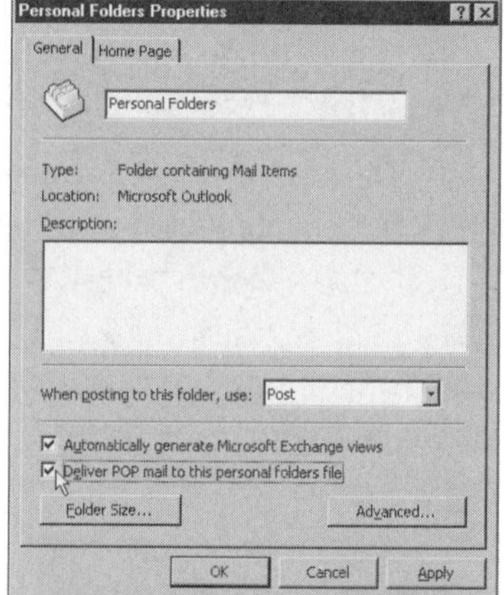

7. Click the Advanced button, and change the name of the Personal Folders file so you can differentiate it easily. Then click OK.

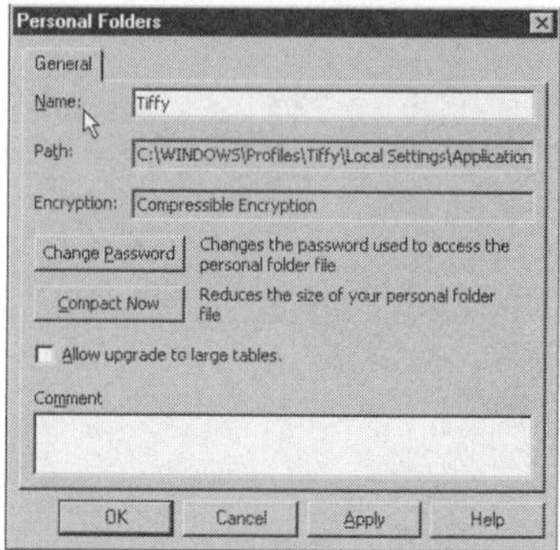

8. Click OK to close the Personal Folders Properties dialog box. If you see a message about exiting and restarting Outlook, click OK.

9. On the File menu, click Exit.

10. Restart Outlook. If a message tells you that your delivery location has changed and your shortcuts might need to be re-created, click Yes.

11. In the Folder list, right-click the Personal Folders file that *doesn't* say Outlook Today, and click Properties. Check the properties to be sure this is the Personal Folders file you want to close. ▶

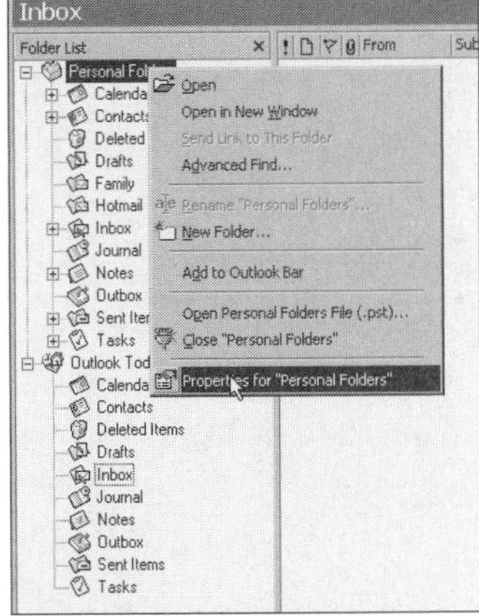


12. Click the Advanced button, and look at the path to this file—it should *not* include the profile name (it probably reads *C:\WINDOWS\LocalSettings\ApplicationData\Microsoft\Outlook\outlook.pst*). Then click Cancel to close both dialog boxes. ▶

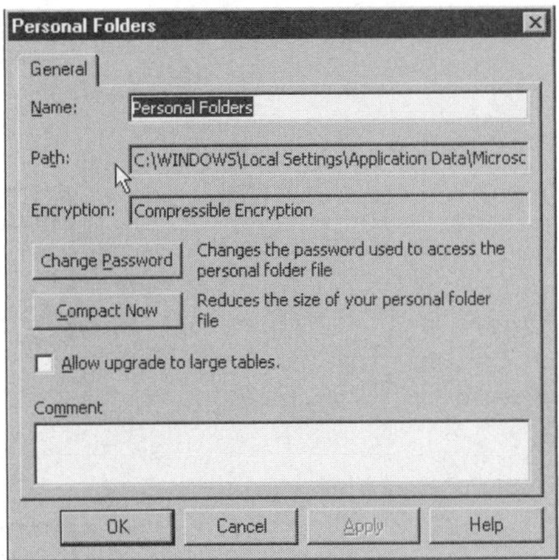


13. In the Folder list, right-click the Personal Folders file that *doesn't* say Outlook Today (the one you just checked to be sure that it *doesn't* include the profile name in the path), and click Close Personal Folders.

This closes the connection between Outlook and the folder. The only Personal Folders file in this user profile is the new Personal Folders file you created. It's password-protected and private, and available only to the user who logs on to Windows with the correct user name and password.

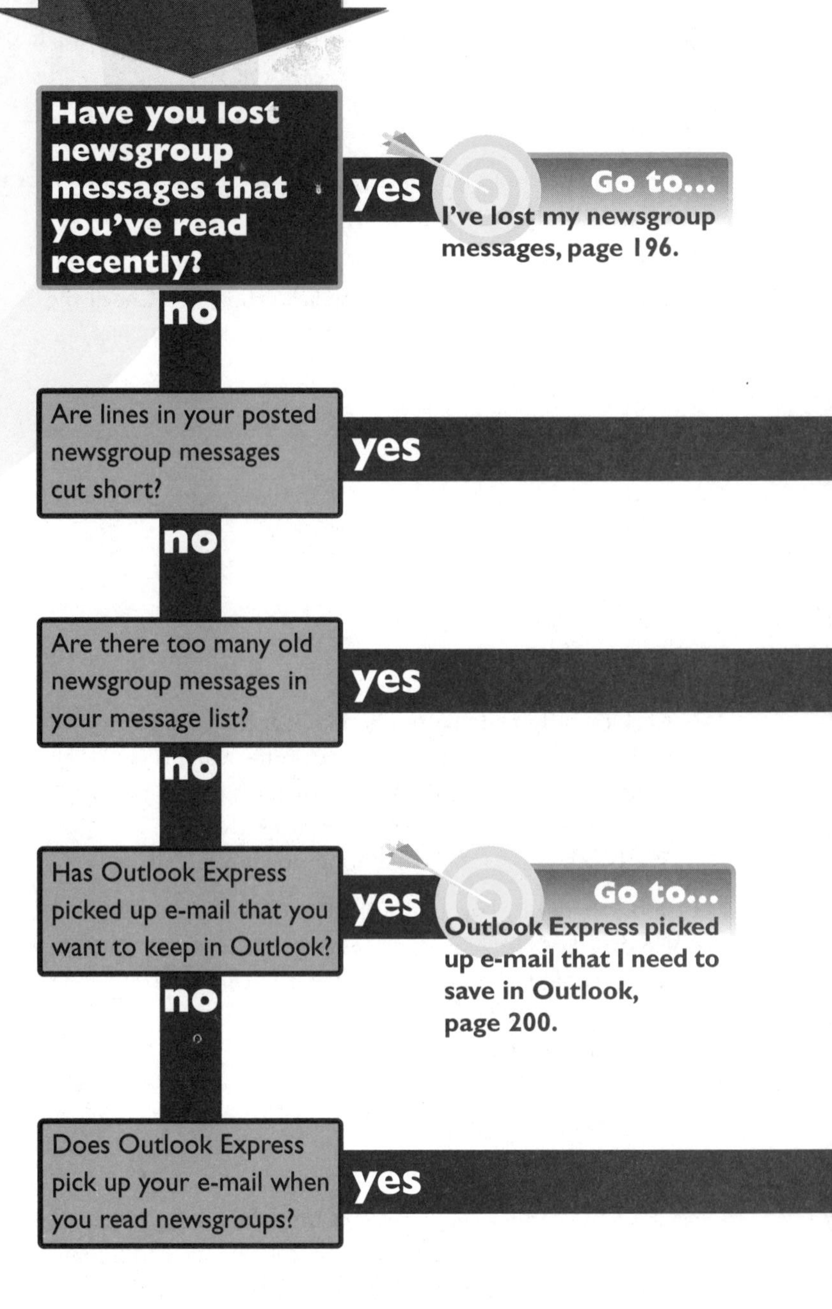
Have you lost newsgroup messages that you've read recently?
yes
Go to...
I've lost my newsgroup messages, page 196.
no
Are lines in your posted newsgroup messages cut short?
yes
no
Are there too many old newsgroup messages in your message list?
yes
no
Has Outlook Express picked up e-mail that you want to keep in Outlook?
yes
Go to...
Outlook Express picked up e-mail that I need to save in Outlook, page 200.
no
Does Outlook Express pick up your e-mail when you read newsgroups?
yes

**If your solution isn't here**
Check the general troubleshooting tips on page xiii.

# Newsgroups

**Go to...**

**The lines in my posted newsgroup messages are cut short, page 197.**

**Go to...**

**My newsgroup message list is too long, page 198.**

**Quick fix**

If you don't want Outlook Express to pick up your e-mail when you go online to read newsgroups:

1. On the Tools menu, click Options.
2. On the General tab, clear the Send And Receive Messages At Startup check box and the Check for New Messages Every check box.
3. Click OK.

# I've lost my newsgroup messages

## Source of the problem

You read several newsgroup messages last week, and when you tried to reread a few of them today, you couldn't find them.

Either the messages are hidden by a filter, or they've been deleted. If they've been hidden by a filter, you can remove the filter. If they've been deleted, you can get them back only by downloading the whole list from the newsgroup again, but you can stop automatically deleting messages in the future.

## How to fix it

### Remove filters

1. In Outlook Express, open a mail folder or a specific newsgroup.
2. On the View menu, point to Current View, and then click Show All Messages. ▶

   If your missing messages don't reappear, they've been deleted from your local files (but you can download all messages from the newsgroup to find them again).

### Stop deleting messages

1. On the Tools menu, click Options.
2. On the Maintenance tab, clear the Delete Read Message Bodies In Newsgroups check box. Your read messages aren't deleted when you quit Outlook Express. ▶
3. Clear the Delete News Messages check box, or change the number of Days After Being Downloaded, to stop or delay automatic cleanup.
4. Click OK to close the dialog box.

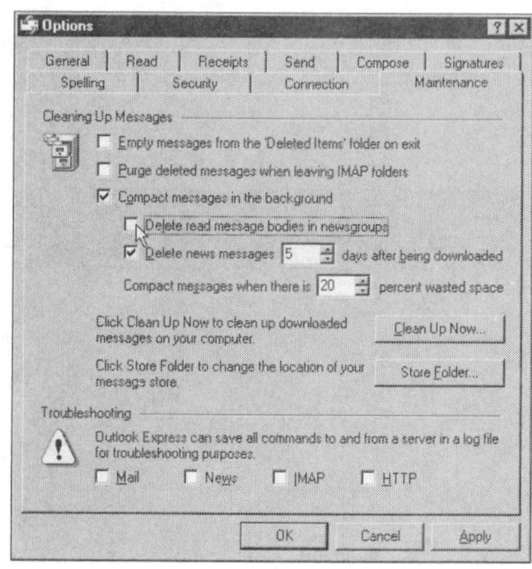

# The lines in my posted newsgroup messages are cut short

## Source of the problem

You posted a message to a newsgroup. Later, when you read your posted message, you saw that the last word in every line had been cut off!

By default, Outlook Express sets the line length of plain text messages at 76 characters per line, but you can change that to a shorter or longer line wrap length. Some news servers don't display more than 80 characters per line, and if your line wrap length has been set to more than 80 characters per line, the extra characters are cut off.

## How to fix it

Reset your line wrap length to 76 or fewer characters per line:

1. On the Tools menu, click Options, and then click the Send tab.
2. Under News Sending Format, click the Plain Text Settings button. ▶

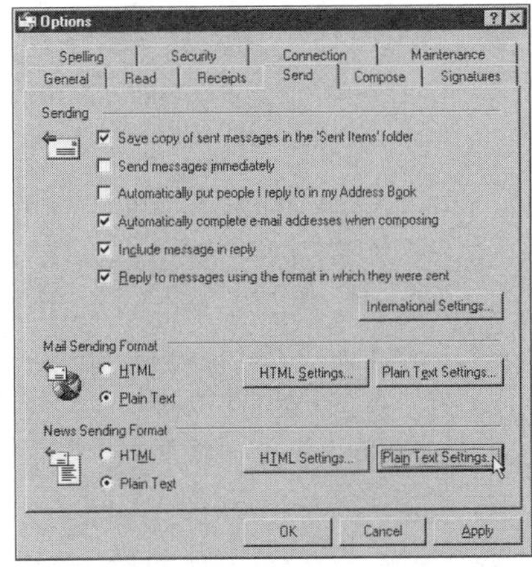

3. In the Plain Text Settings dialog box, in the Automatically Wrap Text At box, type the number of characters at which you want your message lines to wrap. ▶
4. Click OK to close each of the dialog boxes.

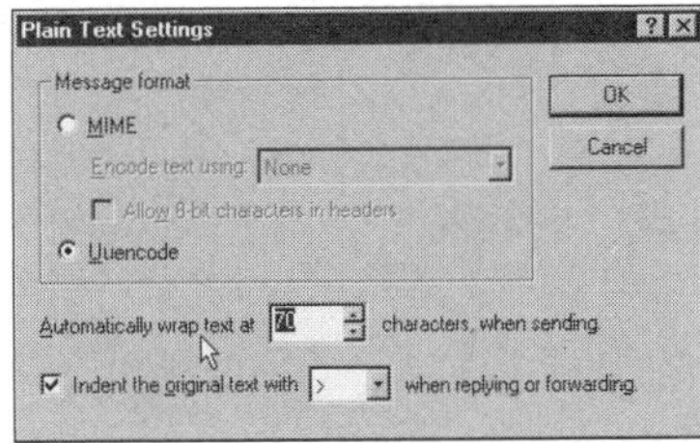

# My newsgroup message list is too long

## Source of the problem

Your newsgroup headers list has hundreds of messages and message headers in it, and it's too long to be useful any more. But when you try to delete old messages and headers, the way you do with your old e-mail messages, they don't delete!

But there are a couple of ways to tell Outlook Express to reduce the length of the list for you: automatically delete old messages on a time schedule, or clean out the list right now.

## How to fix it

### Delete messages on a schedule

1. On the Tools menu, click Options, and then click the Maintenance tab.
2. Select the Delete Read Message Bodies In Newsgroups check box. Messages you've read are deleted when you quit Outlook Express. ▶

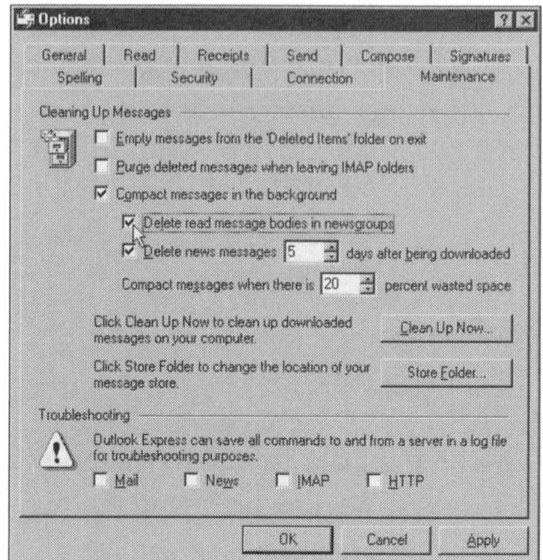


3. Select the Delete News Messages check box. Messages you've downloaded are automatically deleted the specified number of days after you downloaded them.
4. Click OK.

## Delete all messages (or messages and headers) right now

1. On the Tools menu, click Options, and then click the Maintenance tab.
2. On the Maintenance tab, click the Clean Up Now button. ▶

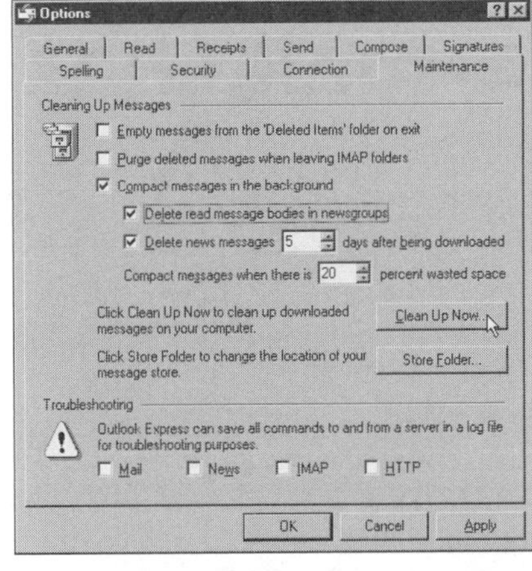


3. In the Local File Cleanup dialog box, click the Browse button.
4. In the Outlook Express dialog box, click either a news server or a specific newsgroup (if you click the news server, all the newsgroups you're subscribed to on that news server are cleaned up), and then click OK. ▶

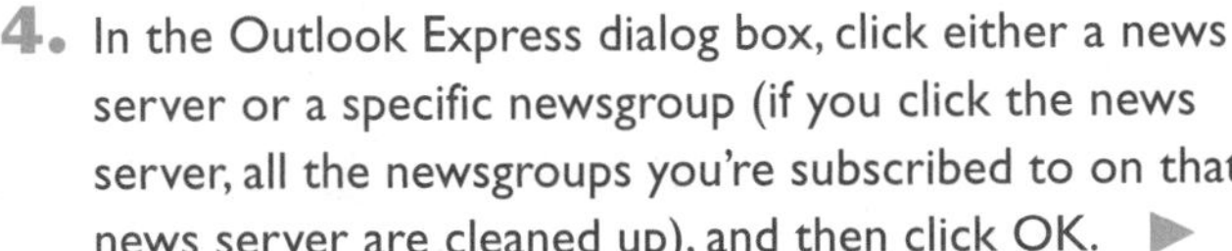

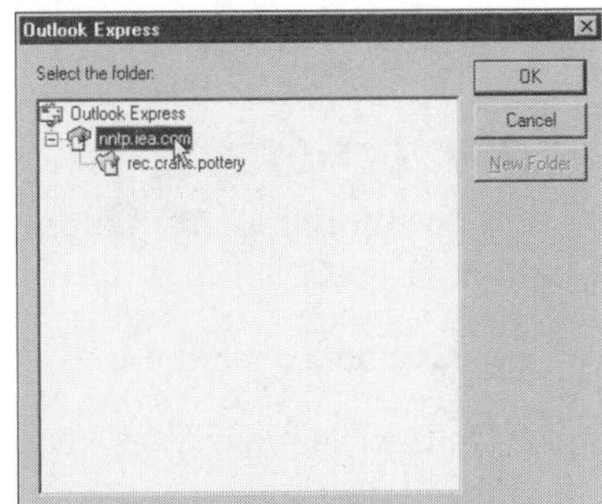


5. With the news server or newsgroup name in the Local File(s) For box:
   - Click the Delete button to delete all messages and headers. ▶
   - Click the Remove Messages button to delete downloaded messages but leave the headers.
6. When asked whether you're sure you want to delete all locally cached messages, click Yes.
7. Click Close and then OK to close all open dialog boxes.

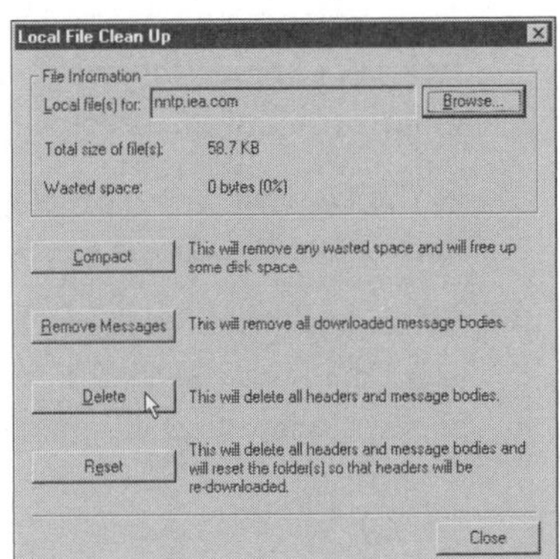

# Outlook Express picked up e-mail that I need to save in Outlook

## Source of the problem

You visited a newsgroup, and while you were online with the newsgroup, Outlook Express unexpectedly picked up your waiting e-mail. You normally pick up your e-mail with Outlook, and you don't want to have to look for your e-mail messages in two different programs.

## How to fix it

Import the messages into Outlook from Outlook Express:

1. In Outlook, open the Inbox folder.
2. On the File menu, click Import and Export.
3. In the Import And Export Wizard dialog box, click Import Internet Mail And Addresses, and then click Next. ▶
4. In the Outlook Import Tool dialog box, click Outlook Express 4.x, 5.
5. Select the Import Mail check box, and clear the Import Address Book and Import Rules check boxes. ▶

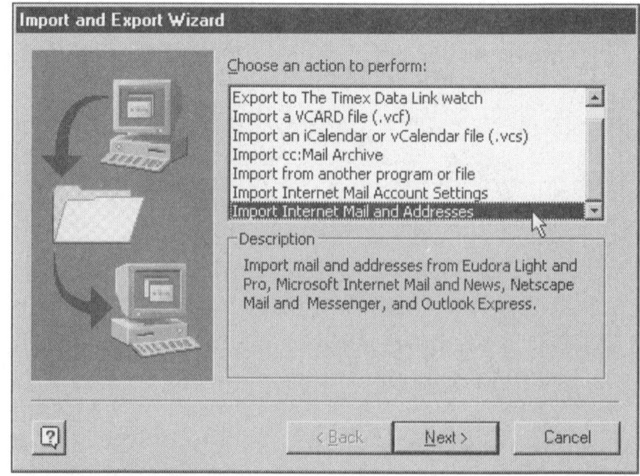


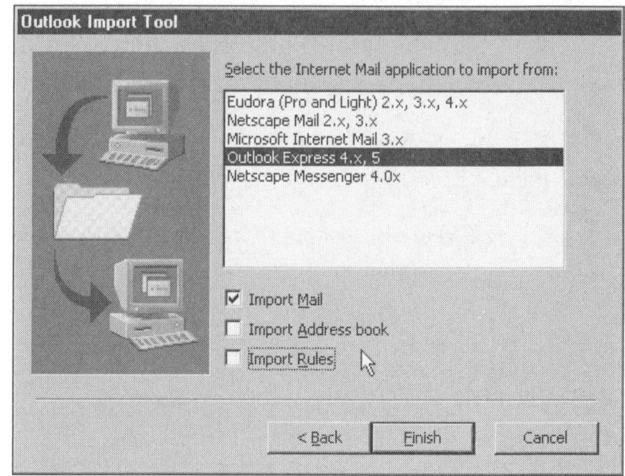

6. Click Finish.

7. In the Import Summary dialog box, click OK (if you click Save In Inbox, an extra message appears in your Inbox that tells you how many messages were imported).

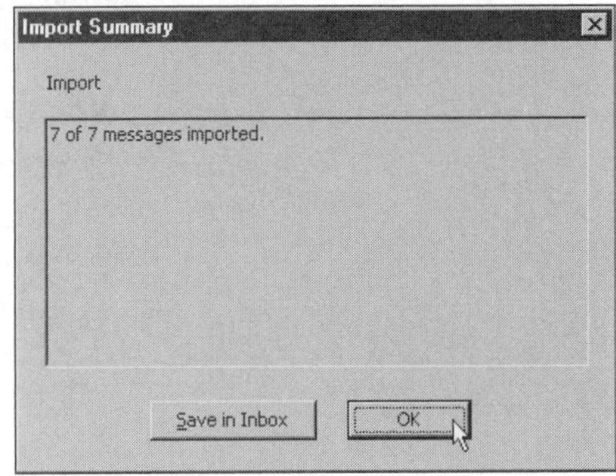


Copies of the messages in all your Outlook Express mail folders are imported into the matching-name folder or subfolder in Outlook, or into the Inbox if there's no matching-name subfolder in Outlook.

If you want to avoid copying duplicates of these messages into Outlook in the future, open Outlook Express and delete the messages you just imported.

## If you want to know more about importing mail from Outlook Express

If you have more than one identity in Outlook Express, only the messages in the most recently opened identity's mail folders are imported. If you want to import messages from a specific Outlook Express identity, open Outlook Express in that identity before you import the messages into Outlook. It doesn't matter whether Outlook Express is open or closed during the import process.

Any messages that were sent to you in Rich Text format will have their original Rich Text formatting restored when you open them in Outlook—even though when you open the same message in Outlook Express, the formatting is ignored and you see only the plain text message.

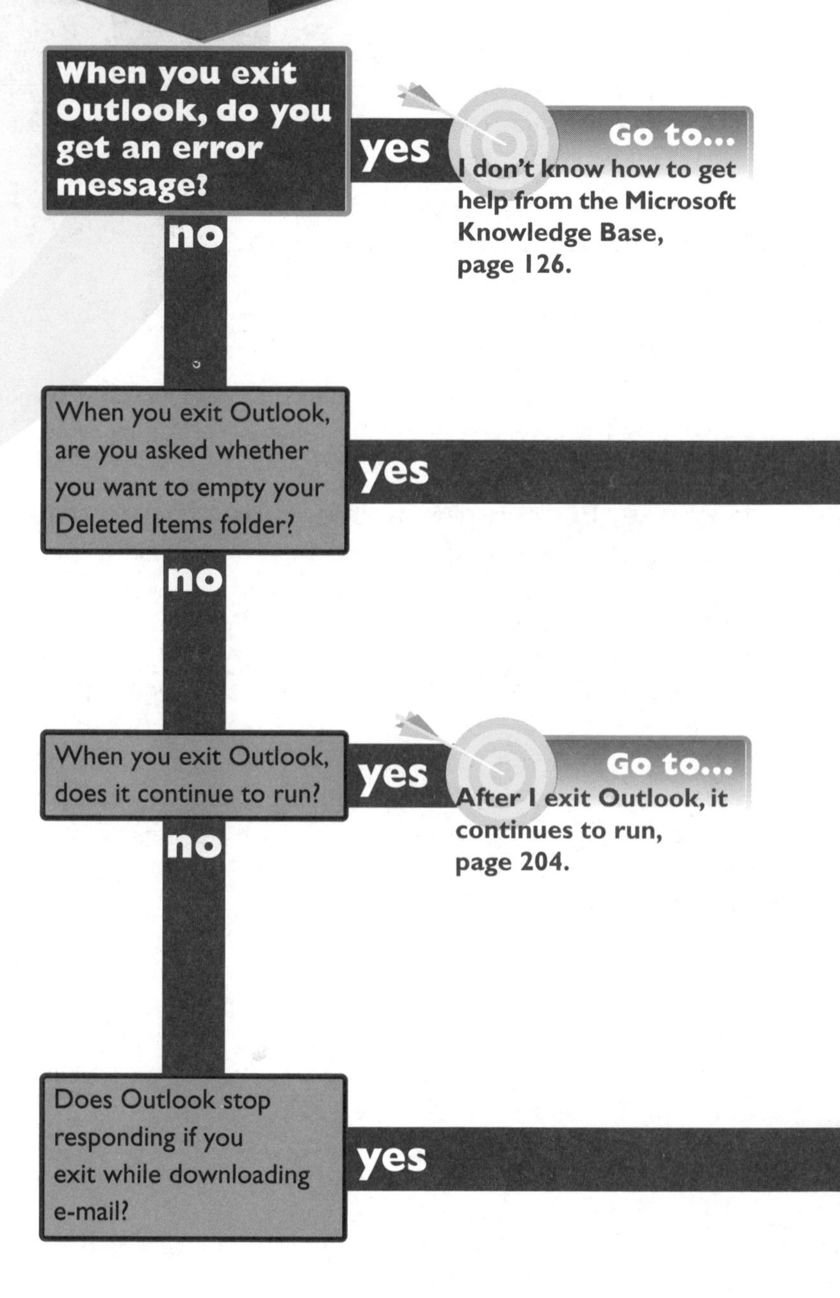
When you exit Outlook, do you get an error message?
yes
Go to...
I don't know how to get help from the Microsoft Knowledge Base, page 126.
no
When you exit Outlook, are you asked whether you want to empty your Deleted Items folder?
yes
no
When you exit Outlook, does it continue to run?
yes
Go to...
After I exit Outlook, it continues to run, page 204.
no
Does Outlook stop responding if you exit while downloading e-mail?
yes

### Quick fix

If you find it bothersome to be asked whether you want to empty your Deleted Items folder every time you close Outlook, a quick change to one setting will put a stop to the bothersome messages. Your deleted items will remain in your Deleted Items folder until you delete them.

1. On the Tools menu, click Options.
2. On the Other tab, under General, clear the Empty The Deleted Items folder Upon Exiting check box.
3. Click OK.

### Go to...

**If I exit Outlook while downloading e-mail, Outlook hangs, page 205.**

**If your solution isn't here**

Check this related chapter:

Error messages, page 122

Or see the general troubleshooting tips on page xiii.

# After I exit Outlook, it continues to run

## Source of the problem

You've got several programs open and your computer is running low on available memory, so you decide to quit a few programs, including Outlook. But Outlook doesn't quit; it continues to run and use a portion of that currently scarce available memory.

Outlook can continue to run under these circumstances:

- If you have an Outlook item, such as an e-mail message, still open and minimized
- If a Visual Basic for Applications (VBA) or a Visual Basic (VB) program is using Outlook data
- If you're running an Office program that's attempting to record an entry in the Outlook Journal
- If you have Symantec WinFax Pro version 9.02 installed

**Tip**

If you're running Symantec WinFax Pro version 9.02 (this is not the Symantec Fax Starter Edition that came with Outlook, but a full version that you got from WinFax), you need to update to a newer version of WinFax from Symantec, Inc., at *www.symantec.com/techsupp/files*.

## How to fix it

Quit Outlook, check to see whether Outlook or any programs that might be using Outlook are still running, and then quit them.

1. On the File menu, click Exit to quit Outlook.
2. Press Ctrl+Alt+Del to open the Close Program dialog box.
3. In the Close Program dialog box, check the list of programs for any reference to Outlook (such as Inbox—Microsoft Outlook). In the list, you'll also see what other programs are still running that might be using Outlook and keeping it open.
4. Click the name of the program (for example, Inbox—Microsoft Outlook), and then click the End Task button.
5. Click Cancel to close the Close Program dialog box.

**Warning**

Don't click the Shut Down button—you'll quit Windows while programs are still running, and that creates a mess for Windows.

# If I exit Outlook while downloading e-mail, Outlook hangs

## Source of the problem

You just got back to the office after a week-long vacation, and you're in the middle of a long e-mail download (lots of e-mail arrived while you were gone). You don't want to wait for the e-mail to download at the moment, so you quit Outlook (or you might have inadvertently clicked the X button and quit Outlook). Outlook stops cold. It won't respond to anything you click or press—it just hangs.

This is called a "known problem" in Outlook, which means it's a bug. If you attempt to quit Outlook (in the Internet Mail Only configuration) while a large background e-mail download is in progress, Outlook might stop responding.

## How to fix it

1. Press Ctrl+Alt+Del.
   Be sure you press all three keys together, and press them just once (if you press them repeatedly, you'll shut down Windows).
2. In the Close Program dialog box, click Inbox—Microsoft Outlook, and then click the End Task button to quit Outlook.
3. Start Outlook again, and wait to pick up your e-mail until you have the time to completely download all the waiting e-mail.

**Tip**

To prevent this bug from biting you, always wait for all your messages to be downloaded (wait until you see the message that says Delivery Complete) before you quit Outlook.

If you know you've got a few messages that you really need to download right away, you can switch to Corporate/Workgroup configuration and use Remote Mail to download those important messages. Let the unimportant messages wait until you've got more time.

If you don't know how to switch your configuration, see the solution to "I don't know how to switch my configuration," on page 20.

**Warning**

Don't click the Shut Down button—you'll quit Windows while programs are still running, and that creates a mess for Windows.

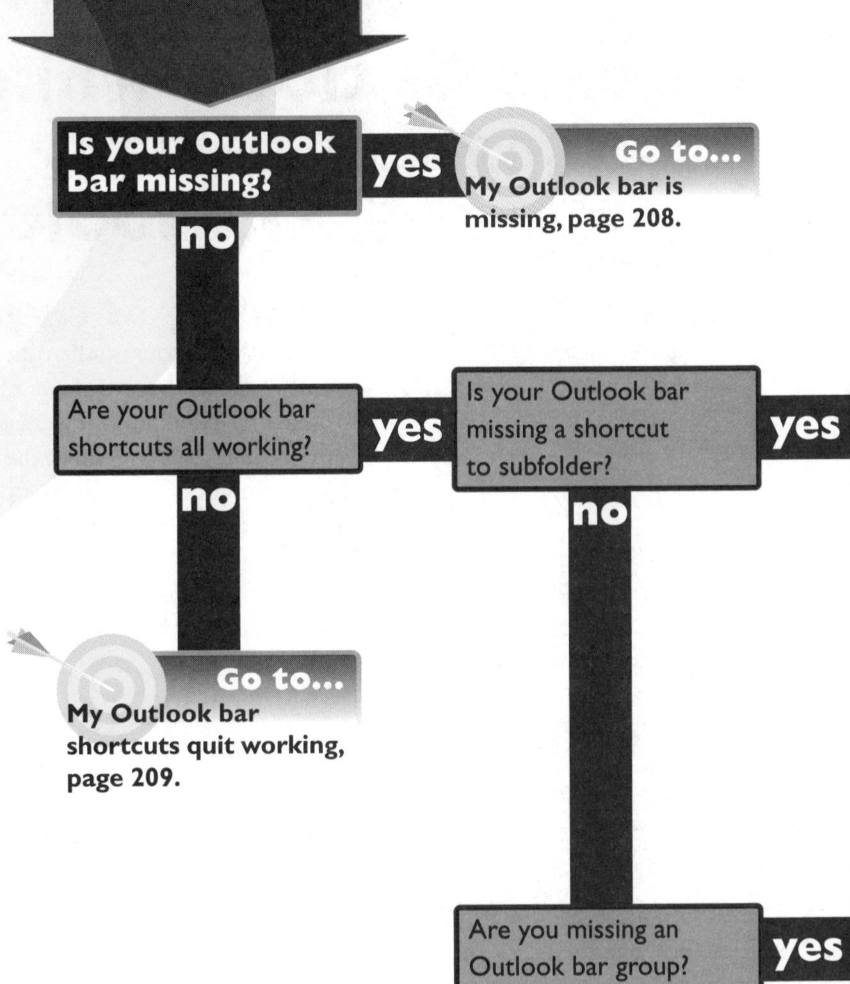

Is your Outlook bar missing?
yes
Go to...
My Outlook bar is missing, page 208.
no
Are your Outlook bar shortcuts all working?
yes
Is your Outlook bar missing a shortcut to subfolder?
yes
no
no
Go to...
My Outlook bar shortcuts quit working, page 209.
Are you missing an Outlook bar group?
yes

**Quick fix**

In both Outlook and Outlook Express, all of your Outlook folders are listed in the folder list. To create an Outlook bar shortcut for an Outlook folder:

1. In Outlook, on the View menu, click Folder List. In Outlook Express, on the View menu, click Layout, and then select the Folder List check box and click OK.
2. In the Folder list, display the folder (or subfolder) you want to create a shortcut for.
3. Right-click the folder and click Add To Outlook Bar.

**Go to...**

**One of my Outlook bar groups is missing, page 210.**

**If your solution isn't here**

Check the general troubleshooting tips on page xiii.

# My Outlook bar is missing

## Source of the problem

You were clicking around in Outlook, experimenting with changing your layout and views, and you lost your Outlook bar. Or, you never knew that there was an Outlook bar in Outlook Express until you saw it on your neighbor's computer, and you can't figure out how to display it in your computer.

You can quickly display (or hide) the Outlook bar in both Outlook and Outlook Express.

## Outlook 2000 How to fix it

On the View menu, click Outlook Bar. ▶

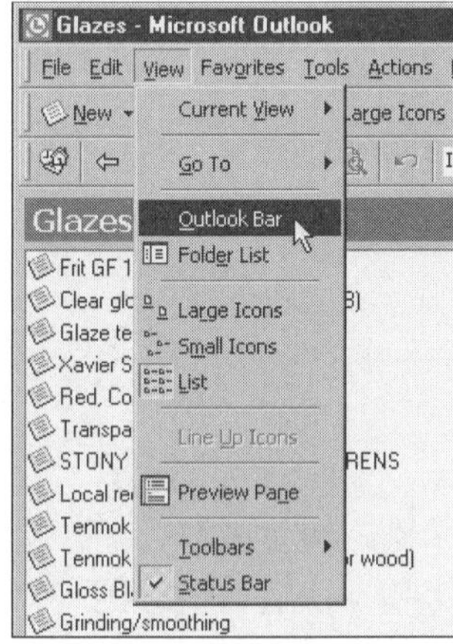

## How to fix it

1. On the View menu, click Layout.
2. In the Windows Layout Properties dialog box, select the Outlook Bar check box. ▶

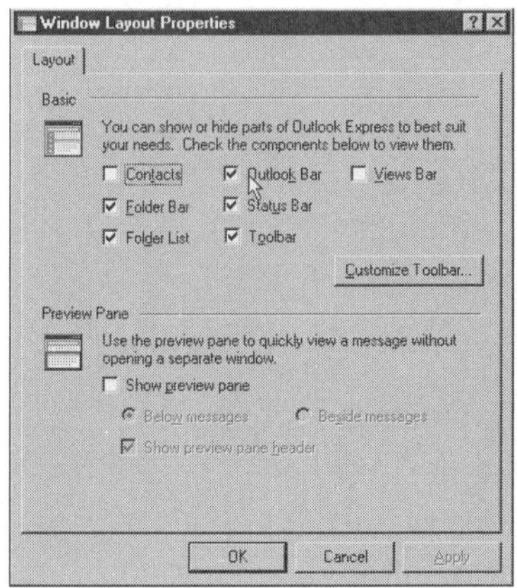

# My Outlook bar shortcuts quit working

## Source of the problem

You started Outlook and then clicked on a shortcut in your Outlook bar, and nothing happened.

The Outlook bar file is probably corrupted, but you can fix it by rebuilding the Outlook bar (unfortunately, rebuilding the Outlook bar returns it to the default build, and all your custom shortcuts are removed).

## How to fix it

1. Click the Windows Start button, point to Find, and then click Files And Folders.
2. In the Named box, type **outlook.exe**.
3. Be sure your hard disk (probably C:) is in the Look In box, select the Include Subfolders check box, and then click Find Now. ▶

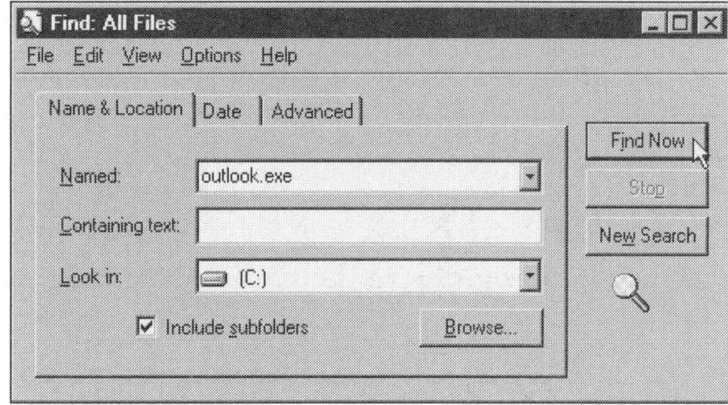


4. When the Find Files dialog box locates the file and stops searching, write down the path to the file (you need to type it in the next step). The default path is **"C:\Program Files\Microsoft Office\Office\outlook.exe"** (including the quotes).
5. Close the Find Files dialog box.
6. Click Start, and then click Run.
7. In the Open box, type the complete path that you noted in step 4, including the file name.
8. Following the file name, type a single space, and then type **/ResetOutlookBar**. ▶

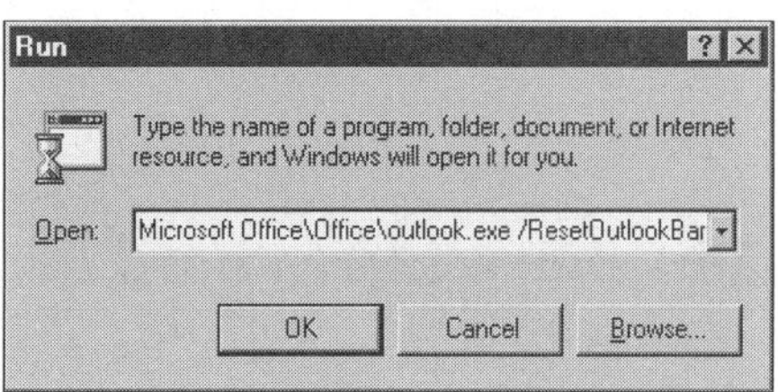


9. Click OK.

If this doesn't fix your Outlook bar, follow the procedure again, but in step 8, type **CleanViews** instead of ResetOutlookBar. The CleanViews procedure restores default views as well as the default Outlook bar (which means you'll probably lose your customized views).

**Tip**

Be sure you type the single space between the file name and the forward slash, and type the upper- and lowercase letters, as shown.

# One of my Outlook bar groups is missing

## Source of the problem

In your colleague's copy of Outlook 2000, in the Outlook bar, there's a group named Other Shortcuts. This Outlook bar group has shortcut icons that open lists of files and folders on the hard disk (rather than Outlook data). This Outlook bar group seems very useful, but you can't find it in your copy of Outlook.

If you installed Outlook 2000 by itself, rather than as a part of the Office 2000 suite, the Other Shortcuts group (or another group) might not have been created. Or, someone might have been practicing creating and deleting Outlook bar groups and deleted your Other Shortcuts group. But that's okay—you can create a new group yourself, and you can name it Other Shortcuts or any name you like.

## How to fix it

First, add a new group to the Outlook bar. Then, add shortcuts to the new group.

### Add a new group to the Outlook bar

1. Right-click in the Outlook bar and click Add New Group.
2. Type the name you want (**Other Shortcuts** or another name). The name you type replaces the highlighted name "new group." ▶

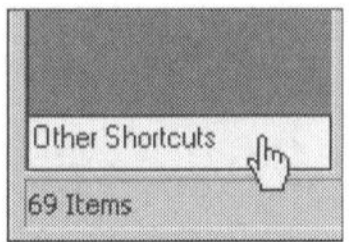


3. Press Enter.

### Add shortcuts to hard disk folders and files to the new group

1. Click the New Group button to open the new group, which is empty.
2. Right-click in the Outlook bar, below the New Group button, and click Outlook Bar Shortcut.

3. In the Add To Outlook bar dialog box, in the Look In box, click File System. ▶

   Your hard disk file system, beginning with the My Computer icon, appears in the list in the big box.

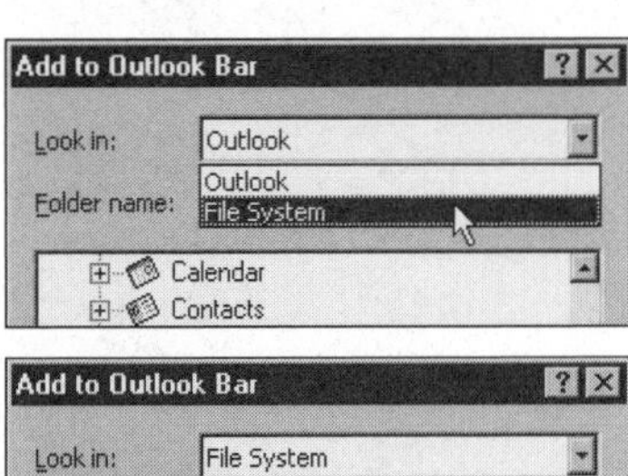


4. Click the My Computer icon, and then click OK. ▶

   The My Computer icon shortcut is added to your Outlook bar. You can click the My Computer icon in the Outlook bar and navigate from there to any folder or file on your hard disk.

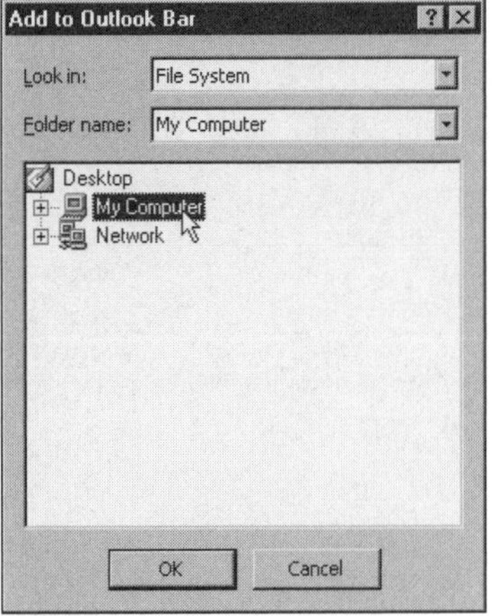


5. Repeat steps 1–4 to add shortcuts to folders and subfolders on your hard disk. In step 4, click the small plus symbol next to the computer icon to open the list of drives in the computer, and click the small plus symbol next to a drive to open lists of folders on that drive. Keep opening folders and subfolders until you find the subfolder you want to add to your Outlook bar. Click the subfolder name, and then click OK. ▶

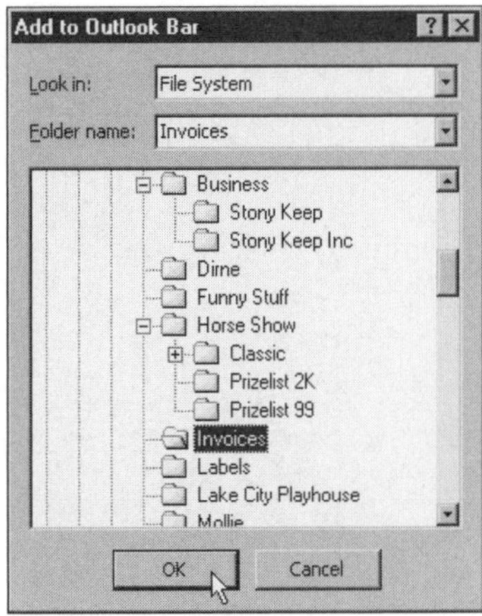


**Tip**

To add a file shortcut to your Outlook bar, click Folder Shortcut in the Outlook bar to display the list of subfolders and files in that folder. Navigate through the file system in the Outlook window until you locate the file for which you want to create a shortcut. Drag the file's icon from the list to the Outlook bar.

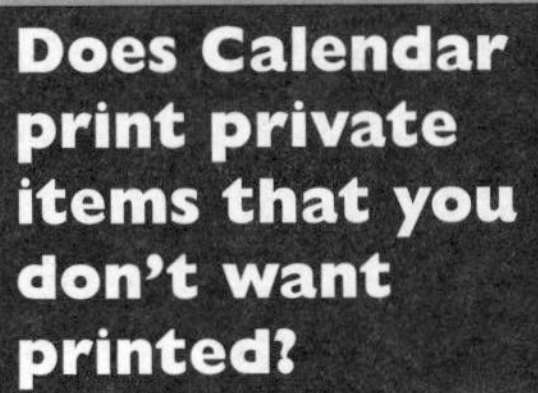

**Does Calendar print private items that you don't want printed?**

yes

no

Does your printer fail to print complete Calendar pages?

yes — **Go to...** **My printer doesn't print all the pages of my Calendar, page 214.**

no

Is text in a printed Calendar week or month cut short?

yes — **Go to...** **The text in my printed calendar is cut short, page 216.**

no

In a printed month, can you print just the dates that you want?

yes — Can you print a list of your contacts?

yes

no

**Quick fix**

There are two reasons why you might get single contacts printed instead of a list: in the Print dialog box, the Memo Style is selected; or, a single contact is selected, and in the Print dialog box, the Only Selected Items option is clicked.

In the Print dialog box, be sure that your selections under both Print Style and Print Range match what you select or display in the Contacts window.

no

**Go to...** **Outlook prints more dates on the page than I want, page 219.**

**If your solution isn't here**
Check the general troubleshooting tips on page xiii.

**Quick fix**

In the Print dialog box, select the Hide Details Of Private Appointments check box. Any appointment or event in which you selected the Private check box will be printed as "Private Appointment."

Can you print a Contacts phone list that includes addresses?

**yes**

Can you print a list of just specific contacts?

**no**

**Go to...**

**I need a Phone List that includes addresses, page 220.**

**no**

**Quick fix**

Filter your view to show only those items that you want to print, and in the Print dialog box, click the All Items option.

Or, use the Shift or Ctrl key to select the specific contacts you want to include in the printed list, and in the Print dialog box, click the Only Selected Items option.

# My printer doesn't print all the pages of my Calendar

## Source of the problem

You set up your Calendar to print six months of appointments. You send it to the printer, and your printer prints one, or maybe two, pages and then quits. Your printer has plenty of paper, so what's the problem?

There are two likely possibilities: your printer doesn't have enough memory to print what you want, or you need to set the complete date range for printing.

## How to fix it

### Printer memory

If you choose to print a special Page Size, such as one of the Franklin Day Planner or Day Runner styles, some printers don't have the memory to print complete pages. They print as much as they can and then quit (you get an "Overrun" error notification from some printers).

To find out whether printer memory is the problem, try printing your pages using a very simple page size, such as Letter or Letter Half.

To set a different page size:

1. On the File menu, point to Page Setup, and then click the print style you want.
2. On the Paper tab, under Page, in the Size list, click one of the sizes at the top of the list. ▶
3. Click the Print button.
4. In the Print dialog box, click OK.

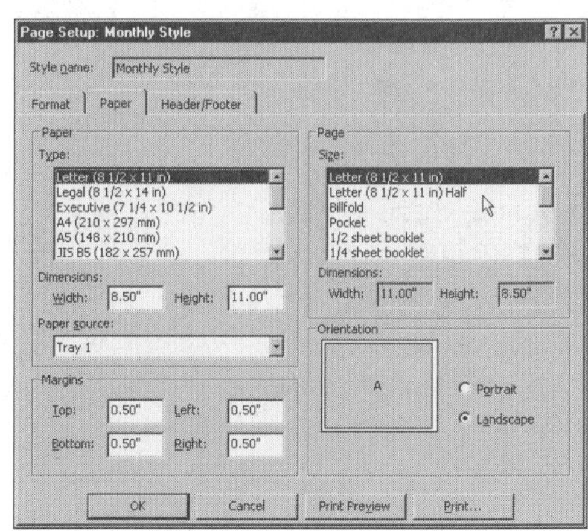


If the simpler page sizes print without problems, you can either stick with simpler pages, print to a different printer, or get more memory for your printer.

### Date range

Another reason your printer might be not be printing all the pages you want is the Print Range (the date range) you set in the Print dialog box.

If you want to print, for example, monthly calendar pages for the entire year 2001, you need to specify the entire range of months.

To specify the dates for the print range:

1. On the File menu, click Print.
2. In the Print dialog box, under Print Range, click the arrow next to the Start box, and click the date on which you want the printed calendar to start. (If the Start date is far in the future, it might be faster to type the date in the Start box—for example, **Jan 1 2001**.) ▶

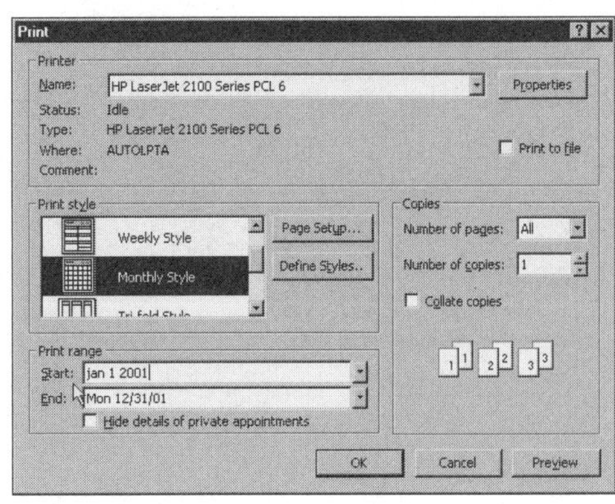


3. Use the same technique to set the date in the End box. For example, if you want to print calendar pages for the entire year, enter **Dec 31 2001** in the End box.
4. Click the Preview button to check your pages before you print them.
5. In the Print Preview window, on the toolbar, click the Multiple Pages button to see all the pages. ▶

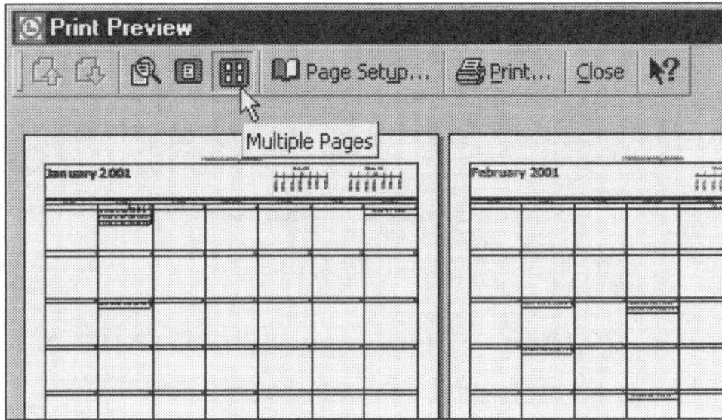


6. If you're ready to print the pages, click the Print button on the Print Preview window toolbar, and then click OK in the Print dialog box.
7. If you need to make more layout changes, such as removing the TaskPad and Notes areas, click the Page Setup button on the toolbar. After you make your changes in the Page Setup dialog box, click the Print button, and then click OK in the Print dialog box.

**Tip**

To print a completely empty calendar to distribute to others in your group, create a new Calendar subfolder and print the new calendar without creating any appointments or events in it.

# The text in my printed calendar is cut short

## Source of the problem

After you print your calendar pages, you notice that the last few characters or words in some of your appointment entries are cut off. The problem is that Outlook can print only as much text as will fit in each date's box.

## How to fix it

There are three techniques you can try that might fix this problem. You can decrease the font size in the printed page, print from a view with AutoPreview turned on, or print the calendar larger on the page.

### Decrease the font size

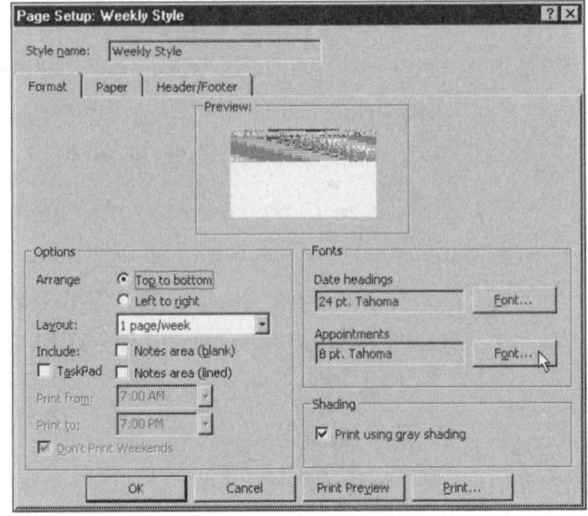


1. On the File menu, point to Page Setup, and click the style you want to print.
2. On the Format tab, under Fonts, click the Font button for Appointments. ▶
3. Click a new Font Size, and click OK in each dialog box to close it.

   The smallest font size you can select is 8 points, but you can force the font size smaller by typing the number you want in the Size box. A font size of 5 or 6 points is awfully small, but it might work for you. If not, try one of the other two techniques.

### Turn on AutoPreview

If AutoPreview is turned on in your display view, the Notes in each appointment entry are printed in calendar pages.

1. On the View menu, point to Current View, and click Day/Week/Month View With AutoPreview.
2. When you set up your printed page, use the Daily print style to print the complete text of each entry, with notes. If your notes for a particular appointment are very long, you might need to make that appointment in the Daily view larger (increase the duration of the appointment) so that all the Notes in the entry can be displayed in the printed page.

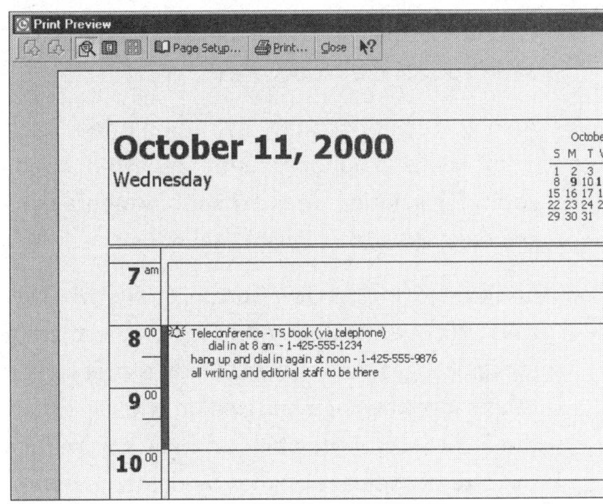


**Tip**

Whether your display is daily, weekly, or monthly, with AutoPreview view, you see all the appointment notes when you point your mouse at an entry.

## Print the calendar larger

If you print the calendar larger on the Page, by choosing a larger print style and by removing extraneous elements, such as the TaskPad and Notes areas, each date box in the calendar will be larger and capable of holding more text.

1. In the Page Setup dialog box, on the Paper tab, click a larger Page Size and an Orientation that makes best use of the page space.

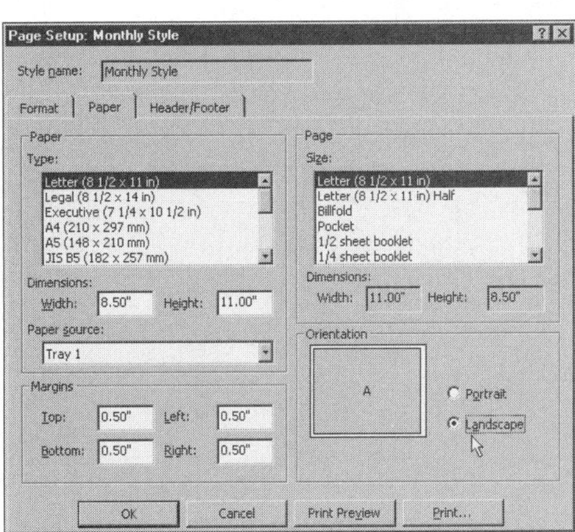

2. On the Format tab, clear the check boxes for TaskPad and the Notes areas.

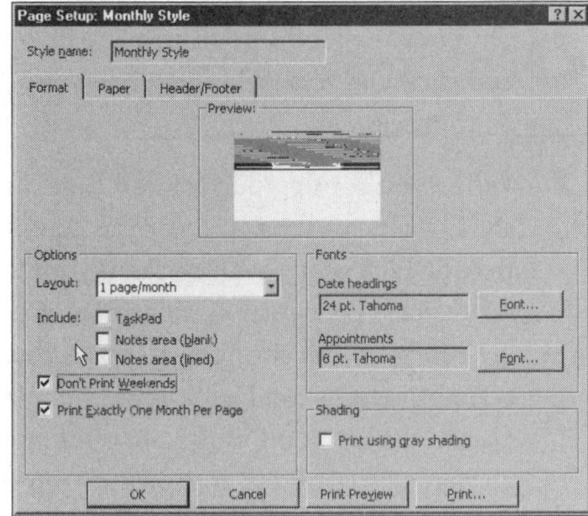


3. Also on the Format tab, if you don't need to print weekend appointments, you can make more room for printing weekday appointments by selecting the Don't Print Weekends check box.
4. Click the Print Preview button to see whether these changes helped and whether there are any more changes you can make. For example, you can change the page margins on the Paper tab in the Page Setup dialog box, and you can reduce the size of the page header by deleting words in the Header boxes on the Header/Footer tab of the Page Setup dialog box.

# Outlook prints more dates on the page than I want

## Source of the problem

You print a calendar month, and in your printed page, all 42 date squares on the page have dates in them (including the last few dates of the previous month and the first few dates of the following month). For clarity and simplicity, you want a month page that shows only the dates for that single month.

## How to fix it

Monthly style prints an entire month, but you can direct Outlook to print only the dates within a single month. For example, instead of printing July 30 through September 2, to fill all the squares on the page with dates, Outlook can print just the dates August 1 through August 31 and leave the remaining squares blank.

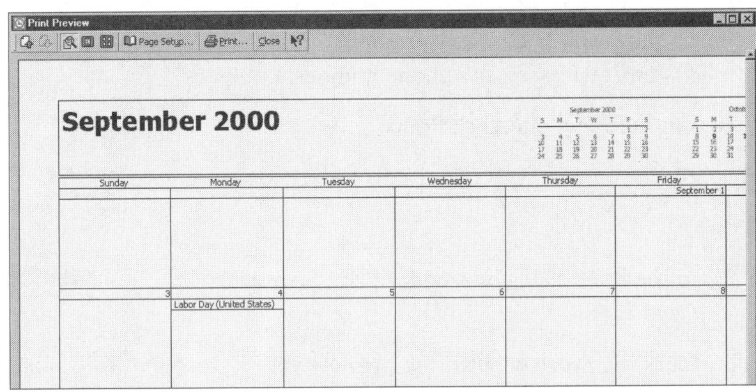


To print the dates for only one month on each page:

1. On the File menu, click Print.
2. In the Print dialog box, under Print Range, set the Start and End dates for your printed pages, and then click the Page Setup button.
3. In the Page Setup dialog box, select the Print Exactly One Month Per Page check box. ▶
4. In the Page Setup dialog box, click the Print Preview button to make sure the pages look the way you want them to before you print them.
5. In the Page Setup dialog box, click the Print button, and in the Print dialog box, click OK.

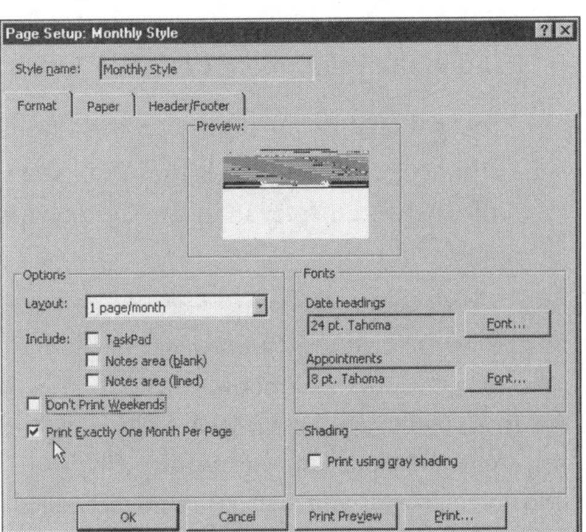

# I need a Phone List that includes addresses

## Source of the problem

You can quickly print a built-in telephone list of your contacts by choosing the Phone Directory Style in the Print dialog box. But the Phone Directory Style list includes only phone numbers, and you can't alter the fields in that print style. You can, however, create your own similar phone list that includes addresses.

## How to fix it

1. In the Contacts folder, set up your Card view to show only the fields you want to print (names, addresses, and phone numbers). ▶

2. On the File menu, click Print.
3. In the Print dialog box, under Print Style, click Card Style. ▶

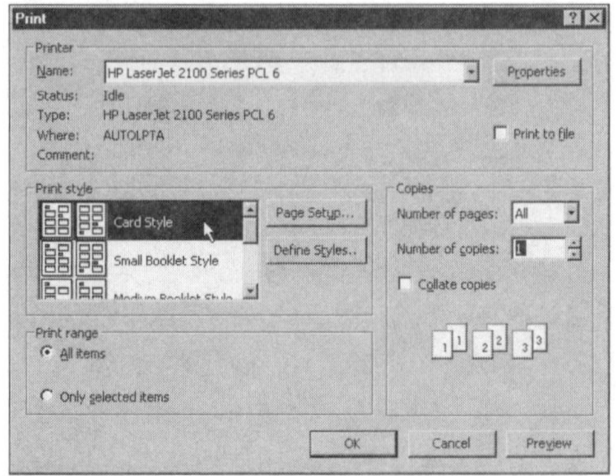


4. Click the Preview button to preview your phone list.
5. If the preview looks good, click the Print button, and in the Print dialog box, click OK.

   You get a printout similar to the Phone Directory style, but it includes all the information displayed in the Outlook window.

### Tip

To change the fields in the Card view, right-click in an empty space in the Contacts window, and click Show Fields. In the Show Fields dialog box, in the Available Fields list, double-click fields you want to include, and in the Show Fields In This Order list, double-click fields you want to remove. Then click OK.

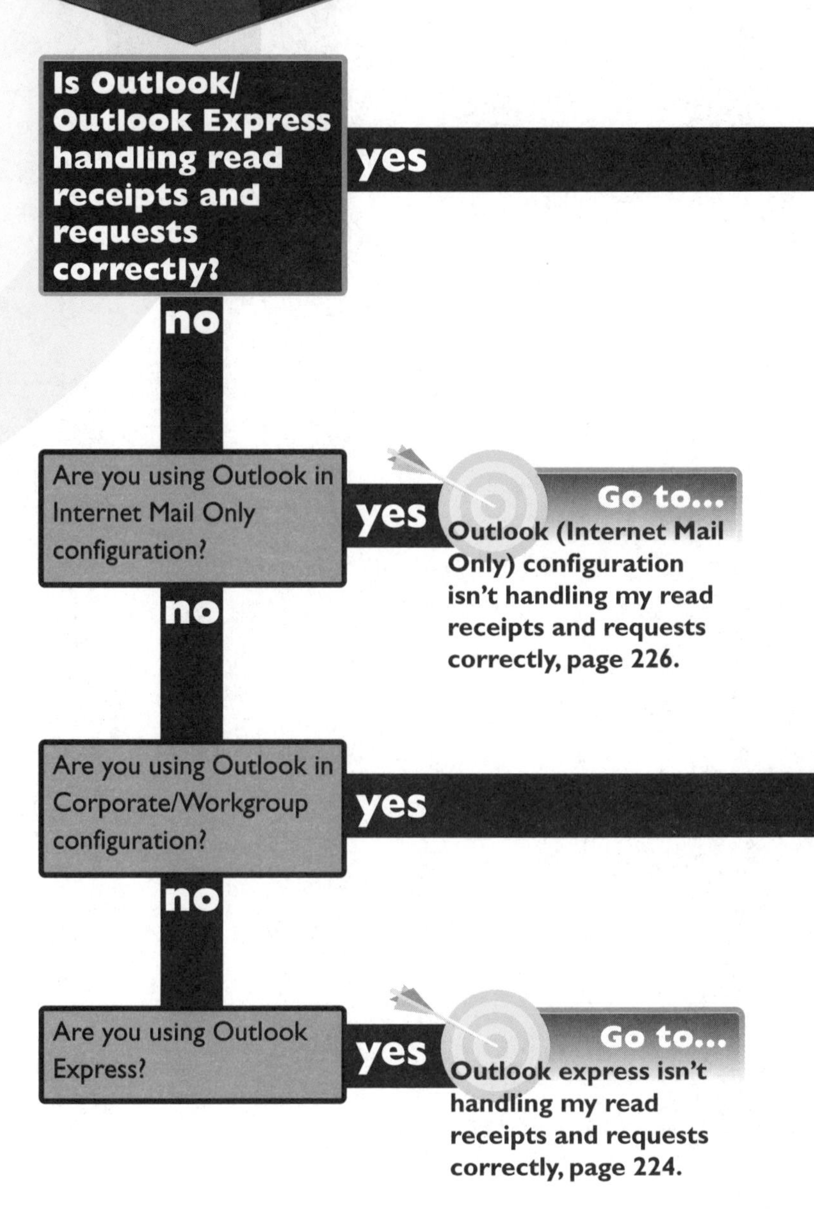
Is Outlook/ Outlook Express handling read receipts and requests correctly?
yes
no
Are you using Outlook in Internet Mail Only configuration?
yes
Go to...
Outlook (Internet Mail Only) configuration isn't handling my read receipts and requests correctly, page 226.
no
Are you using Outlook in Corporate/Workgroup configuration?
yes
no
Are you using Outlook Express?
yes
Go to...
Outlook express isn't handling my read receipts and requests correctly, page 224.

# Read receipts

Are you receiving the read receipts you requested from your receipients?

yes

When you test read receipts by sending yourself a message, do they work correctly?

no

### Quick fix

You might or might not receive read receipts from your correspondents, depending on what mail programs they use and how they have their responses set up. Some mail programs can't respond to read receipt requests at all. Correspondents who use mail programs that can respond to read receipts requests usually have the option of either ignoring read receipt requests altogether or responding to the requests selectively.

It's not a good idea to send read receipt requests to everyone by default, because some people think it's rude. A better idea is to send read receipt requests individually, to colleagues who expect them (or at least don't mind them).

### Go to...

**Outlook (Corporate/ Workgroup) configuration isn't handling my read receipts and requests correctly, page 228.**

no

### Go to...

**When I test read receipts, they don't work right, page 230.**

**If your solution isn't here**

Check the general troubleshooting tips on page xiii.

# Outlook Express isn't handling my read receipts and requests correctly

## Source of the problem

When you send e-mail, there are read receipt messages in your Outbox that go out with your outgoing mail, and it's annoying—you feel as if all these people are checking up on you. Or perhaps you have specific senders (such as your supervisor) whose read receipt requests require responses from you, and you don't know how to set them up without sending responses to everyone.

You also need to control the requests you send. For example, suppose you get an irritated message from a new client asking you to please stop sending read receipt requests to him. You need to be able to change your read receipt request procedures immediately.

## How to fix it

On the Tools menu, click Options, and then click the Receipts tab. ▶

- To ignore all requests, select the Never Send A Read Receipt option.
- To respond to requests individually, select the Notify Me For Each Read Receipt Request option.
- To have Outlook automatically respond to every request, select the Always Send A Read Receipt option.

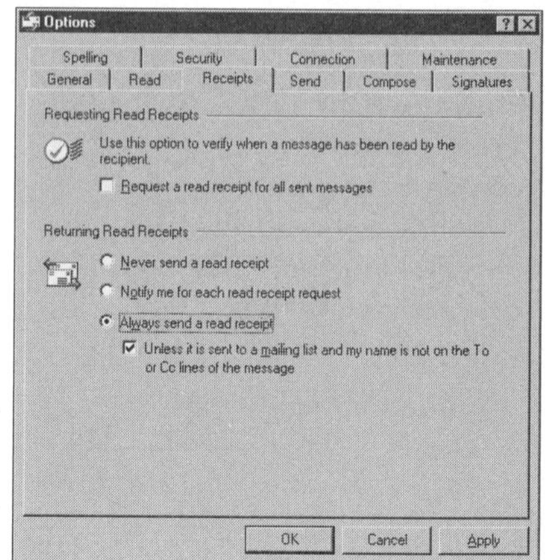

- To request a read receipt for every message you send, select the Request A Read Receipt For All Sent Messages check box.
- To request read receipts only for individual messages, leave the check box clear. Instead, in the new message, on the Tools menu, click Request Read Receipt. ▶

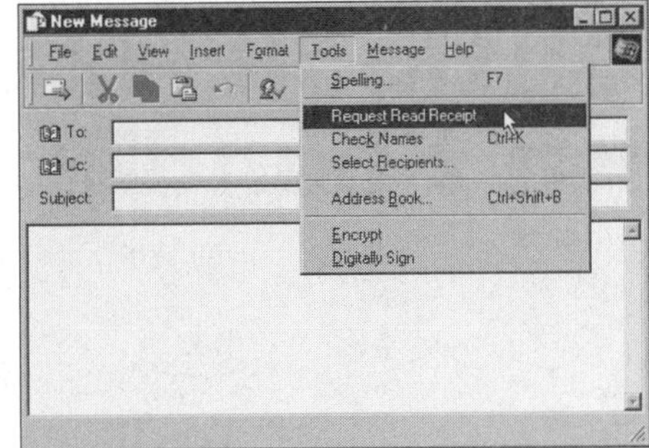


**Tip**

Outlook Express 5 may or may not have Read Receipt capability, depending on your Windows and Internet Explorer versions. If your copy of Outlook Express 5 doesn't have Read Receipts, you can upgrade to Internet Explorer 5.5, free from Microsoft, at *www.microsoft.com/windows/ie/download/*.

# Outlook (Internet Mail Only) isn't handling my read receipts and requests correctly

## Source of the problem

When you send e-mail, there are read receipt messages in your Outbox that go out with your outgoing mail, and it's annoying—you feel as if all these people are checking up on you. Or perhaps you have specific senders (such as your supervisor) whose read receipt requests require responses from you, and you don't know how to set them up without sending responses to everyone.

You also need to control the requests you send. For example, suppose you get an irritated message from a new client asking you to please stop sending read receipt requests to him. You need to be able to change your read receipt request procedures immediately.

## How to fix it

1. On the Tools menu, click Options, and on the Preferences tab, click the E-mail Options button.
2. In the E-mail Options dialog box, click the Tracking Options button. ▶

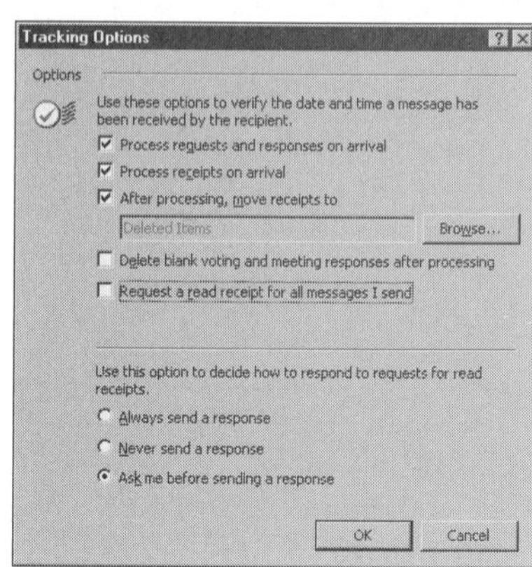


- To ignore all requests, select the Never Send A Response option.
- To respond to requests individually, select the Ask Me Before Sending A Response option.
- To have Outlook automatically respond to every request, select the Always Send A Response option.

- To request a read receipt with every message, select the Request A Read Receipt For All Messages I Send check box.
- To request read receipts for individual messages only, leave the Request A Read Receipt For All Messages I Send check box clear. Instead, in the new message, click the Options button. In the Message Options dialog box, click the Request A Read Receipt For This Message check box, and then click Close. ▶

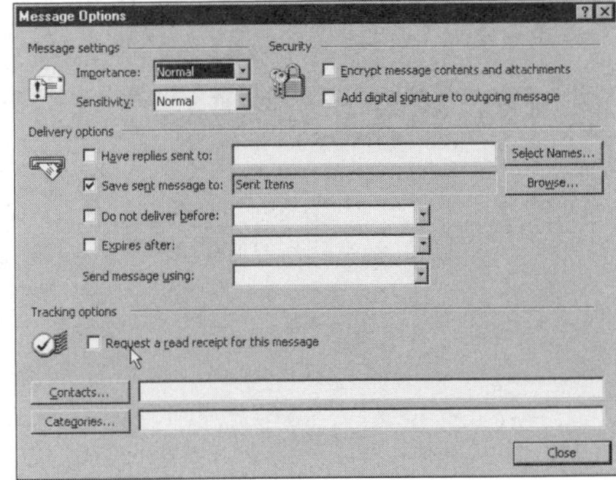

# Outlook (Corporate/ Workgroup) isn't handling my read receipts and requests correctly

## Source of the problem

When you send e-mail, there are read receipt messages in your Outbox that go out with your outgoing mail, and it's annoying—you feel as if all these people are checking up on you. Or perhaps you have specific senders (such as your supervisor) whose read receipt requests require responses from you, and you don't know how to set them up without sending responses to everyone.

You also need to control the requests you send. For example, suppose you get an irritated message from a new client asking you to please stop sending read receipt requests to him. You need to be able to change your read receipt request procedures immediately.

## How to fix it

1. On the Tools menu, click Options, and on the Preferences tab, click the E-mail Options button.
2. In the E-mail Options dialog box, click the Tracking Options button. ▶

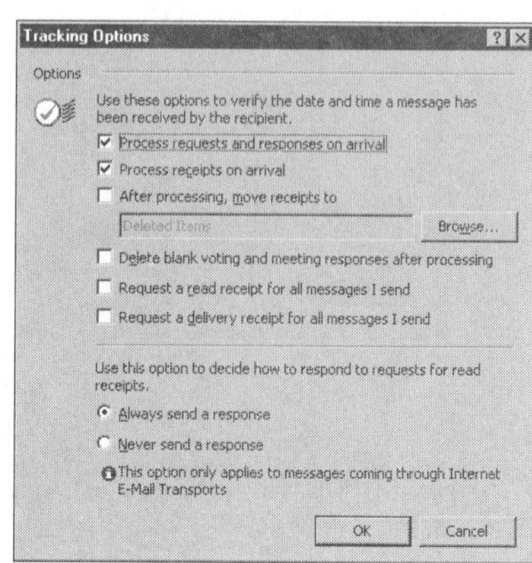


- To ignore all requests, select the Never Send A Response option.
- To respond to every request, select the Always Send A Response option.
- In the Corporate/Workgroup configuration, you can't choose to respond to requests individually—you must respond to all of them or none of them.
- To request a read receipt with every message, select the Request A Read Receipt For All Messages I Send check box.

- To request read receipts for individual messages only, leave the Request A Read Receipt For All Messages I Send check box clear. Instead, in the new message, click the Options button. In the Message Options dialog box, click the Request A Read Receipt For This Message check box, and then click Close. ▶

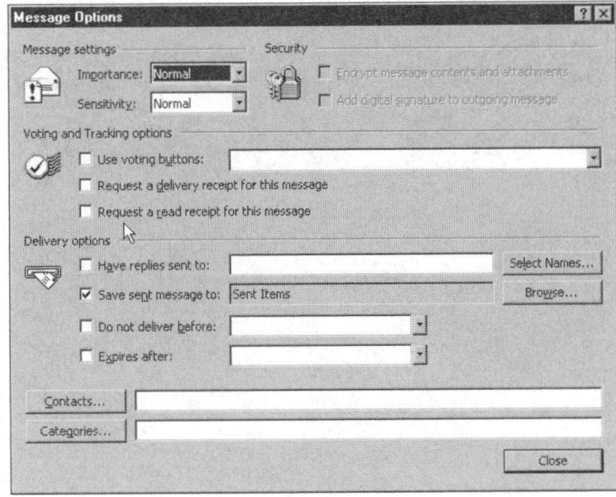

# When I test read receipts, they don't work right

## Source of the problem

You decide to test read receipts in Outlook by sending yourself a message that requests a read receipt. After you send a message, you discover to your dismay that the read receipt for your self-test message is sitting in your Outbox, and no tracking tab appears in the sent message in the Sent Items folder.

## How to fix it

You've tested only half the procedure—the half in which you, the original sender, send the original message with a request for a read receipt.

The second half of the procedure happens when you, the recipient, send mail again (any mail, to anyone). At that point, the read receipt that's sitting in your Outbox is sent with the mail and received by you, the original sender.

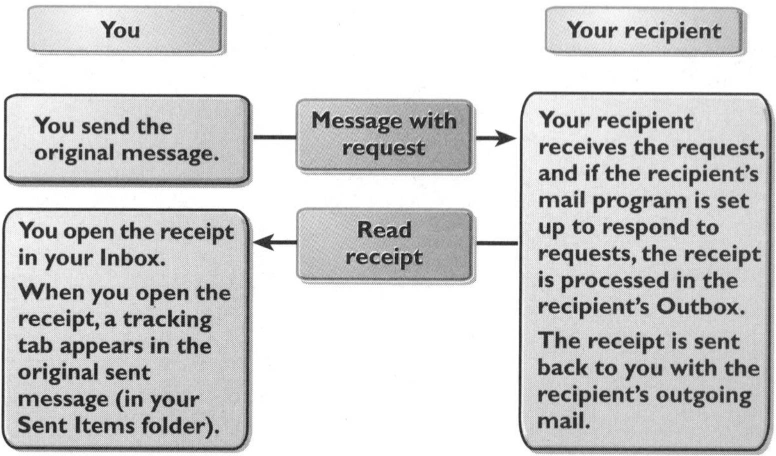

**Is Outlook running?**

yes

Is the appointment or task with the failed reminder saved in a subfolder instead of in the main Calendar or Task folder?

yes

no

no

**Quick fix**

If Outlook is not running, none of your reminders will appear. Next time you turn Outlook on, all of your overdue reminders will pile up on your Windows desktop.

To make sure your reminders appear, keep Outlook running minimized or in the background, all the time.

Are you using Outlook in the Corporate/ Workgroup configuration?

yes

no

After working through the previous solutions, are your reminders still not working?

yes

# Reminders

**Go to...**

**Reminders in my Calendar and Tasks subfolders don't work, page 234.**

**Quick fix**

In the Corporate/Workgroup configuration, if the delivery option for your e-mail service is set to None, your appointment and tasks reminders won't be processed. Also, if you create an appointment or task in a folder that's not where your mail is delivered, the reminder for that appointment or task won't be triggered.

To specify the mail delivery location:

1. On the Tools menu, click Services.
2. On the Delivery tab, make sure that the Deliver New Mail To The Following Location list box is set to the location where you have your mail Inbox. For E-mail, the correct location is Personal Folders, and for network mail the correct location is usually a mailbox in a network post office.
3. Click OK.

If you receive mail in your Personal Folders Inbox and you create an appointment reminder in your Personal Folders Calendar, the reminder is functional; and if your mail is delivered to a network mailbox and you create your appointments and tasks in Outlook folders that are in the network mailbox, your reminders will be functional.

**Quick fix**

It's possible that your Reminders file is damaged.

1. Quit Outlook.
2. Click Start, point to Run, and then type **outlook /cleanreminders** in the Open list box (be sure you type a space between **outlook** and the slash).
3. Click OK.

**If your solution isn't here**

Check these related chapters:

Calendar, page 10

Tasks and TaskPad, page 270

Or see the general troubleshooting tips on page xiii.

# Reminders in my Calendar and Tasks subfolders don't work

## Source of the problem

You've created all your personal appointments—hair cut, dentist, and so forth—in your personal Calendar subfolder, and none of them appear. The source of the problem is that reminders work only from within your main Calendar and Tasks folders (not subfolders).

## How to fix it

If you create a new appointment and see this message when you click Save And Close, you won't get the reminder, because you've made the appointment or task in a Calendar or Tasks subfolder instead of the main Calendar or Tasks folder. ▶

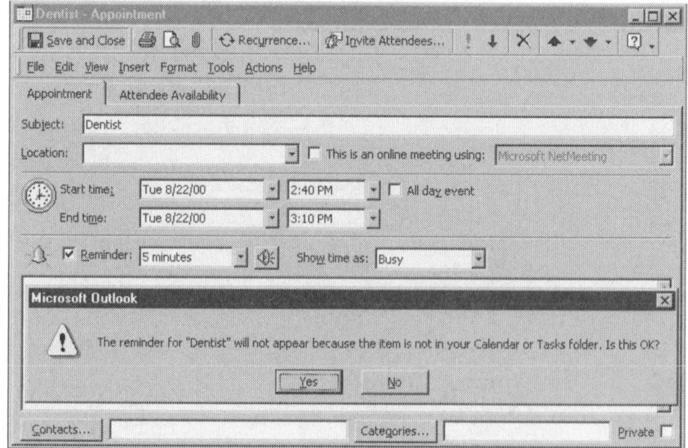


If you click No in the message, the appointment or task isn't saved and the dialog box remains open; but if you click Yes, the appointment is saved. (Don't let the reminder icon in the appointment fool you—you won't get that reminder.)

If you absolutely need to be reminded about an appointment or a task, make sure you save it in your primary Calendar or Tasks folder.

### Tip

If the appointment or task is private, mark the Private check box in the lower-right corner of the dialog box—that hides the item from all eyes but yours.

## If you want to know more about reminders

To change the default reminder times for either Calendar or Tasks, on the Tools menu, click Options, and make the changes on the Preferences tab.

If all your reminders appear too late to get you out of the office in time to make your appointment, you can reset your default reminder time to something much more reasonable—perhaps two hours. If a specific appointment requires a different reminder time—for example, 15 minutes or five hours—you can change the reminder time on the individual Appointment or Task dialog box.

Would you like a reminder to get in touch with a certain contact on a particular morning next month? You can flag a contact for follow-up and be reminded at the date and time you set. To flag a contact for follow-up:

1. Open the contact.
2. On the Actions menu, click Flag For Follow-up.
3. In the Flag To box, select or type a flag note to yourself.
4. In the Due By box, click the arrow, and then click the calendar date when you want to be reminded. A date and time appear in the Due By box.
5. In the Due By box, select the time, and then type the time you prefer. For example, if you want to be reminded at 9:00 that morning, type **9 am**. ▶

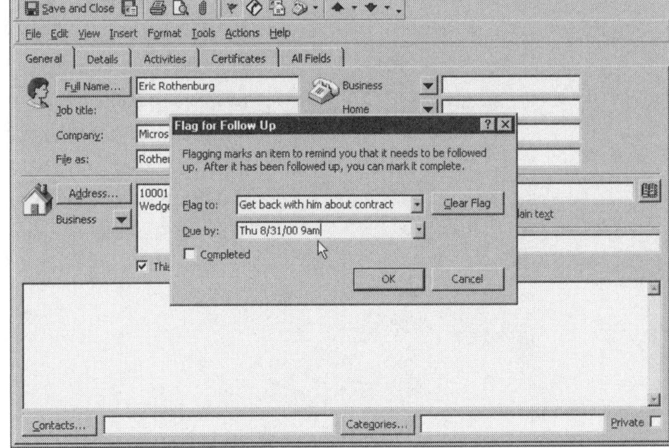


6. Click OK.

If Outlook is running at the reminder time, you get a reminder to contact that person.

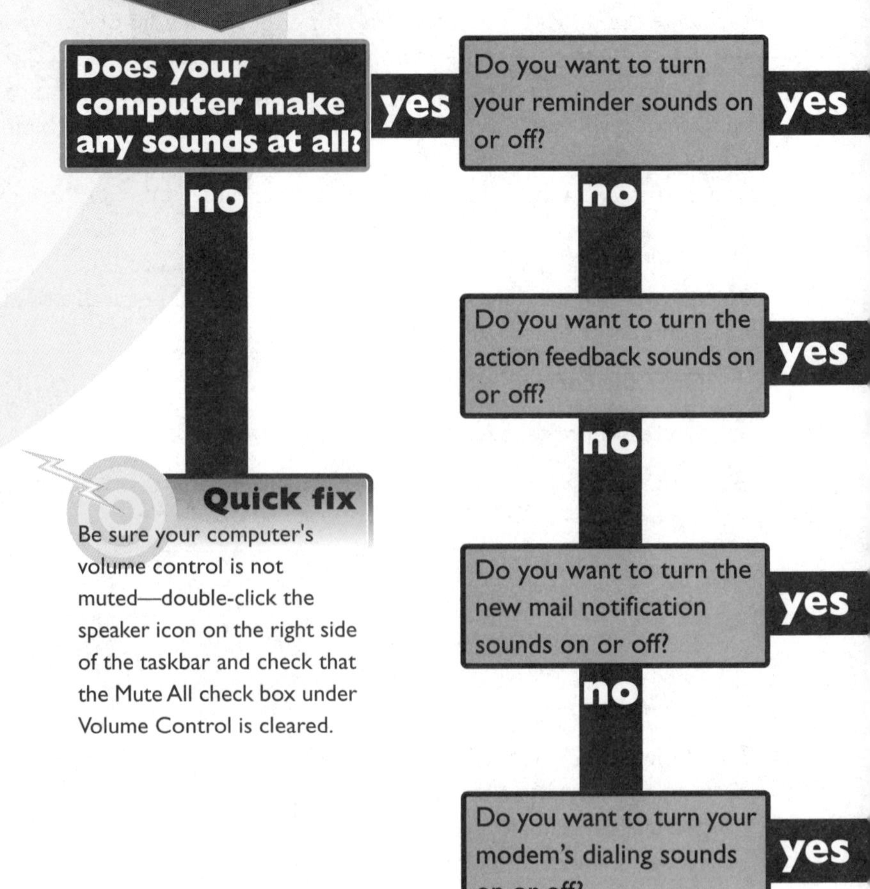
Does your computer make any sounds at all?
yes
no
Do you want to turn your reminder sounds on or off?
yes
no
Do you want to turn the action feedback sounds on or off?
yes
no
Do you want to turn the new mail notification sounds on or off?
yes
no
Do you want to turn your modem's dialing sounds on or off?
yes
Quick fix
Be sure your computer's volume control is not muted—double-click the speaker icon on the right side of the taskbar and check that the Mute All check box under Volume Control is cleared.

# Sounds

**Go to...**
My reminder sounds aren't doing what I want, page 238.

**Go to...**
My action feedback sounds aren't doing what I want, page 239.

**Go to...**
My new mail notification sounds aren't doing what I want, page 240.

**Go to...**
My modem dialing noises aren't doing what I want, page 242.

**If your solution isn't here**
Check the general troubleshooting tips on page xiii.

# My reminder sounds aren't doing what I want

## Source of the problem

The Calendar and Task reminder sounds in Outlook are supposed to alert you to an appointment or task that's due. If you're not being alerted by a sound (and you want to be), there are two places where the sounds might have been turned off. You might have the reminder sound turned off for all tasks, meetings, and events, even though the visual reminder appears, or you might not have Calendar reminders turned on by default, which means you need to remember to enable each appointment's reminder when you create it.

## How to fix it

1. On the Tools menu, click Options.
2. On the Other tab, click the Advanced Options button.
3. In the Advanced Options dialog box, click the Reminder Options button.
4. In the Reminder Options dialog box (shown in the first figure to the right), select the Play Reminder Sound check box to turn reminder sounds on; clear the check box to turn reminder sounds off.
5. Click OK twice to return to the Options dialog box.
6. On the Preferences tab, under Calendar, select the Default Reminder check box to turn Calendar reminders on by default. Clear the check box if you want to set reminders only on specific appointments when you create them. ▶
7. Click OK to close the Options dialog box.

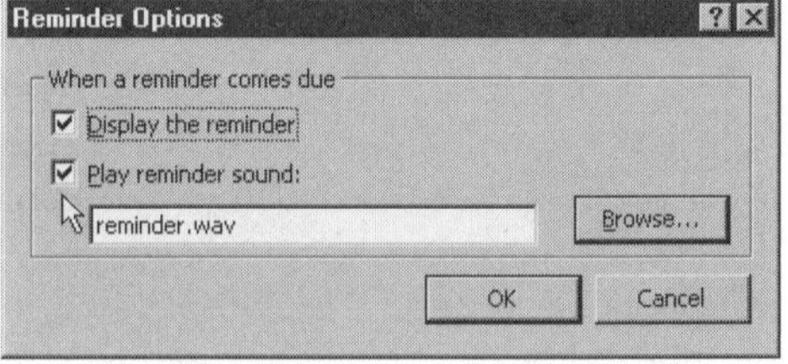


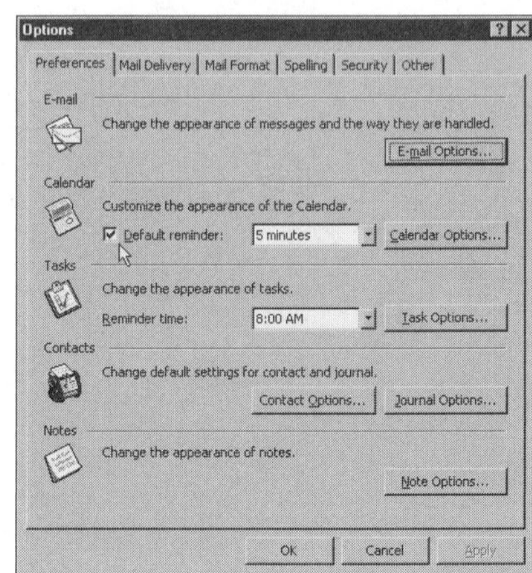

# My action feedback sounds aren't doing what I want

## Source of the problem

When you perform an action in Outlook, such as starting a program or deleting a message (or pressing the wrong key), the action makes a sound by default. If action sounds annoy you, you can turn them off. If someone turned them off and you want to hear them, you can turn them back on.

## How to fix it

1. On the Tools menu, click Options.
2. On the Other tab, click the Advanced Options button.
3. Under General Settings, select or clear the Provide Feedback With Sound check box. ▶
4. Click OK to close each dialog box.

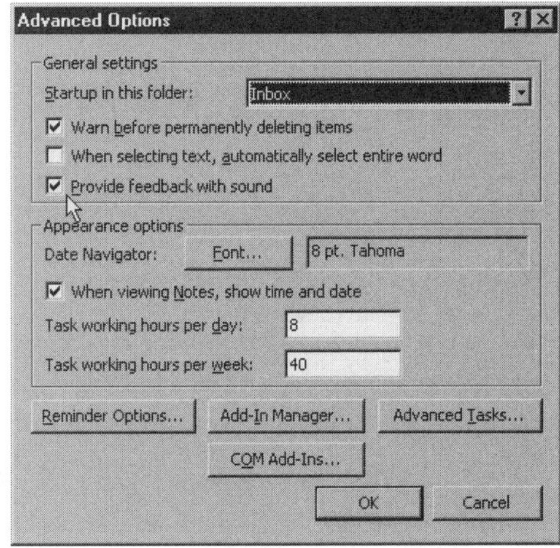


**Tip**

After you select the check box and click OK, you might see a message telling you to download Office Sounds from the Microsoft Office Update web site. Go ahead and download them if you like sounds on your computer—you might find them more interesting than the default Windows sounds, and they're free.

**Tip**

If you have a volume control in the Taskbar, click it once and check whether the Mute check box is selected (for silence) or cleared (for sound).

# My new mail notification sounds aren't doing what I want

## Source of the problem

New mail notification sounds are on by default. I find the sounds annoying because they interrupt my train of thought when new messages arrive. On the other hand, some folks' communications are time-critical, and they need to know the moment a new message arrives. Whether it's silence or sounds you need, if your new mail sounds aren't doing what you want, you can fix them in both Outlook and Outlook Express.

## Outlook 2000 How to fix it

1. On the Tools menu, click Options.
2. Click the Preferences tab.
3. Click the E-mail Options button.
4. In the E-mail Options dialog box, click the Advanced E-mail Options button.
5. In the Advanced E-mail Options dialog box, under When New Items Arrive, select (or clear) the Play A Sound check box. ▶
6. Click OK to close each open dialog box.

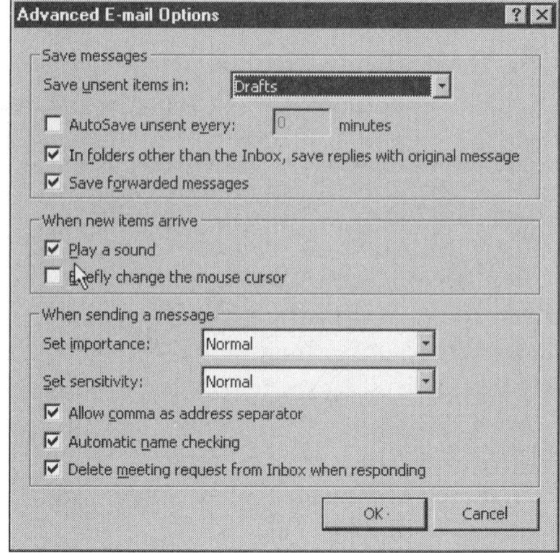

## Outlook Express How to fix it

1. On the Tools menu, click Options.
2. Click the General tab.
3. Under Send/Receive Messages, select (or clear) the Play Sound When New Messages Arrive check box. ▶
4. Click OK to close the dialog box.

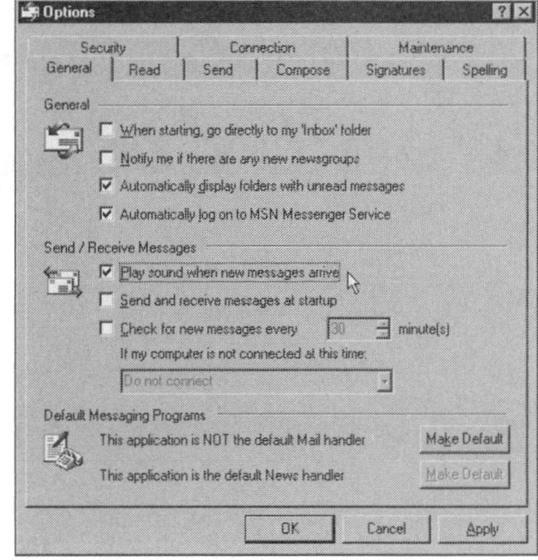

## If you want to know more about sounds

You can change the sound files for various computer events (computer actions that make noises). Sounds accompany events and alerts in Windows and in other programs, such as Excel, Word, and your anti-virus program.

To change a sound, click the Start button on the bottom-left corner of your desktop, click Settings, and then click Control Panel. Double-click the Sounds icon to open the Sounds Properties dialog box.

Click an event in the list of Events, and then click the down arrow on the Name box to select the name of a sound file for that event. To preview the sound, click it and then click the arrow button under Preview. ▶

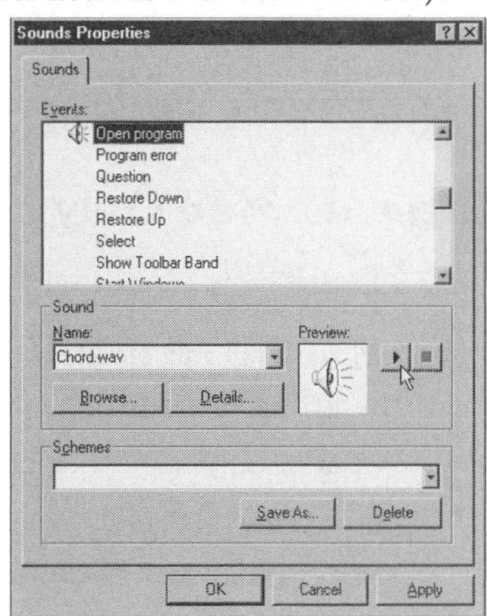

To locate other sounds (such as the Microsoft Office sounds you can download from the Microsoft Web site), click the Browse button and look for *.wav* files in other folders. In the Browse For Sound dialog box, you can preview and select other sounds for your events.

**Note**

If you're using Windows 2000, you'll click the Sounds And Multimedia icon in the Control Panel. In the Sounds And Multimedia Properties dialog box, there will be a right-pointing arrow next to the list box of sound files—click a sound file, and then click the arrow to preview the sound.

# My modem dialing noises aren't doing what I want

## Source of the problem

When you first install and configure a modem, it's nice to hear the dialing noises and the modem static so that you know everything's working the way it should. But those noises can be really irritating after a while. You can turn them off, adjust the volume, or even turn them back on if you need the reassurance of those noises. (If you use Outlook in the Corporate/Workgroup configuration and get your e-mail messages through the network server, modem noises won't be a problem unless you've set up a separate Internet mail account that you dial from your computer.)

## How to fix it

### Internet Mail Only configuration

1. On the Tools menu, click Accounts.
2. On the Mail tab, click your ISP account, and then click the Properties button.
3. In the account's Properties dialog box, on the Connection tab, under Modem, make sure your ISP is selected, and then click the Properties button.
4. In the account name dialog box, on the General tab, under Connect Using, make sure your modem is selected, and then click the Configure button.
5. In the modem's Properties dialog box, on the General tab, slide the Speaker Volume to Off or to a volume level. ▶
6. Click OK or Close to close each open dialog box.

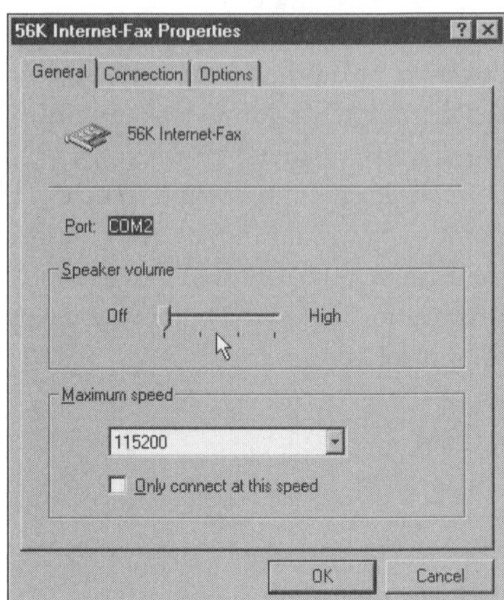

## Outlook 2000 How to fix it

### Corporate/Workgroup configuration

1. On the Tools menu, click Services.
2. On the Services tab, click Internet E-mail, and then click the Properties button. ▶
3. In the account's Properties dialog box, on the Connection tab, under Modem, make sure your ISP is selected, and then click the Properties button.
4. In the account name dialog box, on the General tab, under Connect Using, make sure your modem is selected, and then click the Configure button.
5. In the modem's Properties dialog box, on the General tab, slide the Speaker Volume to Off or to a volume level.
6. Click OK or Close to close each dialog box.

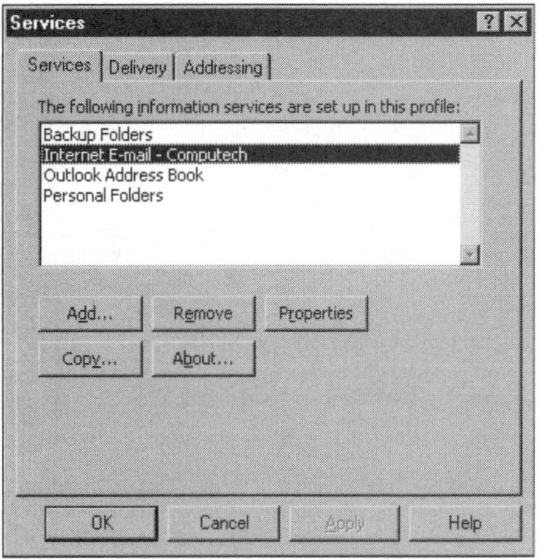


## Outlook Express How to fix it

1. On the Tools menu, click Accounts.
2. On the Mail tab, click your Internet service account name, and then click the Properties button.
3. In the account's Properties dialog box, on the Connection tab, make sure your Internet service account is selected, and then click the Settings button.
4. In the account name dialog box, on the General tab, under Connect Using, make sure your modem is selected, and then click the Configure button.
5. In the modem's Properties dialog box, on the General tab, slide the Speaker Volume to Off or to a volume level.
6. Click OK or Close to close each dialog box.

**Tip**

When you change the volume setting for your modem, that setting applies to both Outlook and Outlook Express (if you are using both).

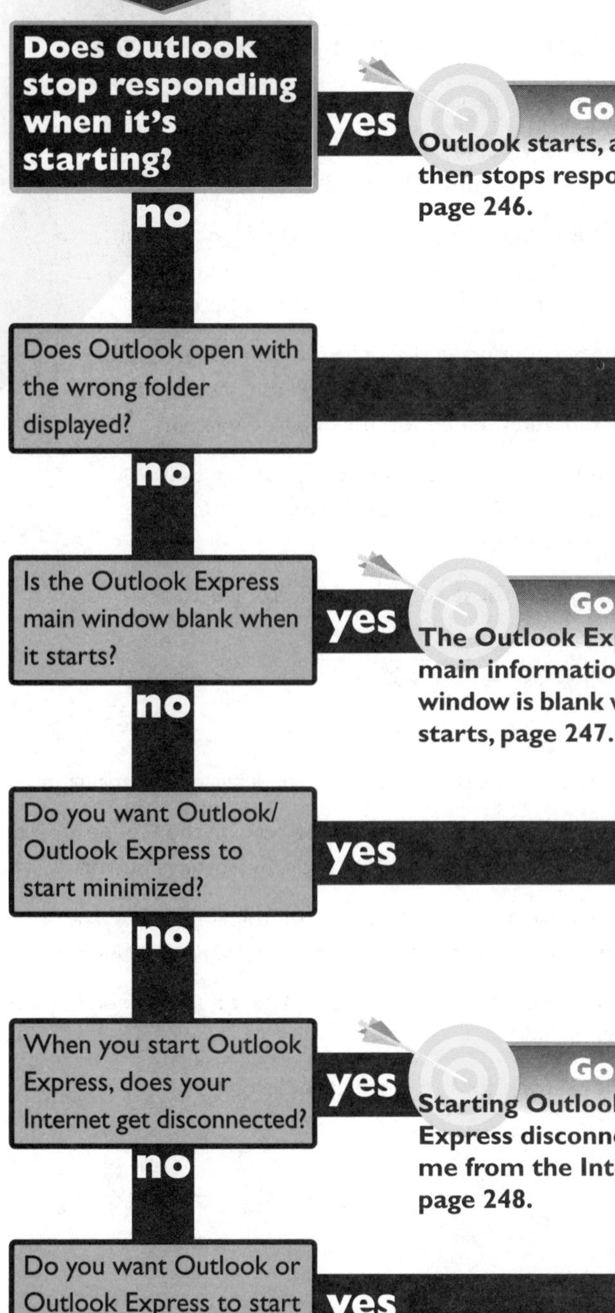

Does Outlook stop responding when it's starting?
yes
Go to...
Outlook starts, and then stops responding, page 246.
no
Does Outlook open with the wrong folder displayed?
no
Is the Outlook Express main window blank when it starts?
yes
Go to...
The Outlook Express main information window is blank when it starts, page 247.
no
Do you want Outlook/ Outlook Express to start minimized?
yes
no
When you start Outlook Express, does your Internet get disconnected?
yes
Go to...
Starting Outlook Express disconnects me from the Internet, page 248.
no
Do you want Outlook or Outlook Express to start automatically when you start Windows?
yes

### Quick fix

To specify which folder you want open when Outlook starts:

1. On the Tools menu, click Options.
2. On the Other tab, click the Advanced Options button.
3. In the Startup In This Folder box, click the folder you want to be open when Outlook starts.

### Quick fix

This start setting must be changed in the shortcut you normally use to start Outlook/Outlook Express. The shorcut can be on your desktop, or it can be in the Windows startup folder. In either case, you have to make this change in a shortcut, not in the original Outlook icon on your desktop.

1. Right-click the Outlook (or Outlook Express) shortcut, and click Properties. If you don't see the Properties command on the shortcut menu, you're clicking the main Outlook icon instead of a shortcut icon. Click the Create Shortcut command to create a shortcut, and then right-click the shortcut icon and click Properties.
2. In the Shortcut To Properties dialog box, on the Shortcut tab, in the Run list box, click Minimized.
3. Click OK.

### Go to...

**Outlook/Outlook Express doesn't start automatically, page 250.**

**If your solution isn't here**

Check the general troubleshooting tips on page xiii.

# Outlook starts, and then stops responding

## Source of the problem

You normally use Outlook with the Preview Pane open for reading e-mail messages, and when you start Outlook, the first thing you normally see is your Inbox with the first message displayed in the Preview Pane. This time, you started Outlook in your normal fashion, and Outlook stopped responding (it "hung") in the middle of startup.

This can happen if the first message in your list (the message Outlook is attempting to display in the Preview Pane) is corrupt and can't be displayed. So how do you get rid of that corrupt e-mail message if Outlook won't respond to your commands?

Start Outlook using the */nopreview* switch, which starts Outlook without the Preview Pane, and then delete the first message without opening it.

## How to fix it

1. Click the Windows Start button, and then click Run.
2. In the Open box, type the path (or click the Browse button and browse) to your *Outlook.exe* file. (The default path is **"C:\Program Files\Microsoft Office\Office\outlook.exe"**, including the quotes.)

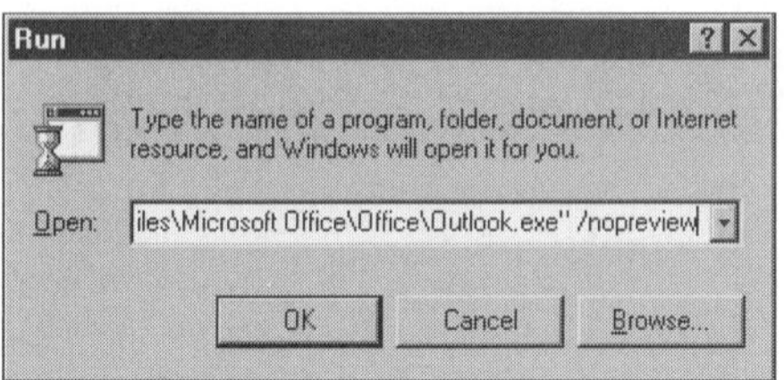


3. In the Open box, following the file name, type a space followed by **/nopreview**.
4. Click OK. Outlook starts without opening the Preview Pane.
5. Delete the first message in the Inbox.

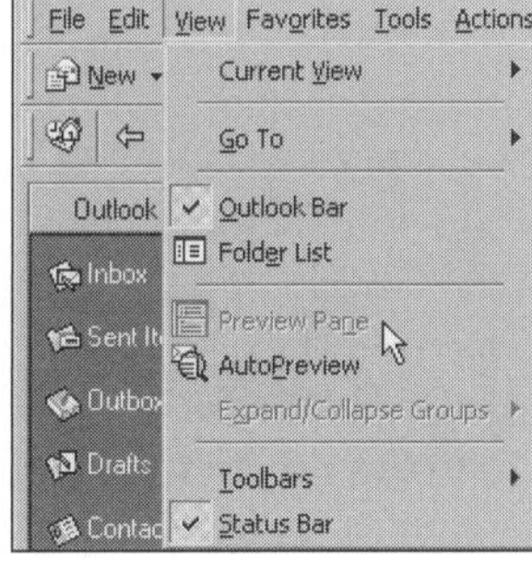


Starting Outlook with the */nopreview* switch disables the Preview Pane completely.

To make the Preview Pane command (on the View menu) available again, exit all copies of Outlook that are open and then restart Outlook normally, without using the */nopreview* switch.

# The Outlook Express main information window is blank when it starts

## Source of the problem

The Outlook Express main information window, which provides startup links to e-mail, newsgroups, and the address book, and a Tip Of The Day window, depends on Active Scripting to function.

If you disabled Active Scripting in Internet Explorer, as a security measure against *.vbs* script–borne viruses, the Outlook Express main information window can't display its information. You can change your Active Scripting to either fully Enabled or Prompt, both of which allow Outlook Express to start normally.

## How to fix it

1. If Outlook Express is running, on the File menu, click Exit.
2. Click Start, point to Settings, and click Control Panel.
3. In the Control Panel, double-click the Internet Options icon.
4. In the Internet Properties dialog box, on the Security tab, click the Custom Level button.
5. In the Security Settings dialog box, under Active Scripting, click either the Enable option or the Prompt option. ▶

   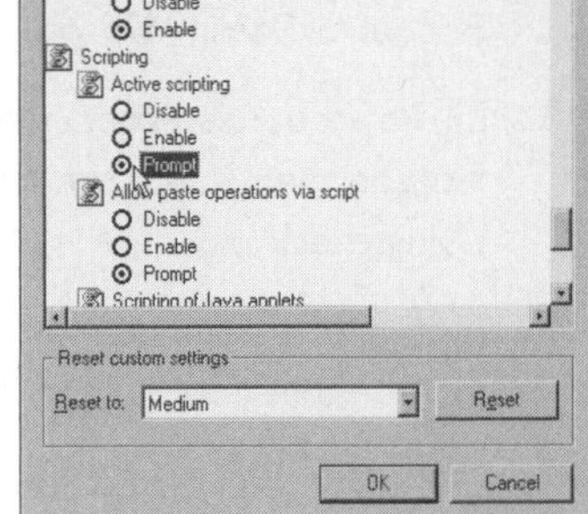
   

   If you click Enabled, Active Scripting is fully enabled for every HTML message and web page you open in any program, which can allow script-borne viruses into your computer if your anti-virus program is not fully updated and scanning everything you open. If you click Prompt, you are asked whether you want to allow scripts to run every time you open an HTML message or web page that uses Active Scripting. This can be annoying, but it's safer than running Active Scripting from untrustworthy sources.
6. When asked whether you're sure you want to change these settings, click Yes.
7. Click OK to close each open dialog box, and then close the Control Panel.

# Starting Outlook Express disconnects me from the Internet

## Source of the problem

Your Internet connection is open for browsing the web. You start Outlook Express—or perhaps Outlook Express is already open and you're trying to send and receive your e-mail—when your Internet connection is unexpectedly disconnected and a new Dial-Up Networking dialog box appears.

If the Dial-Up Networking connection for your e-mail account is different from the Internet connection you use for other reasons (such as browsing the web), the Internet connection is disconnected when you try to connect to your e-mail account. Perhaps the Internet connection for your e-mail account isn't specified in Outlook Express, or you might have upgraded to Windows 98 and your Outlook Express connection settings have been lost.

In either case, all you need to do is reset your Outlook Express connection settings.

## How to fix it

1. Start Outlook Express.
2. On the Tools menu, click Accounts, and then click the Mail tab.
3. Click the first e-mail account, and then click the Properties button. (If there isn't a mail account listed, see E-mail Accounts, Setting Up, pp xxx.)
4. In the account's Properties dialog box, click the Connection tab, and then select the Always Connect To This Account Using check box. ▶

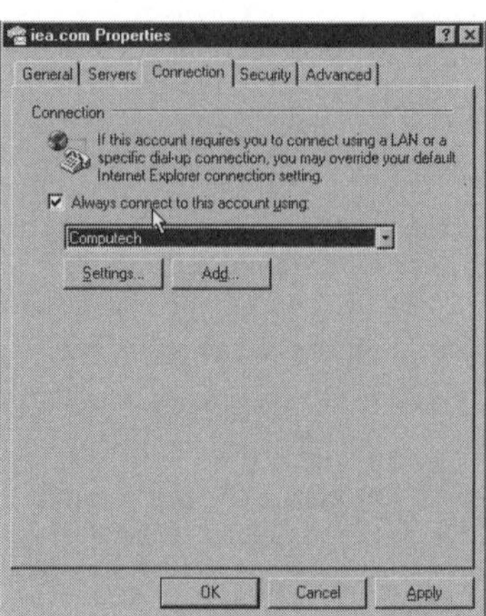


5. In the list of connections, click the Dial-Up Networking connection that you use for this mail account.
6. Click OK to return to the Internet Accounts dialog box. If you have more than one e-mail account, repeat steps 3–5 for each of them.
7. When you finish updating connections, click Close to close the Internet Accounts dialog box.

# Outlook/Outlook Express doesn't start automatically

## Source of the problem

Every day when you turn on your computer, the first thing you do is pick up your e-mail. You are a very efficient person, and having to perform that same double-click every morning seems very inefficient. Wouldn't it be great if your e-mail program could start when you turn on your computer? Well, it can—and it *is* more efficient.

## How to fix it

1. Right-click the Outlook (or Outlook Express) icon on your desktop, and click Create Shortcut.
2. Right-click the new shortcut, and click Copy.
3. Right-click the Windows Start button, and click Explore. The Windows Explorer window opens at the Start Menu folder. Click the small plus sign next to the Start Menu folder and then the small plus sign next to the Programs folder. ▶

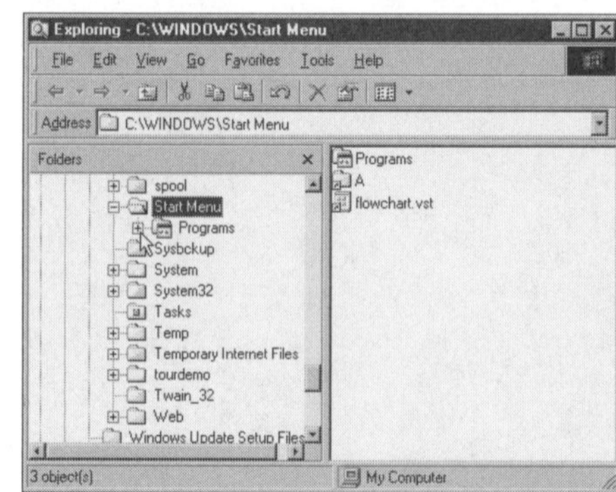

4. Click the StartUp folder icon.
5. Right-click the right pane in the Explorer, and then click Paste Shortcut. ▶

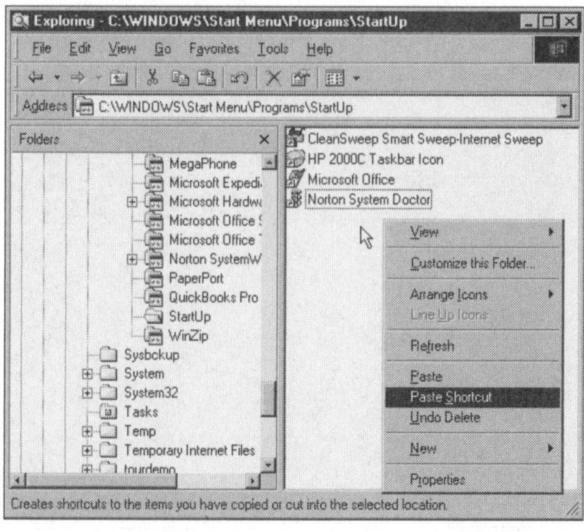

6. Close the Explorer window.

   Whenever you start Windows, Outlook (or Outlook Express) will start in a normal window.

**Tip**

You don't need the new shortcut on your desktop. Right-click the shortcut, and click Delete. When you're asked whether you're sure you want to send the shortcut to the Recycle Bin, click Yes.

# Switchi

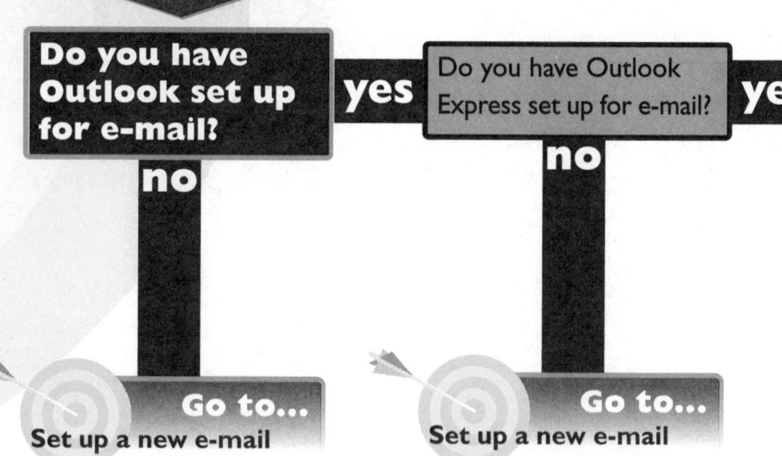
Do you have Outlook set up for e-mail?
yes
Do you have Outlook Express set up for e-mail?
yes
no
no
Go to...
Set up a new e-mail account, page 114.
Go to...
Set up a new e-mail account, page 114.

**If your solution isn't here**
Check these related chapters:
E-mail accounts, page 108
E-mail, addressing messages, page 40
E-mail, importing addresses page 68
Or see the general troubleshooting tips on page xiii.

g e-mail programs

Do you need to have Outlook Express share e-mail addresses?

yes

Are you running Outlook in Internet Mail Only configuration?

yes

**Quick fix**

Outlook in Internet Mail Only configuration can share the address book with Outlook Express, so all the contacts in all of Outlook 2000's Contacts folders are included in the Outlook Express Address Book.

1. Open Outlook Express.
2. On the Tools menu, click Address Book.
3. In the Address Book, click Tools and then Options.
4. In the Options dialog box, click the Share Contact Information option.
5. Click OK.

no

**Quick fix**

If you use Outlook in Corporate/Workgroup configuration, you can periodically import addresses from either program into the other. For more help, see the chapter E-mail, Importing Addresses.

no

Do you want to use Outlook when you send mail through your Web browser or a Web page?

yes

**Quick fix**

To make Outlook the default e-mail program:

1. Open Internet Explorer.
2. Click Tools | Internet.
3. On the Programs tab, in the E-mail list box, select Microsoft Outlook.
4. Click OK.

no

**Quick fix**

To make Outlook Express the default e-mail program:

1. Open Outlook Express.
2. On the Tools menu, click Options.
3. On the General tab, under Default Messaging Programs, click the Make Default button.
4. Click OK.

# Outlook and Outlook Express have different address lists

## Source of the problem

If you use both Outlook and Outlook Express, it's inefficient to have two separate sets of e-mail addresses, because it seems that no matter which program you're using to create a message, the e-mail address you need is sure to be in the other program!

Fortunately, Outlook 2000 in Internet Mail Only configuration can share address books with Outlook Express. All the contacts you enter in any of Outlook 2000's Contacts folders and subfolders are included in the Outlook Express Address Book, and all the contacts you enter in the Outlook Express Address Book can be found in the Outlook Contacts folders and subfolders.

**Tip**

If you're using Outlook in Corporate/Workgroup configuration, see the solution to "Outlook won't share addresses with Outlook Express," on page 256.

## How to fix it

1. Start Outlook Express.
2. On the Tools menu, click Address Book.
3. In the Address Book, on the Tools menu, click Options. ▶
4. In the Options dialog box, click the Share Contact Information option. ▶
5. Click OK.

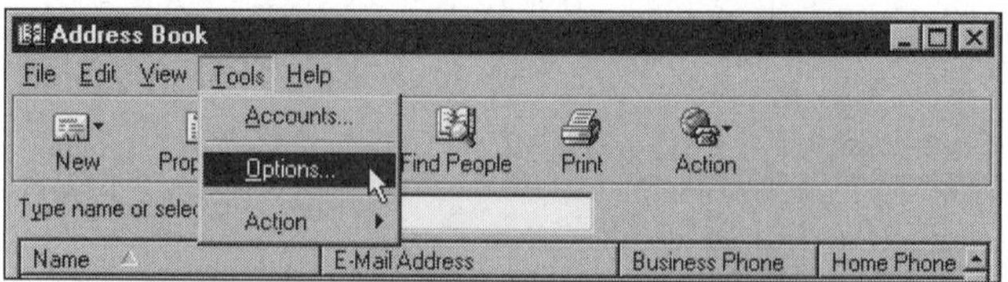


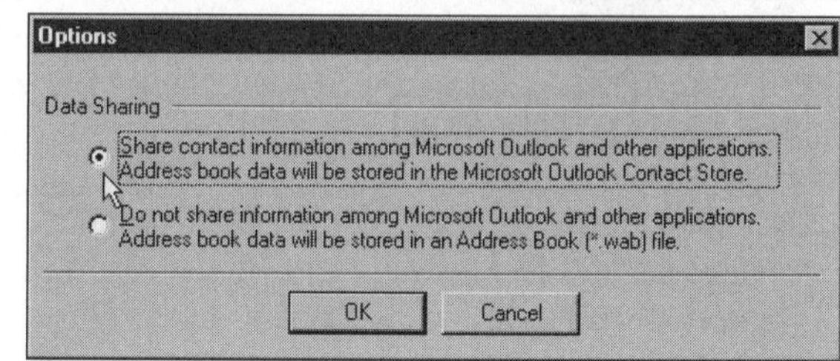

## If you want to know more about shared addresses

When Outlook (in Internet Mail Only configuration) and Outlook Express share contact information, all their contact information is kept in one place—Outlook's Contacts storage area, which is called the Microsoft Outlook Contact Store. The contacts are sorted into the main Contacts folder and any Contacts subfolders you create in Outlook.

If you're wondering how to use, or even see, your Contacts subfolders in Outlook Express, this is how:

1. In Outlook Express, open the Address Book (either click the Address Book button on the toolbar, or click Address Book on the Tools menu).
2. In the Address Book, on the View menu, click Folders And Groups. ▶
3. A list of your Contacts folders and subfolders appears, as shown in the lower-right figure. Click the name of the folder you want to open, and then double-click the name of the contact you want to open.

**Tip**

You can't create or delete Contacts subfolders from within Outlook Express, but whatever changes you make to Outlook's Contacts folders appear immediately in Outlook Express.

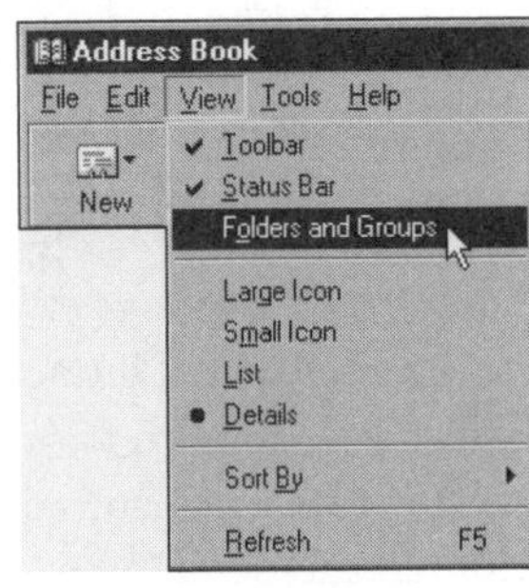


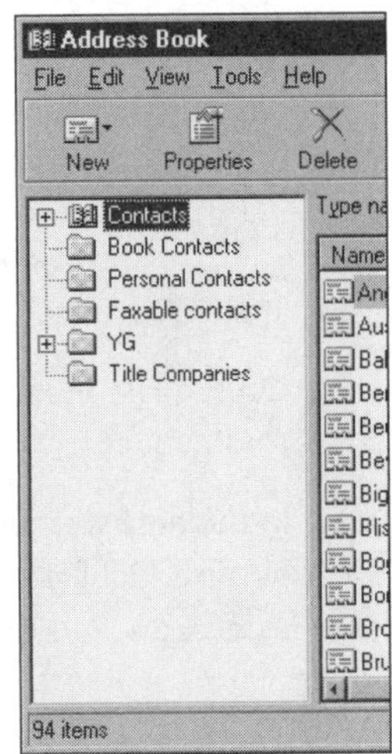


**Tip**

In the Outlook Express Address Book, you can add information (such as names of a contact's children) that you can't add in the Outlook Contacts dialog box. But you can find and use that information in Outlook by switching your Contacts folder to a table-type view and adding the field you want to see to the view.

To add a field to the view, right-click in the row of column headings, and then click Field Chooser. In the box at the top of the Field Chooser, click a category of fields (you'll find Children in the Personal category). Then drag the field you want from the Field Chooser and drop it in the row of column headings. Close the Field Chooser by clicking its close box.

When you're creating a new message in Outlook Express, and you need to send the message to a contact in a subfolder, click the To button in the message. In the Select Recipients dialog box, in the box above the contact names, select the subfolder where you've stored the specific contact's name. Double-click the contact's name to add it to the To box in the message, and continue with your new message.

# Outlook won't share addresses with Outlook Express

## Source of the problem

If you're using Outlook in Corporate/Workgroup configuration, you can't share e-mail addresses between Outlook and Outlook Express. But if you need to have all your e-mail addresses available in both programs, you can periodically import addresses from one program to the other.

Importing contact information into the Outlook Contacts folder from Outlook Express is straightforward, and Outlook's Import And Export Wizard guides you through the process. If you need to go in the other direction—importing contact information into Outlook Express from your Outlook Contacts folder—you must first save the Contacts folder as a text file and then import the text file into Outlook Express.

## How to fix it

### Export contacts from Outlook Express

1. Start Outlook.
2. On the File menu, click Import And Export.
3. In the first step of the Import And Export Wizard, highlight Import Internet Mail And Addresses, and then click Next. ▶
4. In the second wizard step, click Outlook Express 4.x, 5.

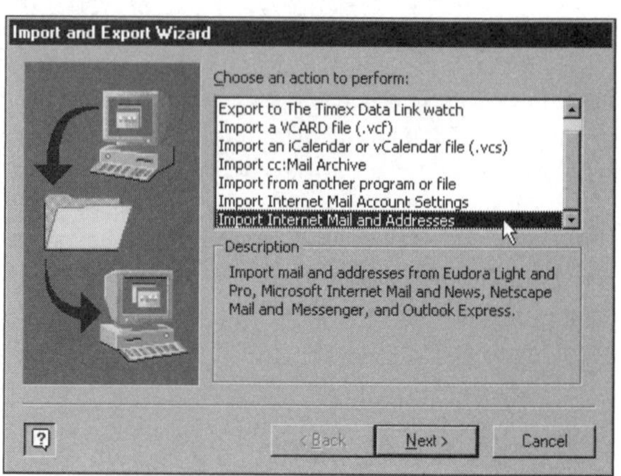

5. Select the Import Address Book check box, and clear the Import Mail and Import Rules dialog boxes. Then click Next. ▶

6. In the third wizard step, click the Outlook Contacts Folder option, and click a duplicates option. Then click Finish.

   Your contacts are imported from Outlook Express into your main Contacts folder in Outlook. After the import process is complete, an Import Summary message tells you how many addresses were imported (if you selected the Do Not Import Duplicates option, some addresses might not be imported).

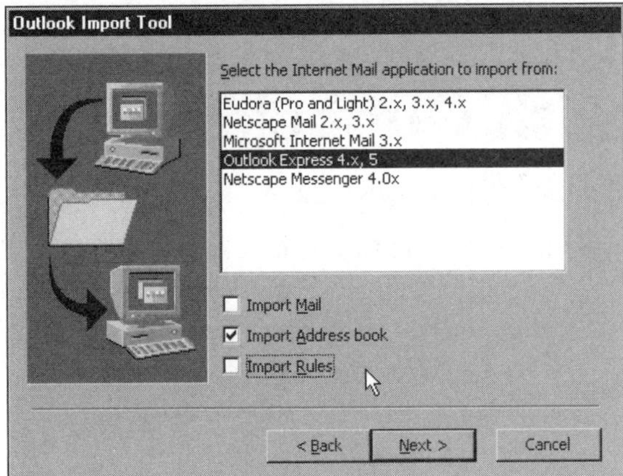


**Tip**

The duplicates option you choose depends on what you need. If you want to compare the information between contact entries in the two programs, click the Allow Duplicates To Be Created option. If you know you're importing more current information, click the Replace Duplicates With Items Imported option. If you import contacts from Outlook Express regularly, click the Do Not Import Duplicates option so that only new contacts will be imported.

## Export contacts from Outlook

1. Start Outlook.
2. On the File menu, click Import And Export.
3. In the Import And Export Wizard dialog box, select Export To A File, and then click Next.
4. In the first Export To A File dialog box, select Comma Separated Values (Windows), and then click Next. ▶

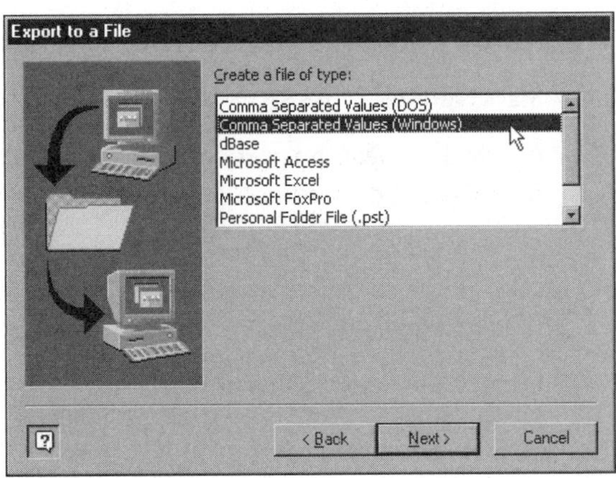


*If this solution didn't solve your problem, go to the next page.*

# Outlook won't share addresses with Outlook Express

*(continued from page 257)*

5. In the second Export To A File dialog box, select the Contacts folder or subfolder you want to export items from, and then click Next. You must create a separate text file for each Contacts folder or subfolder you want to export. ▶

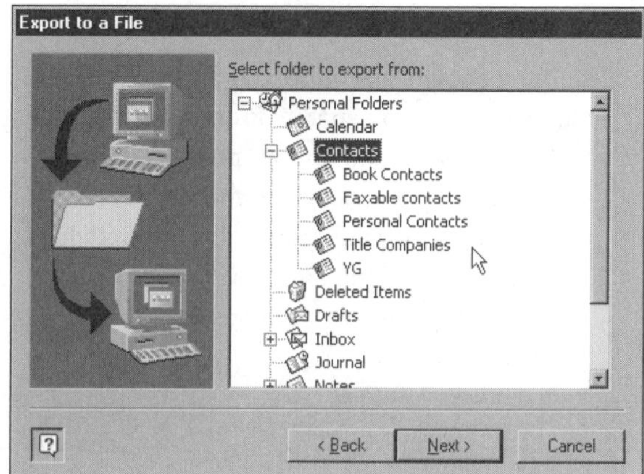


6. In the third Export To A File dialog box, click the Browse button and navigate to a folder where you want to save the text file (make it an easy-to-locate folder so you can find it quickly later).
7. In the Browse dialog box, give the text file a name in the File Name box, and then click OK.
8. Again in the third Export To A File dialog box, click Next.
9. In the final Export To A File dialog box, click Finish.

The text file is created. Next, you import the new Contacts text file into Outlook Express.

## Import contacts into Outlook Express

1. Start Outlook Express.
2. On the File menu, point to Import, and then click Other Address Book.
3. In the Address Book Import Tool dialog box, select Text File (Comma Separated Values), and then click Import. ▶

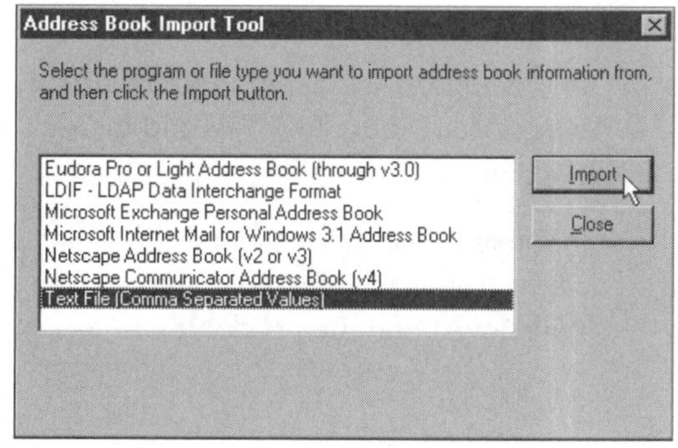


4. In the CSV Import dialog box, click the Browse button.

5. In the Open dialog box, navigate to the folder where you saved the text file earlier.
6. Select the text file, and then click Open.
7. Again in the CSV Import dialog box, click Next.
8. In the next CSV Import dialog box, choose which data fields to import. If you want to import all the data in the Contacts folder, click the Finish button. If you want to limit the imported data (for example, if you want to import only names and phone numbers), clear the check boxes for the fields you don't want, and then click Finish. ▶

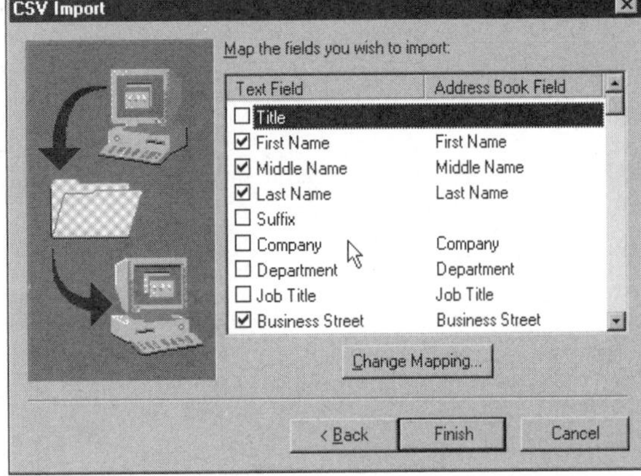


9. When you see an Address Book message that says the import process has completed, click OK.
10. In the Address Book Import Tool dialog box, click Close.

All the contacts in the folder you selected for importing are in the Outlook Express Address Book, ready to use.

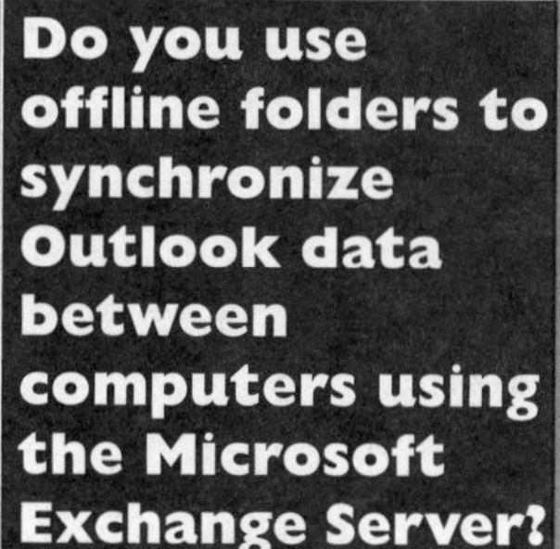

**Do you use offline folders to synchronize Outlook data between computers using the Microsoft Exchange Server?**

yes

no

Do you use Net Folders to synchronize Outlook data between computers?

yes

**If your solution isn't here**
Check the general troubleshooting tips on page xiii.

Are you logging on to the Windows and your local area network correctly?

yes

**Go to...**

**My offline folders aren't synchronizing correctly, page 266.**

no

**Quick fix**

When you turn on your computer and Windows starts, be sure you type your password and click OK. If you click Cancel in the Windows start-up dialog box, Windows will start but you won't be logged onto your computer profile, and you won't have access to your offline folders, file, and passwords list. When you want to synchronize, make sure you're logged on to your local area network; otherwise you won't have access to your Exchange Server mailbox, and you won't be able to synchronize.

Are your subscriber invitations being processed?

yes

Are you getting an error message when you update Net Folders?

yes

**Go to...**

**My Net Folders aren't updating correctly, page 262.**

no

**Quick fix**

If you use Outlook in the Corporate/Workgroup configuration, it's important that an invitation to a subscriber be sent in Rich Text format. Rich Text format sends the invitation with Accept and Decline buttons, and when the new subscriber clicks one of those buttons, your Outlook is able to process the response to the invitation and set up the Net Folders dialog between the folder owner and folder subscriber.

To fix it:

1. In your contact dialog box for the subscriber, double-click the e-mail address.
2. Select the Always Send To This Recipient In Microsoft Outlook Rich Text Format check box.
3. Run the Net Folders Wizard again, using the subscriber contact you just updated.

# My Net Folders aren't updating correctly

## Source of the problem

You and your business partners each work at home, so you can't share a network. But you found a way to share and synchronize Outlook information almost as if you are on a network: you use Net Folders to send Outlook synchronization updates through e-mail.

But lately you've been getting an error message telling you that, for one reason or another, Net Folders is nonfunctional. It's probably something simple and easy to fix.

## How to fix it

This solution covers four common Net Folders error messages. If none of these is the error message you get, visit the Microsoft Knowledge Base and search for a solution to your error message.

### Error message: "Net Folders is unable to send out updates to your folders due to an error. One probable cause is that you have exceeded your server quota."

The shared net folder has exceeded Outlook's 2 MB folder size limitation. You need to reduce the size of the folder. To check the size of the shared net folder:

1. In the Outlook bar or the Folder list, right-click the shared folder.
2. Click Properties.
3. On the General tab, click the Folder Size button.

   The folder size, which includes all the subfolders in the folder, is shown at the top of the dialog box. ▶

4. Close all open dialog boxes.

   You can reduce the size of the shared folder by removing unnecessary subfolders, archiving old data, or removing unnecessary data.

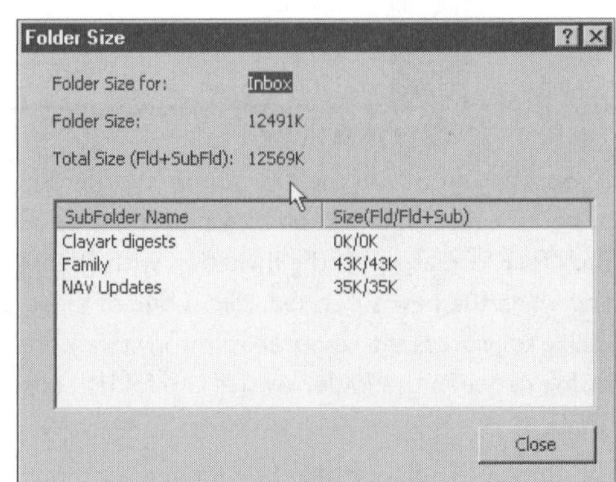

## Error message: "This task cannot be processed at this time."

Net Folder subscriptions cannot be processed if the subscriber's Personal Folders file (where the Net Folders update is delivered) is password-protected. The subscriber needs to remove the password from the shared Personal Folders file.

1. Open the Folder list.
2. Right-click the Outlook Today-Personal Folders file, and click Properties For Personal Folders. ▶

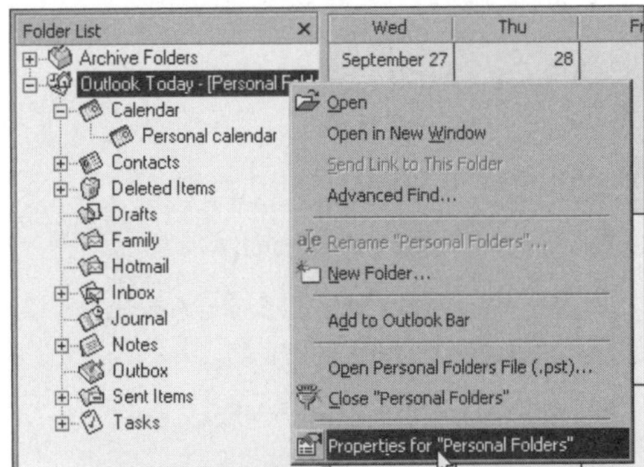


3. On the General tab, click the Advanced button.
4. Click the Change Password button. ▶

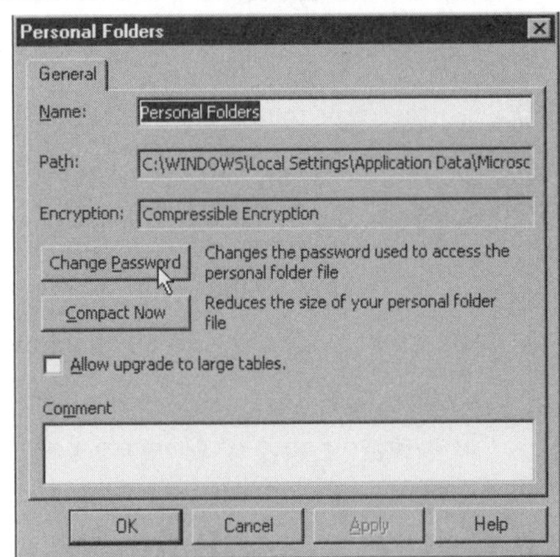


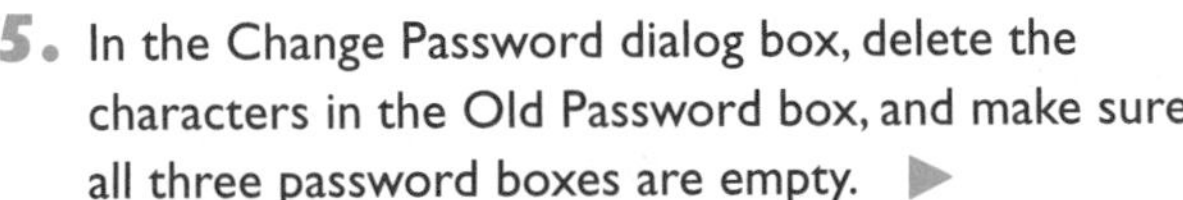

5. In the Change Password dialog box, delete the characters in the Old Password box, and make sure all three password boxes are empty. ▶

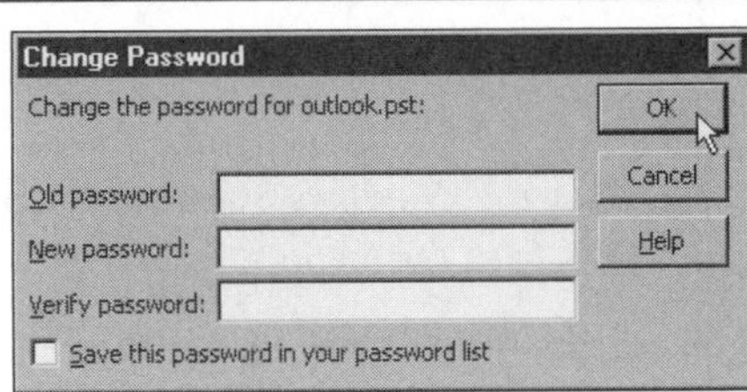


6. Click OK three times to close all the dialog boxes.

## Error message: "The command is not available. See the program documentation about how to use this extension."

Net Folders depends on the Net Folders add-in (which the error message calls an "extension") and a functional Rules Wizard file. Problems with the add-in or Rules Wizard file can cause this error, but you can usually fix this problem by resetting the add-in. If resetting the Net Folders add-in doesn't fix it, the next step to try is replacing the Rules Wizard file.

***If this solution didn't solve your problem, go to the next page.***

# My net folders aren't updating correctly

*(continued from page 263)*

## Reset the add-in

1. On the Tools menu, click Options.
2. On the Other tab, click the Advanced Options button, and then click the Add-In Manager button.
3. Clear the Net Folders check box. ▶

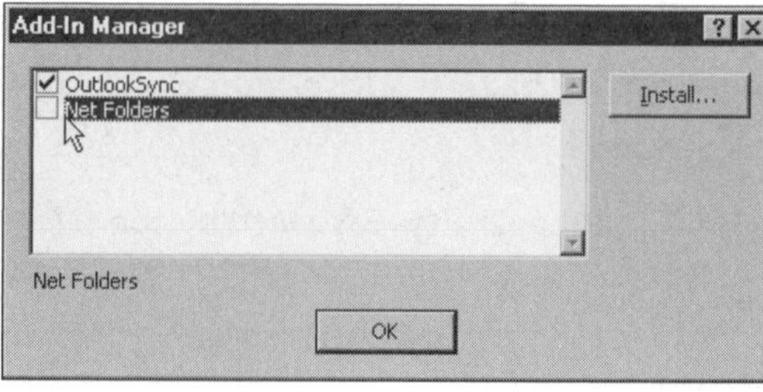


4. Click OK twice to close the dialog boxes.
5. Quit Outlook, and then restart Outlook.
6. On the Tools menu, click Options.
7. On the Other tab, click the Advanced Options button, and then click Add-In Manager.
8. Select the Net Folders check box.
9. Click OK twice to close the dialog boxes.

If resetting the add-in doesn't fix your Net Folders, you might have a damaged Rules Wizard file. To fix it, you need to generate a new rules file.

## Generate a new Rules Wizard file

Generating a new Rules Wizard file wipes out all your existing rules.

1. Click the Windows Start button, point to Find, and click Files Or Folders.
2. In the Named box, type ***.rwz**. ▶

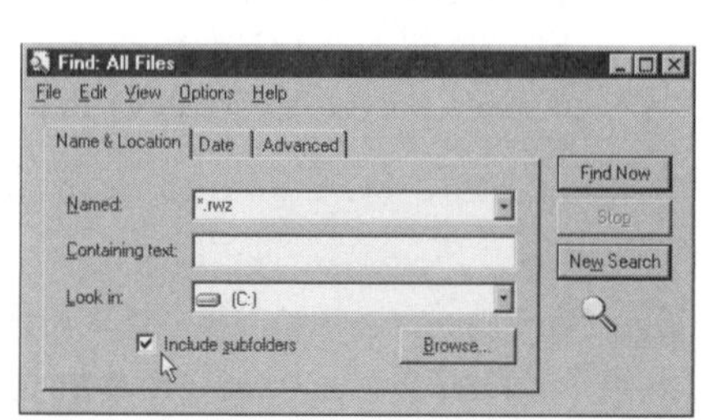


3. Be sure you're searching your entire hard disk, and click the Find Now button.

   The active Rules Wizard file is the one in your current profile path. ▶

4. Right-click the icon for the current file, and click Rename.
5. Replace the extension *rwz* with **old**, and press Enter. ▶

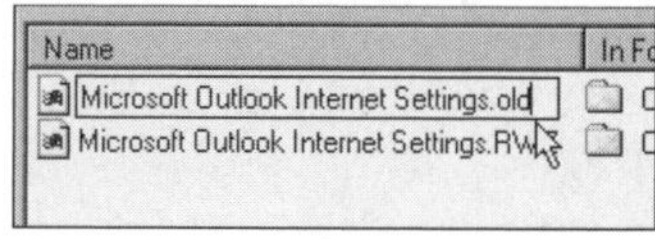

6. Close the Find Files dialog box.

7. To reset the Net Folders add-in again, repeat the steps in the previous section, "Reset the add-in." .

All your existing rules are gone, along with the potentially corrupt Rules Wizard file; however, when you create your first new rule, a new Rules Wizard file is created. If generating a new Rules Wizard file doesn't fix your Net Folders problem, you can recover your old Rules Wizard file by deleting the new Rules Wizard file (with the extension *.rwz*) and then searching for files named **.old*. When you locate the original Rules Wizard file you renamed in steps 4 and 5, change its extension back to **rwz** and all your old rules will work again.

## Error message: "The Net Folder which is administered by <folder owner> is no longer sending you updates. If you have any questions, please contact the administrator of this net folder."

You might get this error because your ISP or one of your subscribers' ISPs has turned off Autoreplies to the Internet at the mail server. (Some ISPs turn off this feature to cut down on the propagation of e-mail viruses.)

You can find out whether Autoreplies is turned off at one of the ISPs between you and your subscribers by sending a read receipt request to your subscribers.

1. Create a new message, addressed to all your subscribers. Tell them that you need to receive read receipts from them.

   If they have read receipt responses turned off, they need to turn responses on and let you know so you can resend this message to them.

2. In the new message, on the File menu, click Properties.

3. Select the Read Receipt Requested check box. ▶

4. Click OK, and send the message.

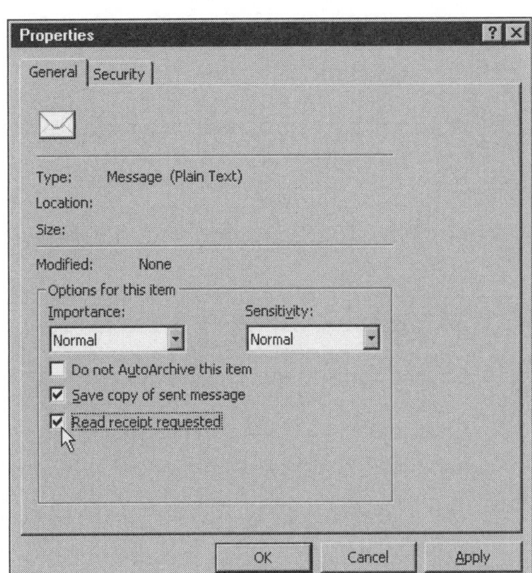


If you don't get a read receipt from one or more subscribers, the subscriber's ISP might have Autoreplies turned off. If you don't get a read receipt from any subscribers, your ISP might have Autoreplies turned off. Contact the suspect ISP to ask whether Autoreplies can be turned on for a specific account.

# My offline folders aren't synchronizing correctly

## Source of the problem

You use Outlook on a corporate network that uses the Microsoft Exchange Server as the mail server. You know Outlook is set up to use offline folders and to synchronize those offline folders, but lately it seems as if your synchronization is not working correctly. There are several possible reasons why your offline folders might not be synchronizing. The best way to figure out what's wrong is to start with the easiest solution and work through different solutions until the problem is fixed.

## How to fix it

Work through these troubleshooting procedures one-by-one to see whether you can find and fix the problem yourself. If, after you work through the procedures in this solution, synchronization still doesn't work, see your network administrator.

Items you'll check in these procedures include:

- Profile and delivery settings
- Automatic synchronization settings
- Potential damage to offline folders
- Potential damage to Exchange Server support files

### Profile and delivery settings

1. On the Tools menu, click Services.
2. On the Services tab, be sure that your profile includes Microsoft Exchange Server. ▶
3. On the Delivery tab, in the Deliver New Mail To The Following Location box, be sure you see "Mailboxes — <*your account name*>."

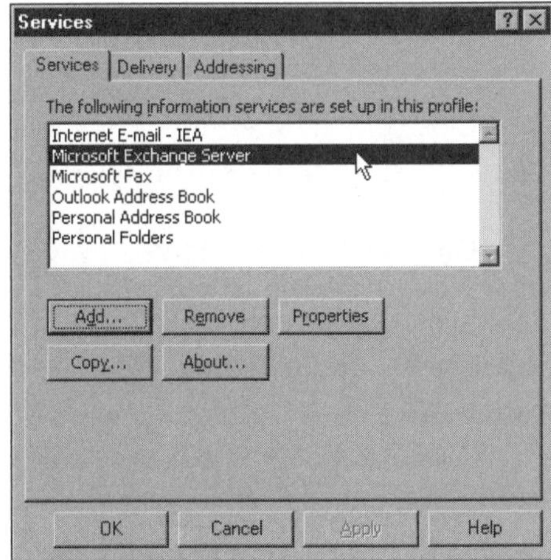

If your profile doesn't include Microsoft Exchange Server, or your mail is not delivered to the correct mailbox, make these changes and see whether your synchronization problems are solved. If not, move on to the next procedure in the checklist.

## Automatic synchronization settings

1. On the Tools menu, click Options.
2. On the Mail Services tab, select the Enable Offline Access check box.
3. Select the When Online, Synchronize With All Folders Upon Exiting check box.

These check boxes set Outlook to synchronize all offline folders every time you go online and every time you quit Outlook. If these check boxes are not marked, select them and see whether your synchronization problems are solved. If not, move on to the next procedure in the checklist.

## Potential damage to offline folders

Your problem might be a damaged offline folder (*.ost*) file. To fix a damaged file, you replace it with a new one.

1. Quit any open programs.
2. Click the Windows Start button, point to Find, and click Files Or Folders.
3. In the Named box, type ***.ost**.
4. Be sure you're searching your entire hard disk, and click the Find Now button. ▶

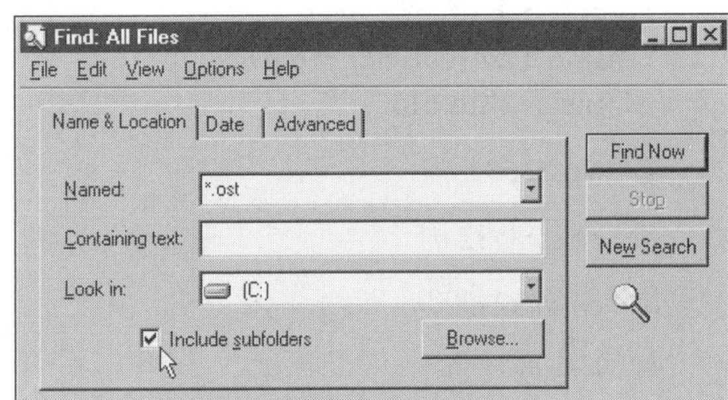


5. Right-click the *.ost* file icon, and click Rename.
6. Replace the extension *ost* with **old**, and press Enter.
7. Close the Find Files dialog box.
8. Start Outlook.
9. On the Tools menu, point to Synchronize, and click All Folders.

Synchronizing all folders (as in step 9) creates a new offline folder (*.ost*) file. You won't lose or damage any information doing this, because your offline folder file is just a replication of the information that's stored in your Exchange Server mailbox.

***If this solution didn't solve your problem, go to the next page.***

# My offline folders aren't synchronizing correctly

*(continued from page 267)*

If this fixes your synchronization problems, great—stop here. If not, move on to the last procedure in the checklist.

**Tip**

If you want to clean up your hard disk, feel free to delete the old offline folder file (the one you renamed **.old**).

## Potential damage to Exchange Server support files

If you still can't synchronize your offline files, you might be working with damaged Microsoft Exchange Server support files. To fix this, you remove your Exchange Server support files and replace the deleted files with fresh Outlook files by reinstalling Office 2000.

1. Click the Windows Start button, point to Programs, and click Windows Explorer.
2. Navigate to the Windows\System folder. ▶
3. Locate each of these files, and rename it by replacing the *dll* extension with **old**.

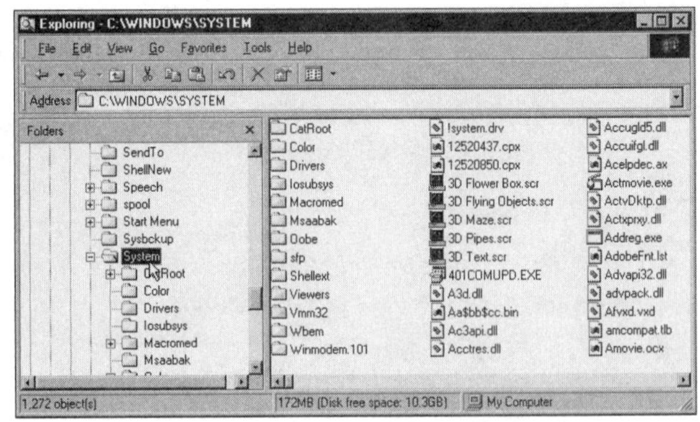


- *emsabp32.dll*
- *emsmdb32.dll*
- *emsui32.dll*
- *emsuix32.dll*

When you rename a file with a new extension, your programs won't be able

**Tip**

To rename a file, either right-click the file and click Rename, or click the file name twice (not a double-click).

to find and use that file, but the file will still be in your system. If you need to reinstall the file, all you have to do is replace the original extension in the file name.

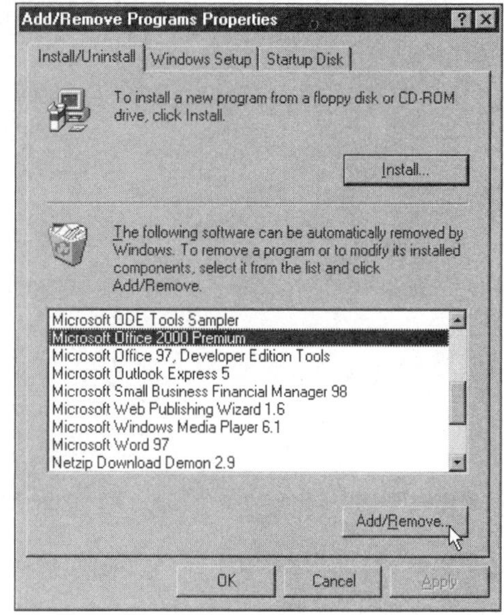


4. Click the Windows Start button, point to Settings, and click Control Panel.
5. In the Control Panel, double-click Add/Remove Programs.
6. In the Add/Remove Programs dialog box, on the Install/Uninstall tab, click Microsoft Office 2000, and click Add/Remove.
7. In the Microsoft Office 2000 Maintenance Mode dialog box, click the Repair Office icon.
8. In the Reinstall/Repair Microsoft Office 2000 dialog box, click the Reinstall Office option, and click Finish.

If this fixes your synchronization problems, terrific. If not, contact your network administrator. Your synchronization problem might be something your network administrator needs to fix.

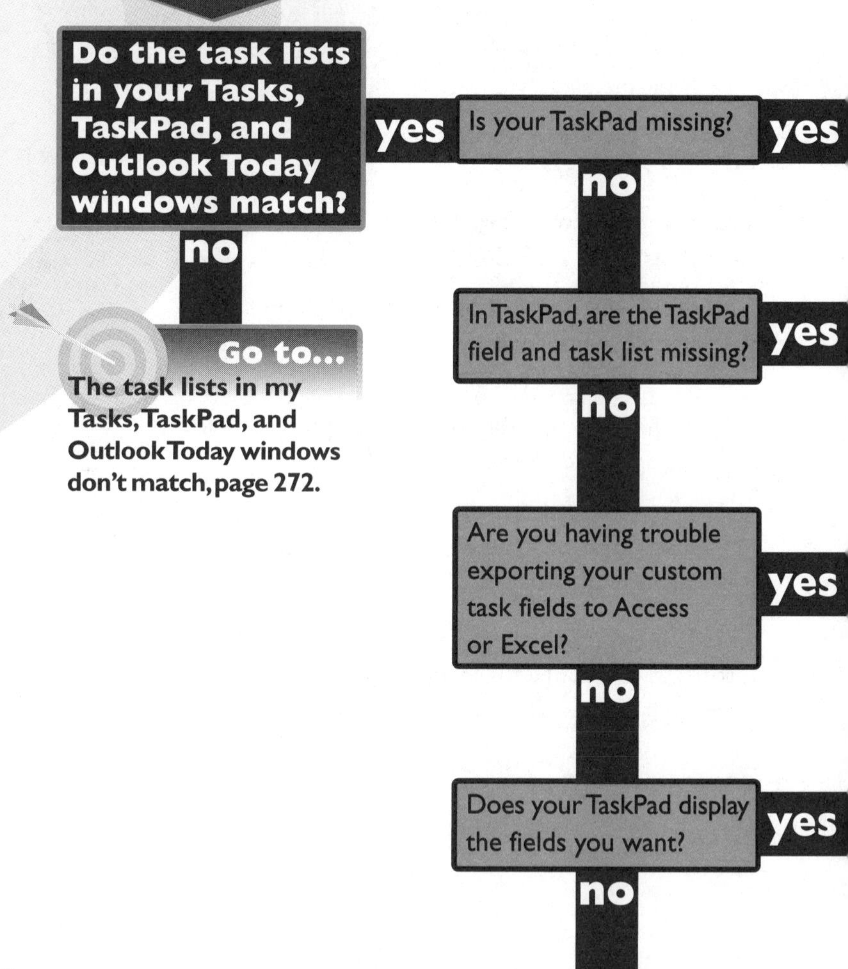
Do the task lists in your Tasks, TaskPad, and Outlook Today windows match?
yes
no
Is your TaskPad missing?
yes
no
In TaskPad, are the TaskPad field and task list missing?
yes
no
Are you having trouble exporting your custom task fields to Access or Excel?
yes
no
Does your TaskPad display the fields you want?
yes
no

**Go to...**

**The task lists in my Tasks, TaskPad, and Outlook Today windows don't match, page 272.**

## Quick fix

1. Click in the TaskPad's column headings, click Field Chooser.
2. In the list box at the top of the Field Chooser, select a category of fields. The category All Task Fields contains all the appropriate fields for the TaskPad.
3. From the Field Chooser, drag a field name button to the TaskPad and drop it on the row of TaskPad column headings.
4. Close the Field Chooser by clicking its X close button.

# asks and TaskPad

**Go to...**

**The Calendar is not showing the TaskPad, page 14.**

**Go to...**

**In TaskPad, the TaskPad field and task list are missing, page 274.**

**Go to...**

**I can't export custom fields to an Access database, page 166.**

Do you want to change the column labels in your TaskPad or Tasks folder?

**yes**

**Quick fix**

1. Right-click the column label you don't like, and click Format Columns.
2. In the Format Columns dialog box, in the Label box, type the column label you would rather have.
3. Click OK.

**If your solution isn't here**
Check these related chapters:
Importing and exporting, page 162
Calendar, page 10
Or see the general troubleshooting tips on page xiii.

# The task lists in my Tasks, TaskPad, and Outlook Today windows don't match

## Source of the problem

The task lists in your TaskPad, Outlook Today window, and main Tasks folder are all the same list. If you see different lists, it's because you have different views and possibly filters displayed in those windows.

Even though it's useful to be able to maintain different task lists in these different tasks folders (for example, you might want to display only your most critical tasks in the TaskPad and Outlook Today task list, but display all your tasks in the main Tasks folder), it's disconcerting and misleading if you don't see the list you expect.

**Tip**

The Outlook Today window and TaskPad display tasks from only the main Tasks folder. They won't display tasks from any tasks subfolders you create.

## How to fix it

Each task list offers a slightly different set of built-in views and a slightly different technique for choosing the view you want.

### Change the Tasks folder view

In the main Tasks folder, or Tasks subfolders you create, you can choose built-in views, customize existing views, and create new views.

- On the View menu, point to Current View, and click a view from the list of views available. ▶

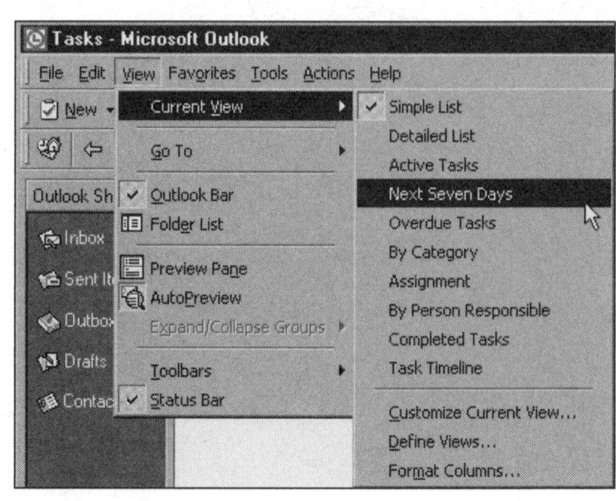


- If you want to alter an existing view, click Customize Current View instead. In the View Summary dialog box, make changes to the view that's currently displayed.
- If you want to create a new custom view, click Define Views instead. In the Define Views dialog box, click the New button, type a name for the new view and click Table, and then build your new view in the View Summary dialog box.

## Change the TaskPad view

In the TaskPad, you can select from among only a handful of built-in views.

1. Open the Calendar, and be sure the TaskPad is displayed.
2. On the view menu, point to TaskPad view, and click a built-in view. ▶

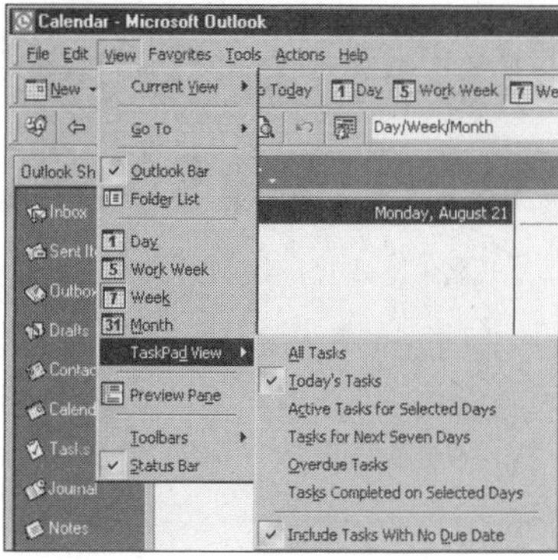


## Change the Outlook Today task view

In the Outlook Today window, you can select from among only a handful of built-in views for your task list.

1. Open the Outlook Today window.
2. Click the Customize Outlook Today button. ▶
3. In the Customize Outlook Today window, under Tasks, click options for what you want to display in the Outlook Today tasks list.

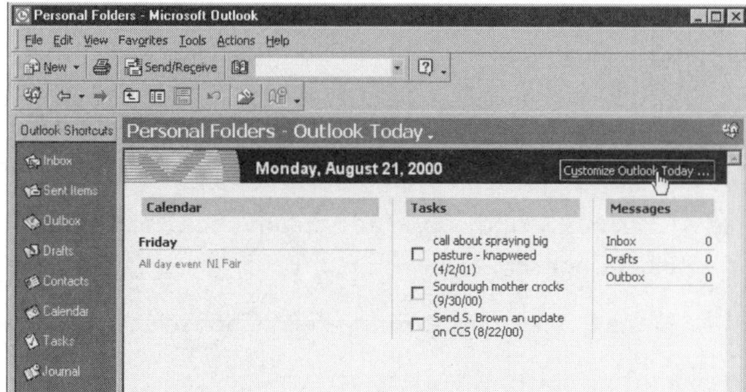


4. Click the Save Changes button. ▶

   The Outlook Today window returns, with your new tasks view displayed.

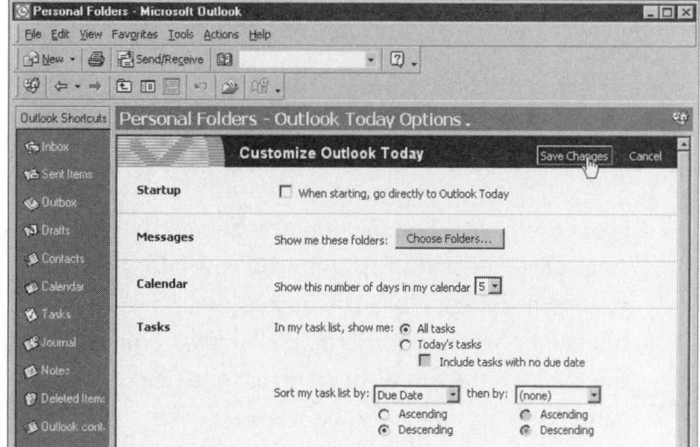

# In TaskPad, the TaskPad field and task list are missing

## Source of the problem

You've been clicking and dragging in the Calendar, learning how to change and customize your Calendar view, and you've inadvertently lost your task list by dragging the field out of the row of TaskPad field labels. No problem—it's easy to replace the missing field.

**Tip**

The trick here is the field label, TaskPad. It's really the Subject field, with an altered label.

## How to fix it

1. Open the Calendar in Daily or Weekly view so that TaskPad is displayed.
2. Click in any of the TaskPad's column headings, and then click Field Chooser.
3. In the box at the top of the Field Chooser, click All Task Fields. ▶

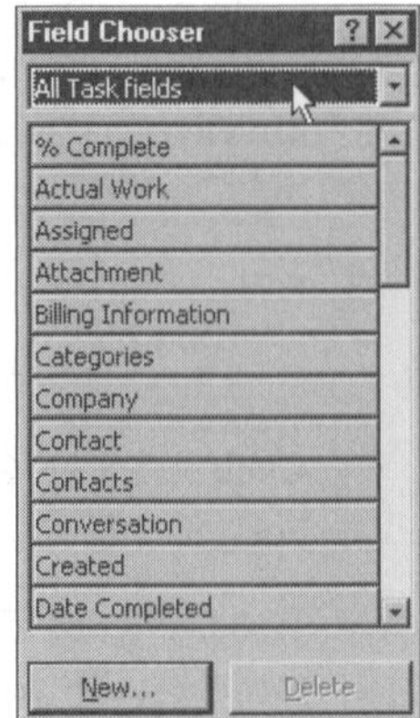


4. From the Field Chooser, drag the Subject button to the TaskPad and drop it on the row of TaskPad column headings. Move the button along the row of column headings until the red arrows point to the spot where you want to insert the field name. ▶

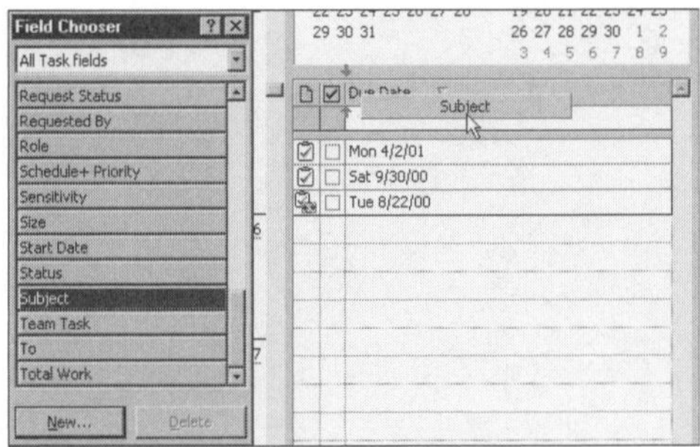

5. Close the Field Chooser by clicking its X close button.

   When you drop the subject Field, it doesn't immediately look like your original TaskPad field, because the TaskPad field is, in reality, the Subject field with an altered label.

6. Right-click the Subject heading button, and click Format Columns.

7. In the Format Columns dialog box, in the Label box, highlight the word Subject, and type the word **TaskPad** to replace it. ▶

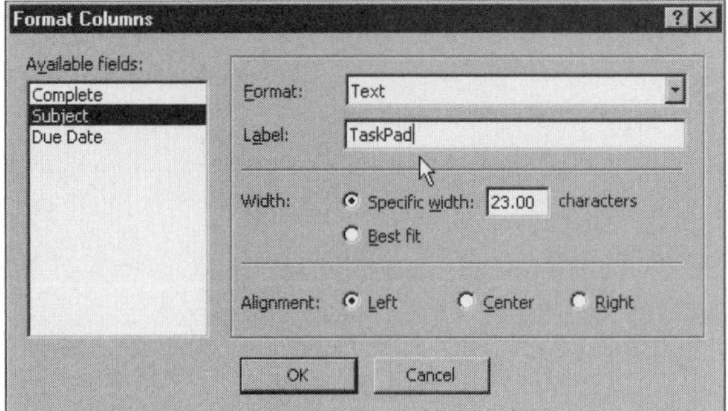


8. Click OK.

   Now your TaskPad looks the way it did when you first installed Outlook.

## If you want to know more about Tasks displays

Task items usually need notes in the Notes field, such as a phone number or an order quantity, to remind you of exactly what that task entails. You can use the Field Chooser to display the Notes field in your Tasks window, but the Notes field displays only four or five words of your note. A more useful way to display your Notes is to turn on AutoPreview in the folder display.

Right-click in an empty space in the Tasks window and click AutoPreview. Every task that has notes recorded will display up to three lines of notes in blue type in that task row. ▶

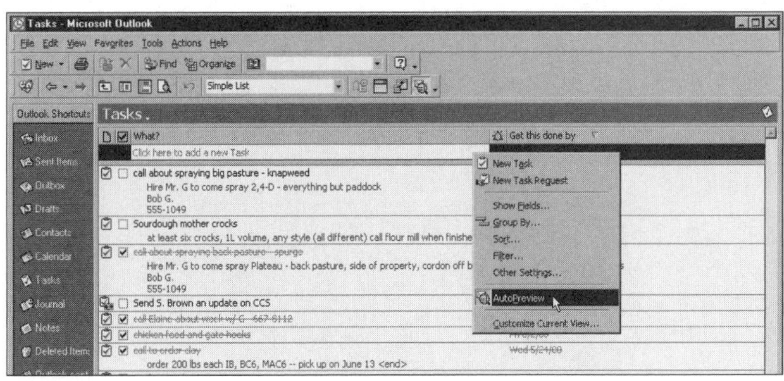

# Index

## F

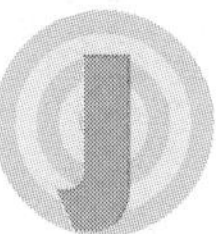

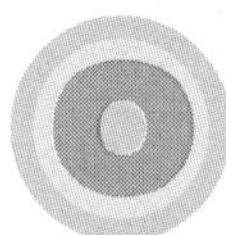

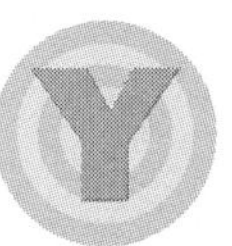

# About the author

Julia Kelly, cybergirl in cowspace, ex-jet jockey, and former mad scientist, has also done time as a stable cleaner, hardware-store cashier/barrista, theme park candy girl, veterinary cat-holder, Caribbean pilot, graduate student, and teacher of diverse topics.

She currently lives on her farm in north Idaho, where she writes books, teaches classes, builds databases, and shovels snow. When she's not at her computer, she's escaping from electrons in her pottery studio, barn, or garden.

The manuscript for this book was prepared and galleyed using Microsoft Word 2000. Pages were composed using Adobe PageMaker 6.52 with text in ACaslon Regular and display type in Gill Sans Composed pages were delivered to the printer as electronic prepress files.

**Cover designer**

Landor Associates

**Interior graphic designer**

James D. Kramer

**Principal compositors**

Jimmie Young
Robert Place

**Principal proofreader**

Jeanne Dittman

**Indexer**

Sherry Massey

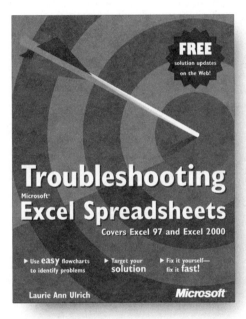